ADAPTIVE COACHING

ADAPTIVE COACHING

Second Edition

The Art and Practice of a
Client-Centered Approach to
Performance Improvement

Terry R. Bacon, PhD • Laurie Voss, PhD

NICHOLAS BREALEY
INTERNATIONAL

BOSTON • LONDON

First published by Nicholas Brealey International, an imprint of Nicholas Brealey Publishing, in 2012.

20 Park Plaza, Suite 1115A	3-5 Spafield Street, Clerkenwell
Boston, MA 02116, USA	London, EC1R 4QB, UK
Tel: + 617-523-3801	Tel: +44 (0)20 7239 0360
Fax: + 617-523-3708	Fax: +44 (0)20 7239 0370

www.nicholasbrealey.com

Printed in the United States of America

16 15 14 13 12   1 2 3 4 5

ISBN: 978-1-90483-824-1
E-ISBN: 978-1-85788-472-2

Library of Congress Cataloging-in-Publication Data
Bacon, Terry R.
Adaptive coaching : the art and practice of a client-centered approach to performance improvement / by Terry R. Bacon and Laurie Voss. -- 2nd ed.
     p. cm.
Includes bibliographical references and index.
1. Executive coaching. I. Voss, Laurie. II. Title.
HD30.4.B33 2012
658.3'124--dc23
                    2011035270

CONTENTS

ACKNOWLEDGMENTS

Much has happened in the world of coaching since 2003, when *Adaptive Coaching* was first published. It would be fair to say that coaching grew up. More organizations have adopted coaching as a fundamental tool for professional and executive development, more coaching certification programs have emerged, more coaches have hung out their shingles, more research has been done on coaching, and much more has been written about coaching. What had been a respectable but fledgling leadership development practice has become substantially more mainstream, more accepted, more valued, and more scrutinized—as it should be when billions of dollars are spent annually on it.

We based the first edition of *Adaptive Coaching* on research results from the Coaching Effectiveness Survey (CES), which was developed by Lore International Institute in the early 2000s. We now have more than three times the data we had when we wrote the first edition and are pleased to say that the conclusions we drew from the data while writing the first edition have been confirmed in our latest round of analyses. Some percentages have changed slightly, but the need for an adaptive approach to coaching is as strong as ever. The gaps remain between how people want to be coached and how they are coached and between what coaches perceive about the process and what clients perceive.

A book of this nature is not merely the product of two minds but is the result of years of accumulated experience and the thoughts and contributions of hundreds of people, not least of whom are the countless professionals, executives, and managers we have coached in more than three decades of experience as coaches, educators, mentors, and managers. We therefore begin by thanking the many coaching clients with whom we have worked during the course of our careers. Without their concerns, needs, problems, questions, challenges, and confidence in us, we would know very little about coaching. The plain fact is that without the thousands of dialogues we have had with them, we would not have understood what successful coaching looks like or how critical it is to be adaptive to our clients' needs and preferences.

We also acknowledge the help we've received from our many colleagues in Lore International Institute and Korn/Ferry International (Korn/Ferry acquired Lore in 2008). When we became part of Korn/Ferry, we joined an extensive group of global consultants and professionals whose expertise in assessment, leadership development, enterprise learning, recruiting, and other aspects of talent management opened new avenues of exploration for us and gave us additional insights into the art and science of developing people through coaching. We are particularly indebted to Kevin Cashman and Janet Feldman, formerly of Leader-Source (which was also acquired by Korn/Ferry). Kevin and Janet have devoted years of their professional lives to executive coaching, most often at the highest levels of client organizations. Their Executive-to-Leader Institute, in particular, is a groundbreaking approach to developing leaders through a very comprehensive program of executive coaching. They gave us numerous insights into coaching from the inside out and the outside in, which we have included in part 3 of this book. Kevin and Janet are extraordinary professionals and have become good friends to us. Many thanks to them.

We would also like to express our gratitude and appreciation to the men and women of Lominger, which became part of Korn/Ferry in 2006. Ken DeMeuse, Kim Ruyle, Guangrong Dai, and others have been insightful, especially regarding leadership competencies, assessment, and research. Terry would like to thank his fellow gurus in Korn/Ferry, particularly Bob Eichinger and Dana Landis, who offered such an array of insights that it is difficult to determine what has been most helpful. These thought leaders, along with Kevin Cashman and Janet Feldman, have been for us a virtual think tank on talent management, leadership development, and coaching.

PERMISSIONS

We would like to thank the authors and publishers who have granted us permission to include lengthy quotations from their works: Kevin Cashman (2008), *Leadership from the Inside Out: Becoming a Leader for Life*; Larissa MacFarquhar (2002), "The Better Boss," in *The New Yorker*; Steven Berglas (2002), "The Very Real Dangers of Executive Coaching," in *Harvard Business Review*; Charles O'Reilly III and Jeffrey Pfeffer (2000), *Hidden Value: How Great Companies Achieve Extraordinary Results with Ordinary People*; David Bohm (1996), *On Dialogue*; Lester Tobias (1996), "Coaching Executives," in *Consulting Psychology Journal*; Deborah Flick (1998), *From Debate to Dialogue*; and David Bohm, Donald Factor, and Peter Garrett (1991), "Dialogue: A Proposal."

A WORD ABOUT PRONOUNS

Throughout this book, we have tried to avoid the awkward use of dual pronouns: *he/she, his/her, him/her,* and *himself/herself.* Although these constructions attempt to be inclusive, they are a clumsy use of English. Instead, we have varied our pronoun use, sometimes referring to coaches or clients as he and sometimes as she. Our pronoun choices are random and are meant to illustrate that, insofar as our discussion of coaching is concerned, the gender of the coaches and clients is largely irrelevant.

ABOUT THE AUTHORS

TERRY R. BACON is the scholar-in-residence emeritus in the Korn/Ferry Institute, which is part of the research and intellectual property development arm of Korn/Ferry International. Prior to this role, he was founder, president, and CEO of Lore International Institute, an executive development firm that provided executive coaching, assessment, and education to major corporations around the world. In more than thirty years as an educator and consultant, he has developed scores of training programs, worked with hundreds of clients, and coached more than one thousand executives globally.

He has a B.S. in general engineering from the United States Military Academy at West Point (class of 1969) and a PhD in literary studies from The American University in Washington, D.C. He has also studied business at Roosevelt University; psychology and counseling at Goddard College; leadership at Stanford University; sales management at the University of Chicago; strategic planning at the Wharton School of Business, University of Pennsylvania; and leading professional service firms at the Harvard Business School.

He is a prolific writer and speaker. In addition to *Adaptive Coaching*, he has written or co-written *Selling to Major Accounts* (1999); *Winning Behavior: What the Smartest, Most Successful Companies Do Differently* (2003); *The Behavioral Advantage: What the Smartest, Most Successful Companies Do Differently to Win in the B2B Arena* (2004); *Powerful Proposals* (2005); *What People Want: A Manager's Guide to Building Relationships that Work* (2006); *The Elements of Power: Lessons on Leadership and Influence* (2011); and *Elements of Influence: The Art of Getting Others to Follow Your Lead* (2011). In recent years, his speaking engagements have included talks on the essence of leadership, leadership in challenging times, respect, accountability, what people want, going global, developing business internationally, leading with a global mind-set, behavioral differentiation, global account leadership, developing your c-suite, nondirective coaching, measuring coaching effectiveness, and the ideological foundations of adaptive coaching.

In addition to his professional role, he is the chairman of the Fort Lewis College Foundation Board, president of Music in the Mountains (a summer classical music festival in Durango, Colorado), and a member of the advisory boards of the Durango Arts Center and Friends of the Fort Lewis College Theatre. He lives in Colorado and Hawaii.

His thoughts on power, influence, leadership, coaching, and other topics appear on his websites: *www.terryrbacon.com*, *www.booksbyterryrbacon.com*, and *www.theelementsofpower.com*. For the past four years, *Leadership Excellence* has named him one of the "Top 100 Thinkers on Leadership in the World."

LAURIE VOSS is managing principal and global lead for executive coaching at Korn/Ferry International. In 2001, Terry hired Laurie with an official job title of "Ghost Writer." One of her first assignments in the Lore Research Institute was to write a research brief about the benefits of executive coaching. A trend in leadership development and talent management began to take shape and companies hired firms like Lore to deliver more consistent and economical coaching services. Laurie's entre to the field corresponded perfectly with this organizational trend, and over the course of ten years she moved from research to proposal writing to coach recruiting to operations to sales and back again, full circle, to research. This path was formed when Lore was selected by a Fortune 500 company to be the exclusive vendor of executive coaching worldwide.

The first priority for the client and the firm was to recruit coaches to serve several hundred executives in five geographic theaters. After eight months, two thousand phone hours, and one hundred fifty certification days, Laurie and a global team recruited, certified, and oriented more than two hundred coaches for their global delivery network. The opportunity to learn from hundreds of seasoned coaches—many successful, retired, business leaders—is perhaps the best definition we can identify for "accelerated development." It's the very best of on-the-job and just-in-time training. Learning from and interacting with this elite group of professional development experts created a foundation from which Laurie moved into an additional operational role to implement the global contract and build a team that could develop the technological infrastructure (including online time and expense entry) and measurement approaches to understand the benefits of executive coaching.

After four years of operations, Laurie moved into sales and currently holds the thought leadership and sales role as global lead for executive coaching at Korn/Ferry International. As a thought leader in executive coaching she has been exploring, writing, and learning more about what drives lasting value for individuals and organizations. In the past ten years, she has co-authored more than thirty responses to very large coaching RFPs and written two hundred proposals, two published articles, and now this book. A decade of fieldwork led her from ghost writer to co-author.

Any good coach understands the importance of recognition, so she is compelled to send the biggest shout out to her husband, Shane Voss, and daughters Hailey and Lainey. Hailey was just one when the first edition of *Adaptive Coaching* was printed, and now she's jumping horses, texting, using Skype, and wearing mascara. Lainey has truly been with Laurie every step of the way. She was born a few years into Laurie's executive coaching career, and she has had to listen to many calls in the car, wait while Laurie sent emails while walking the dogs, and hunt Laurie down (once) while she was hiding in a dark closet to finish a conference call. Lainey is an avid soccer player, a tenacious climber, and the true fan of which everyone should have at least one.

INTRODUCTION

In the first edition of *Adaptive Coaching*, we cited these facts from *The War for Talent* (Michaels, Handfield-Jones, and Axelrod, 2001):

- Ninety-nine percent of corporate officers believe that their pool of managerial talent will need to be stronger three years from now.

- Fifty-four percent of corporate officers report that their inability to cultivate strong executive leadership from their people is a "huge" or "major" obstacle to their company's success.

- Fifty-seven percent of managers believe that their company does not develop their people quickly and effectively.

- Fifty-seven percent of managers who intend to seek new jobs with new companies name insufficient development and learning opportunities as "critical" or "very important" reasons for leaving.

The authors of *The War for Talent* derived these statistics from a series of McKinsey-sponsored studies conducted in 1997 and 2000 with more than one hundred large and midsized U.S. companies. The ten thousand respondents in these studies included corporate officers, senior managers, midlevel executives, and HR executives (pp. 4, 97–98). The real war for talent was not so much a war among corporate combatants raiding each other's fiefdoms for executive plunder, although it was often practiced as such. It was really a war of the imagination and the will to envision and implement new and better ways to develop and retain existing talent. A decade ago, businesses were coming to recognize that they could not simply recruit their way to victory. Winning the war for talent meant winning on the home front by developing more skillful, more sustained, more effective means of helping good people grow into their current assignments, and into the challenges of their next assignments, and the ones after that.

To wage the war for talent largely outside your organization was to chase a chimera. In *Hidden Value: How Great Companies Achieve Extraordinary Results with Ordinary People*, authors Charles A. O'Reilly III and Jeffrey Pfeffer (2000) offer a compelling, commonsense argument for developing talent within your organization:

> *Of course, companies that want to succeed need great people, and recruitment, selection, and retention are obviously important. But companies need something else that is even more important and often more difficult to obtain: cultures and systems in which these great people can actually use their talents, and, even better, management practices that produce extraordinary results from almost everybody. The unfortunate mathematical fact is that only ten percent of the people are going to be in the top ten percent. So, companies have a choice. They can all chase the same supposed talent. Or, they can do something even more useful and much more difficult to copy—build an organization that helps make it possible for regular folks to perform as if they were in the top ten percent. (pp. 1–2)*

Arguments like these—and the fact that the war for talent was a real and threatening phenomenon—led to the rise of talent management as a subject of intense focus in human resources departments throughout the business world. Today, talent management is of the utmost importance, not only to HR executives but to corporate strategists and senior executives in companies across the globe, who have come to realize that the key to sustained high performance is attracting and retaining key talent. And this challenge has not diminished in the past decade. In fact, it's gotten greater. Consider these facts from Deloitte's "Talent Edge 2020" (April 2011):

- "As the economy improves, only 35 percent of employees surveyed in 2011 expect to remain with their current employer. The remaining two-thirds are actively or passively testing the job market." (p. 1)

- "The nearly two out of three employees surveyed who are exploring their career options have strong, negative views about the job employers are doing to create challenging career paths and to open up advancement opportunities." (p. 1)

- "Very few employees define their employers' overall talent efforts as 'world-class' or even 'very good'—and the same lack of confidence holds true when it comes to key talent retention strategies." (p. 2)

As the war for talent continues and companies struggle to retain their key talent, they are increasingly turning to coaching as a principal means of developing their existing people, both to provide career path opportunities and also to produce extraordinary results from almost everybody. In the first edition, we argued that coaching had become one of the hottest movements in professional development since the early 1990s, and that argument is even more true today. Several years ago, an American Management Association (2008) survey reported that 60 percent of North American companies regularly use coaching for high-potential employees and 42 percent make regular use of executive coaching, figures that have likely increased by 2012. By some estimates, there are now more than 150,000 people in the developed world who call themselves executive coaches—and that number pales beside the hundreds of thousands of executives, managers, supervisors, and other professionals in thousands of companies worldwide whose jobs include coaching others. This extraordinary burst of coaching activity has generated an accompanying explosion of coaching literature. A look at the Amazon.com listing under "business coaching" reveals nearly 2,000 books (and on "coaching" nearly 15,000), most written since 1995 and some written by sports coaches, military leaders, and others with only a peripheral connection to business.

Businesses moved to coaching as the limitations of traditional classroom training became more and more obvious. Lack of transfer in learning and lack of sustained behavioral change pointed toward the need for more individualized, more engaged, more context-specific learning. Coaching seemed to provide a solution to the human and systemic challenges posed by the new business paradigm:

- Real-time, on-time learning

- Individualized learning

- Integrated learning to help people negotiate the demands of their work with the demands of their lives

- Sustained attention to progress and development to foster genuine change

- Accelerated learning for a rapidly changing business environment

- A changed role for managers in the new learning organization

The coaching literature that emerged both responded to and drove these expectations—in many cases to absurd extremes. The literature was replete with grandiose claims about personal growth and transformation, improved quality of life, spiritual renewal, wildly enhanced productivity, unleashed human potential, enhanced creativity, heightened self-confidence, and having it all faster and easier with the help of a devoted coach. Leading the charge were sports coaches like Don Shula and Rick Pitino, who cashed in on their fame. Pitino, coach of the Louisville Cardinals men's basketball team and formerly coach of the Kentucky Wildcats when they won the NCAA title, wrote a 1998 book called *Success Is a Choice: Ten Steps to Overachieving in Business and Life*. The blurb on the back cover read, "Make Rick Pitino your personal coach and achieve more than you ever thought possible." Shula co-authored two books with Ken Blanchard titled *Everyone's a Coach* (Blanchard and Shula, 1995) and *The Little Book of Coaching: Motivating People to Be Winners* (2001). While some readers may have enjoyed the sports anecdotes, these books offered little beyond the standard platitudes about leadership and motivation. They reduced coaching to cheerleading and the coach to a dynamic dispenser of wisdom. Moreover, they misplaced the responsibility for successful coaching interventions. In *Everyone's a Coach*, Blanchard and Shula argued that "beliefs are what make things happen. Beliefs come true. Inadequate beliefs are setups for inadequate performance. And it's the coach's—the leader's—beliefs that are the most important; they become self-fulfilling" (p. 29). In their perspective, coaching is all about leading and motivating others, and the people being coached change through the strength of a paternalistic coach's vision, energy, and charisma. In this reductio ad absurdum, which shows little insight into human development, clients simply follow the leader. They accept the coach's direction because the coach knows best, and they bear no responsibility for their own development. As such, these books were works of staggering oversimplification.

There is only the loosest affiliation between athletic coaching and business practice, and a number of better works on coaching were quick to dissociate the meanings they attached to coaching in business from what is practiced in sports. While applications of coaching vary widely depending on the context and the client, coaching in business contexts can generally be defined as an informed dialogue whose purpose is the facilitation of new skills, possibilities, and insights in the interest of individual learning and organizational advancement. Coaching is anchored in a trust relationship best characterized by listening, observing, questioning, joint problem solving, and action planning. Business coaching is largely not about the processes more commonly associated with sports coaching—advice giving, training, instruction, exhortation, rewards, and punishments—although, to be sure, some business clients do want advice, direction, and motivational speeches.

As the coaching boom gained momentum, the literature began to reflect a shift from its roots in the organizational changes of the late 1980s when managers saw the need to let go of their old command-and-control styles and become more developmental in their orientation. Companies needed and expected more of their employees, and coaching emerged as a way to get it. However, as outsourcing became more prevalent in the 1990s, the locus of coaching shifted away from managers—at least in the literature. Though it is often not clearly specified, the most recent coaching literature is more geared toward the external executive coach, the coach-for-hire whose functions range from extended one-on-one coaching with a high-level executive to the coaching of an entire executive team. As the demand and cost for such services escalated, so did the claims about what coaching could achieve.

The truth is that in spite of all the excitement, there remains a huge gap between rhetoric and reality. First, the McKinsey studies indicate that coaching, combined with performance feedback, ranks among the most significant drivers of talent development, but before coaching can be useful in organizations employees must have an honest appraisal of their performance, and according to the War for Talent survey "only 35 percent of individuals feel their company tells them openly and candidly where they stand." (Michaels et al 2001) Research on coaching effectiveness conducted by Lore International Institute (now part of Korn/Ferry International) also shows a significant gap between what companies and clients expect from coaching and what it actually does for them. From 1996 through 2011, Lore (Korn/Ferry) conducted an extensive survey of coaching effectiveness within Fortune 500 companies. Our database now includes assessments from more than twenty thousand coaching clients. Here are some of the data that indicate the need for dramatic improvements in alignment between the expectations for coaching and its effectiveness:

- Fifty-seven percent of clients say they would like more coaching than they are currently getting.

- Sixty percent of clients say they would like better coaching than they are currently getting.

- Fifty-six percent of clients report that the coaching they receive is often not focused on the right things and does not help them learn exactly what they should do differently to be more effective.

- Forty-five percent of clients report that coaching sessions with their current coach have not had much positive impact on their work performance.

For all the vaunted claims about the potential of coaching advanced in the hundreds of books on the topic, these outcomes are dismal. How many of us would purchase a product that had only a 45 percent likelihood of doing what it was purported to do?

Second, who receives coaching from whom? Companies can afford outside coaches for senior executives, but the need for developmental coaching extends throughout the entire organization. External coaches should be used at executive levels where objective outside help can be most beneficial, as well as for special cases at lower levels. However, all employees deserve the opportunity to improve their skills, so education and coaching should be part of the fabric of a company. In most companies, managers throughout the organization provide the bulk of the coaching, but, as our research on coaching effectiveness reveals, the grassroots work of developing managers as coaches remains far from finished. Furthermore, many of the people who sell themselves as coaches do a poor job of it. We hear time and again from companies that they have been disappointed by much of the coaching their leaders have received from external coaches. Coaches of both sorts—internal and external—need to continue to refine their skills to adapt to the coaching situations in which they find themselves.

Coaching holds much promise, but there is a serious need to improve on what it currently delivers. Improvement will come only from a sober and realistic look at what coaching can and cannot do, not from hyperbolic and suspect claims. Coaches must be clear and realistic about what they are offering and why. They must hold the line about what coaching is and is not. And clients must be encouraged to be thoughtful in defining what they want and need. Once the ground rules are set, clients and coaches can determine what falls in the realm of coaching and what may more properly belong in other kinds of helping situations, such as psychotherapy, family therapy, formal education, spiritual guidance, human resources functions, or even legal intervention. The coach can often serve quite usefully as a conduit to other kinds of helping interventions. The coach can also define fully what coaching can provide, such as gathering and interpreting performance feedback; career planning for personal and professional development; improving interpersonal and leadership or management skills; mediating team relationships; analyzing career roadblocks and setbacks; uncovering blind spots and assumptions that limit the client's abilities; helping clients stick with and assess progress on an agenda; and serving as a confidential, disinterested sounding board to deliberate on alternative courses of action and business strategies.

In the first edition of *Adaptive Coaching*, we noted that in spite of the vast potential for coaching, in reality there is only the skimpiest of empirical evidence for what happens in the relationship, why it happens, and what makes it effective or ineffective. Most of the published research, we said, could be found only within the relatively narrow confines of doctoral dissertations. Instead, most coaching theory and practices reside in the vivid anecdotal accounts of successful practitioners, where all kinds of variables from personal charisma to the halo effect of receiving special attention from a coach cloud a genuine understanding of the dynamics and techniques of good coaching.

That picture has changed dramatically since our first edition. In the past decade, hundreds of research studies have been done on coaching, and the literature now abounds with serious, scholarly work on the philosophy of coaching, the various approaches to coaching, and the effects of coaching. But if the coaching industry once suffered from a paucity of research and inquiry, it now may suffer from such a profusion of opinions, approaches, and statistics that practitioners can find the field more confusing than reassuring (Campone, 2008, pp. 91–102). Much of the recent research on coaching theory and practice has been based on applying psychological theories to the practice of coaching, including Carl Rogers's person-centered approach, cognitive psychology, behavioral psychology, developmental psychology and adult learning theory, family therapy, social psychology, emotional intelligence, positive psychology, and even psychotherapy. There are so many schools of thought, it begs the question whether there is a right approach to coaching people in the world of work. In chapters 13 and 14, we present some of the key concepts of these psychological approaches to coaching and note the value they can bring to coaches.

We believe there isn't a single right approach to every coaching client, in every situation, for any issue or opportunity the client might be facing, just as there is no single, proven approach to therapy that is effective with each client every time. Moreover, our own research, conducted over the past twenty years, confirms this conclusion. What we have learned, by listening carefully to the wants and needs of coaching clients and by analyzing their responses to our Coaching Effectiveness Survey, is that effective coaching must first and foremost be adaptive. By this we mean that coaches must be skilled at adapting their methods, techniques, and approaches to the needs of their clients—both personally and contextually. Throughout this book, we will report some of the tens of thousands of responses we've heard from coaching clients to the question "What could your coach do to be more effective?" Their answers indicate a crying need for coaches to be more adaptive. Here are a few representative responses:

- Use different coaching styles; ask more questions.

- Become more patient during coaching sessions and take more time for the concerns of those who are being coached.

- Release your own agenda.

- Be more open in helping the coachee develop his ideas rather than providing him direction.

- Help the person being coached to consider the culture and what will actually work in the organization rather than a pure view of what is best in a vacuum but may not fly in practice.

- Take more time to find out the history of the individual (what he has done, good and not so good, his experience).

- Be more open in helping me develop my ideas rather than providing me with direction.

- In my opinion, it is important to view coaching more as a part of a long-term development process, instead of a way to solve specific performance problems.

- Ask the coachees more where they see improvement potential by themselves. Match their point of view with her observations and work out individual development plans with defined tasks, milestones, and feedback loops together with the coachees.

Although the first principle of coaching espoused in most of the coaching literature is to do all the things these respondents call for, many coaches still consistently fail in the fundamentals of listening, empathizing, probing, and contextualizing even when they think that's what they are doing. Instead they revert to advice giving, problem solving, and theorizing. This is not simply a coaching shortcoming as much as it is a human tendency in all kinds of helping situations, a tendency to want to fix the problem. All of us have grown up with an implicit model of coaching that is fundamentally flawed.

We have learned how to help others while receiving instruction, advice, and guidance from our parents, schoolteachers, religious leaders, scoutmasters, dance teachers, music instructors, friends—and athletic coaches—who, for the most part, take a highly directive and authoritarian approach. John Goodlad's (1984) research, in *A Place Called School*, established clearly that teachers teach the way they were taught, not the way they were taught to teach. The same can be said about the difficulties anyone faces in a helping relationship. The challenge is to unlearn that deeply embedded, directive model of helping in favor of one that is more mutual, more collaborative, and more centered on the needs and preferences of the other person. Our research tells us that most corporate coaches prefer to use a directive approach, whereas more than half of clients want their coaches to use a nondirective approach. Furthermore, in training coaches through role plays, we have found that many coaches prematurely decide what the client's issues are, direct the conversation according to that assumption, and frequently discover later that they were wrong.

What many coaches lack are frameworks for understanding what it means to adapt to the client. The admonition to adapt is clear enough, but absent a sense of what the alternatives are, coaches revert to the style and approach with which they are most comfortable. To elaborate further, we will frame our approach to adaptive coaching with three concepts: the two-minds model, a taxonomy of coaching styles, and the use of dialogue—each of which will be explored more fully in subsequent chapters.

THE TWO-MINDS MODEL

At the outset of a coaching relationship, there are enormous differences between the coach's perspective and the client's perspective. As figures 1 and 2 illustrate, each has a very different set of experiences, expectations, assumptions, and perhaps values and beliefs. For the coach to build trust with the client, there must be enough alignment in their mindsets for the client to feel that the coach understands him and his circumstances, is sympathetic toward him, is genuinely interested in helping him, is credible as a helper, is on his side, and can be trusted. This is a tall order, especially when the coach and client are members of the same organization, when the coach has some role relationship with the client (such as his boss), and

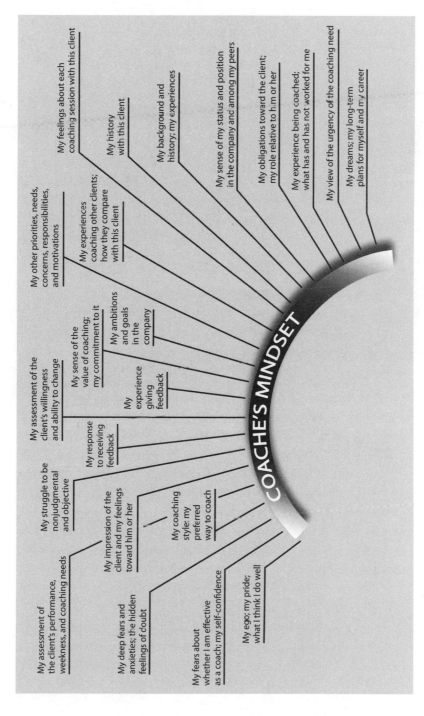

Figure 1: The Coach's Mindset

COACHE'S MINDSET

My assessment of the client's performance, weekness, and coaching needs

My feelings about each coaching session with this client

My history with this client

My background and history; my experiences

My sense of my status and position in the company and among my peers

My obligations toward the client; my role relative to him or her

My experience being coached; what has and has not worked for me

My view of the urgency of the coaching need

My dreams; my long-term plans for myself and my career

My other priorities, needs, concerns, responsibilities, and motivations

My experiences coaching other clients; how they compare with this client

My ambitions and goals in the company

My sense of the value of coaching; my commitment to it

My experience giving feedback

My assessment of the client's willingness and ability to change

My response to receiving feedback

My struggle to be nonjudgmental and objective

My impression of the client and my feelings toward him or her

My coaching style; my preferred way to coach

My deep fears and anxieties; the hidden feelings of doubt

My fears about whether I am effective as a coach; my self-confidence

My ego; my pride; what I think I do well

Figure 2: The Client's Mindset

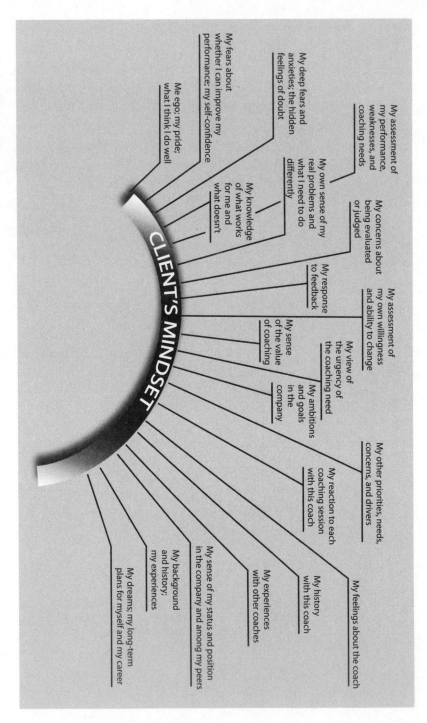

when the client's career prospects depend to some extent on the outcomes of the coaching.

It's fair to say that most of the coaching that takes place in business organizations is boss (coach) to direct report (client). To achieve successful coaching, the boss has to work hard to establish a coaching relationship that is productive and useful in the client's eyes. Because of the power difference, this is not easy. Recognizing how difficult it is, some companies set up coaching programs where the coach is not a client's boss but is instead a peer, an unrelated manager, an HR professional, or an outside coach. Even under these conditions, however, coaching will only be effective to the extent that the coach can understand and reflect the client's mindset. The coach's first task in building a relationship is to gain alignment between her mindset and the client's. Metaphorically, this means moving the two minds closer together.

How do coaches do this? Essentially, through a nonthreatening discussion—asking questions, clarifying assumptions, listening carefully, and sharing their own perspectives. Coaches have to know how to open and sustain coaching relationships through the right kinds of questions, suggestions, and observations. They have to be aware of differences and also aware that they need to gain alignment on some fundamental things—like how the client wants to be coached, what has worked for the client in the past and what hasn't, and so on. Too often, coaches short-circuit this phase of the coaching relationship and fail thereafter to create a space in the dialogue for differences and alignment to emerge. In the next chapter, we will examine more fully how coaches can adapt to a client's context in order to gain alignment between their mind-set and their client's.

COACHING STYLE PREFERENCES— A TAXONOMY

In our coaching experience, we have noticed that some clients want to be given advice and direction; others (most others, in fact) prefer the coach to ask questions and guide but not direct them. We came to see this as a fundamental distinction in coaching preferences, and we labeled these diametrically opposed approaches *directive* and *nondirective*. We also observed that most coaches naturally use a more directive approach; however, most clients prefer a nondirective approach, which may explain why so many clients feel that the coaching they receive is not helpful.

We also noticed that some clients want to be coached only when a particular need arises; others want a longer-term relationship with their coaches and to be coached regularly, with development plans guiding what amounts to a program. As we explored these differences in preference, we called them *circumstantial* and *programmatic*. Finally, we observed that some clients want coaching only about specific, task-related work issues, like how to conduct a meeting, how to use a piece of equipment or software, or how to build stronger relationships with customers. Other coaching clients want their coaches to take a more holistic view of their development and help them think about their careers and perhaps even personal problems. We came to call these distinctions *specific* and *holistic*.

As we explored these distinctions, we realized that they formed different coaching approaches or styles, and this led us to create the coaching styles taxonomy that we explore in chapter 5. The coaching effectiveness survey we developed to test this model showed that it was a valid way of understanding how different coaches approached coaching and how different clients responded to coaching. We learned that the most effective coaching occurs when coaches adapt their approach to their clients' preferences. In chapters 3 through 5, we explore how to assess a client's needs and coaching style preferences and adapt to them.

DIALOGUE

What drives adaptive coaching is the ongoing dialogue between a coach and a client. The term *dialogue* acquired a specialized meaning in the early 1990s when British physicist and philosopher David Bohm used it to describe a multifaceted process that helps groups of people explore their perceptions and assumptions and deepen communication and understanding. Bohm felt that many of the world's problems occurred because people talk at cross-purposes, don't examine their assumptions, are unaware of how their perceptions influence their thought processes, and try to prevail in conversations by imposing their "truth" on others. Bohm's (1996) concept of dialogue pushes against popular understandings of the role of empathy in coaching. While we tend to think about the outcome of empathy as a merger of one person's perspective with another's (the cliché of walking in another person's shoes), dialogue elevates the importance of difference as a key to reaching new understandings:

> *When one person says something, the other person does not in general respond with exactly the same meaning as that seen by the first person. Rather, the meanings are only similar and not identical. Thus, when the second person replies, the first person sees a difference between what he meant to say and what the other person understood. On considering this difference, he may then be able to see something new, which is relevant both to his own views and to those of the other person. And so it can go back and forth, with the continual emergence of a new content that is common to both participants. Thus, in a dialogue, each person does not attempt to make common certain ideas or items of information that are already known to him. Rather, it may be said that the two people are making something in common, i.e., creating something new together. (p. 2)*

Bohm's concept of dialogue puts the coaching relationship at the center of the activity. It suggests that every coaching situation involves the co-construction of a narrative of the client's experience in terms of the issues that are the focus of the coaching. The narrative is constructed to make sense of the client's experience in a more coherent way than the client felt at the time. The coach doesn't know the ending of the story. In fact, at the beginning of a coaching relationship, the coach doesn't really know the beginning. The coach can't know everything about the client; can't know what the real issues are; and can't know how the client will respond, how hard the client will work, what exigencies will help or hinder the client, or how the story they construct will turn out. However, the coach has the ability to influence the outcomes, which gives the coach a unique role as both a character in the story and a co-creator of its meaning. The coach can't dictate the outcome—but through the dialogue, the coach and client attempt together to influence the outcome through the meanings they attach to the story. Actually, the art of coaching is to exert only enough influence to help the real participants in the story tell their own tales and shape their own destinies. We will explore Bohm's concept of dialogue more fully in chapter 7 to show how managing the ongoing dialogue is a coach's most fundamental skill.

AN OVERVIEW OF THE BOOK

To help readers explore adaptive coaching, we have divided the book into four parts. Part 1, Assessing Clients' Needs, explores how coaches discover what their clients really need and adapt their coaching style and approach to their clients. As you will see, this is no trivial matter. Clients often don't know what they really need, and coaches who jump too quickly to conclusions about what clients need are often wrong. Determining clients' real needs requires patience, multiple sources of information, and skillful exploration. In this part of the book, we also discuss the differences between coaching and therapy, and we introduce a taxonomy of coaching style preferences that can help coaches adapt to the needs and wants of the people they are trying to help.

Chapter 1 discusses the various contexts of coaching and how those contexts are important in establishing a coaching relationship, creating a "contract" between coach and client, and assessing the client's real needs.

Chapter 2 introduces several fundamental adaptive coaching concepts and illustrates how you and your clients can negotiate your expectations of the coaching process and intended outcomes so that you are both comfortable with the process and your roles in it.

Chapter 3 presents a concept we call the needs compass. There are four primary sources of information about clients' needs and opportunities. To uncover someone's real needs and opportunities, you should seek information from all four sources.

Chapter 4 addresses how you discover the client's real issues—the problems or opportunities that often lie below the surface of the "presenting problem." Surfacing the real issues—and therefore handling the real problems—is one of the art forms in effective coaching. A lengthy coaching dialogue in this chapter illustrates this process.

Finally, chapter 5 elaborates on our coaching styles taxonomy and explores how coaches can adapt to different client preferences. We elaborate here on the differences between directive versus nondirective coaching, programmatic versus circumstantial coaching, and specific versus holistic coaching. This chapter includes many of the responses we received from coaching clients when we asked them what their coaches could do to be more effective.

Part 2, Practicing Adaptive Coaching, addresses the art and skill coaches need to initiate coaching, manage the coaching dialogue, and conclude coaching successfully. The aim of these chapters is to help coaches increase their flexibility in using a range of coaching skills.

Chapter 6 discusses how you initiate a coaching relationship, prepare for the first coaching session, conduct the first session, explore the client's needs, initiate a personal development plan, and open subsequent sessions. The beginning of a coaching relationship is critical. As Alexander Clark said, "Let us watch well our beginnings, and results will manage themselves."

Chapter 7 elaborates on the art of managing the coaching dialogue and includes a lengthy illustration of dialogue in action. Few coaching skills are as important as managing the dialogue. As we observe in this chapter, coaching can be powerful—indeed, life changing—if the journey is interesting, the discoveries unexpected, and the insights actionable. Or the journey can be dull, uninspiring, and empty. The art and skill of the coach makes the difference.

Chapter 8 discusses two fundamental coaching skills—listening and questioning. Although this will be familiar territory for many readers, we offer some insights on listening and questioning that may be new to some readers, including using "Columbo" questions, listening with your eyes and your heart, following the bread crumb trail, and going through the open doors. These are critical skills for anyone who coaches others.

Chapter 9 talks about how you should share your observations with clients. Here we discuss how to give effective feedback; how to solicit feedback on clients from others; how to reframe your client's perceptions, including how to differ with them; and how to reflect your perceptions of clients in ways that can be insightful for them.

Chapter 10 describes effective means of telling clients what you think by advising or teaching them, by confronting them, and by encouraging them. The chapter also discusses a crucial adaptive coaching technique— the process check. Effective coaching is often a combination of pushing clients by asserting your point of view and pulling clients by encouraging them and continually involving them in the management of the dialogue.

Finally, chapter 11 discusses how you close individual coaching sessions and bring closure to the coaching relationship itself. As there must be good beginnings, so there must also be good endings. The most satisfying coaching relationships end with a sense of accomplishment and quiet celebration.

Part 3, Driving Deep and Lasting Change, goes to the heart of coaching and discusses how coaches can help their clients change their attitudes and behaviors. While parts 1 and 2 of this book focus on the process of coaching, part 3 focuses on the content of coaching and elaborates upon some of the schools of thought we discussed earlier in this introduction. We begin by discussing a coaching metaphor created by our Korn/Ferry colleagues Kevin Cashman and Janet Feldman. They have created a methodology that integrates coaching from the inside out and coaching from the outside in. We will also describe several other approaches to coaching that seek to be transformational by helping clients achieve lasting change.

Chapter 12 describes our four-step change model. As we argue throughout this book, coaching is about initiating change: improving skills, building better relationships, overcoming performance problems, and so on. Much of the change clients seek is behavioral, and it is difficult for adults to alter their behavior significantly. A lifetime of habits is difficult to modify. So in this chapter, we present a framework for guiding change. This framework is an effective way to gauge what will be required for clients to make significant and lasting changes—and to identify what is getting in the way when they can't or won't change.

Chapter 13 discusses transformational coaching, which our colleague Kevin Cashman describes as coaching from the inside out. The essential idea in this chapter is that human development cannot be unanchored from the core of a person's values, beliefs, and sense of purpose. To help clients effect transformational changes, you must help them develop themselves from the inside out. We elaborate on Cashman's ideas in this chapter and also present some of the core concepts of two other transformational approaches to coaching: psychoanalytic and family therapy/systems thinking.

Chapter 14 addresses performance coaching, in which the intent is not so much to transform the client but to improve the client's performance based on assessments, feedback, and other observations of people who work with the client. Cashman describes this as coaching from the outside in. We describe Cashman's approach in some depth and then present the core concepts of other approaches to performance coaching, including the behavioral, cognitive, and appreciative inquiry methods.

Part 4, Becoming an Adaptive Coach, describes the journey coaches take to become adaptive, informed practitioners of coaching.

Chapter 15 describes what we believe is the ideal model for an adaptive coach—an informed practitioner. Informed practitioners are well versed in areas like leadership, organizational dynamics, change, coaching skills, and the various psychological approaches to coaching. Rather than adhere rigidly to one approach, they adapt according to their clients' needs and wishes and use appropriate frameworks and practices from a number of different coaching disciplines.

The final chapter of the book, chapter 16, discusses how coaches are also transformed by the coaching they do—and how completing their own journey is an essential part of the work of coaching and an outcome that makes coaching so rewarding for the coach. In this chapter, we describe some of the exercises we have found most useful for helping coaches in their own journeys of development and transformation. An appendix to the book provides an annotated bibliography of resources we have found useful for coaches. Of the tens of thousands of books that might help coaches become informed practitioners, we believe these are among the best. For all the talk about change in business, politics, and global events, and for all the evidence we see daily of sweeping change in all these arenas, human change at the micro level of the individual is among the most difficult challenges we face. The aim of coaching is to facilitate constructive, self-initiated change one person at a time—not just to ward off catastrophic change imposed from without, but to help individuals maximize their potential and the contributions they can make to the businesses where they invest their passions and their energies. For change of this sort to occur, coaching must become a vastly more adaptive, responsive enterprise. In short, if the clients we coach are to change in the ways they hope, we as coaches must be masters of change as well, starting with ourselves. This book seeks to help in that most personal of transformations.

PART

1

ASSESSING CLIENTS' NEEDS

The most effective coaches adapt their coaching style and approach to every client because every client is different. We became acutely aware of this fact in our research on coaching effectiveness. As we noted in the introduction, since 1996 we have surveyed thousands of coaches and tens of thousands of clients (the people receiving the coaching) in large and smaller corporations in a variety of industries and countries. From these surveys, we learned that different clients prefer to be coached in different ways. We also learned that coaches tend to coach the way they prefer to coach, rather than the way their clients prefer to be coached. The resulting misalignments in coaching preference mean that a large number of clients are frustrated with the coaching they are getting. In fact, nearly half of the clients we surveyed said that their coaching sessions with their current coaches had not had much positive impact on their work performance.

In the first part of this book, we discuss the foundations of adaptive coaching, namely, understanding the context in which coaching takes place, understanding clients' expectations and negotiating a set of shared expectations, using the four primary sources of information to discover clients' needs, triangulating among these sources to uncover the underlying issues that must be resolved for the client to make progress, and, finally, adapting to clients' coaching style preferences.

The purpose of coaching is to help people change. If there is no change, then the coaching has not had any impact. However, coaching does not occur in a vacuum. To facilitate change, you must understand the context in which that change needs to occur, including people's job situations, the organizations they work in, the urgency of their needs, their psychological readiness to change, their history with and expectations of coaching, and their view of and respect for the coach. Clients' openness and willingness to change is shaped by this context. If you fail to understand it, you may use the wrong approach at the wrong time and focus on the wrong issues, which is a formula for failure.

To help clients change, you must not only consider the context in which they work; you must also uncover and address the root causes of their problems. But this raises an important issue: How is coaching different from therapy? In chapter 1, as we discuss the contexts of coaching, we also address this thorny question. In chapter 2, we describe an effective process for understanding clients' expectations of coaching and then negotiating a set of shared expectations. To coach adaptively, you have to be transparent about how the coaching will occur, what you will focus on, how you will help clients, and so on. Surfacing their preferences and changing your approach accordingly is obviously a crucial part of being an adaptive coach. You have to start where your clients are and then continuously adapt to their needs or preferences.

Chapters 3 and 4 address the difficult challenge of discovering your clients' real needs. In our coaching experience, we have found that the presenting problem, what clients say they need help with, is rarely the real one. To discover what clients really need, you have to explore all four points of what we call the *needs compass*: your own observations of clients, clients' perceptions of themselves, others' observations of clients, and clients' work products and performance metrics. The client's real needs emerge through a process of co-discovery in which all sources of information are explored within the context of the client's life and work. Themes and patterns emerge as coaches triangulate from these different sources, and coaches use them to form and test hypotheses about the real issues.

Part 1 ends with a more detailed discussion of the taxonomy of coaching preferences introduced in chapter 1. In chapter 5, we describe the client comments and research findings that helped us distinguish between directive versus nondirective coaching, programmatic and circumstantial coaching, and specific and holistic coaching. This chapter includes suggestions for coaching clients who prefer each of the eight possible coaching styles.

The Contexts of Coaching

*Take more time to explore the backgrounds of the people you coach
and the situational constraints on their behavior.*

*Help the person being coached consider the culture and what will
actually work in the organization rather than [taking] a pure view of
what is best in a vacuum but may not fly in practice.*

*Find out the history of individual coachees (what they have done,
what experiences they've had, what they've done well and not so well,
what education they've had, and so on).*

SUGGESTIONS TO COACHES FROM THE "COACHING EFFECTIVENESS
SURVEY," KORN/FERRY INTERNATIONAL

We have found, in our studies of coaching effectiveness, that
the comments above are representative of how clients expect
coaching to reflect the various personal and organizational
contexts that define their work. It is, of course, impossible to coach anyone
without knowing enough about the client to know which questions to ask,
what avenues to follow, what suggestions make sense, and which options
are appropriate and relevant for the client. Coaching without considering
the context would be no more accurate or useful than following the astro-
logical advice in the Sunday newspaper. This point seems self-evident, yet
in the coaching world a debate has been raging for decades about the importance of context and the kind of background and personal information
the coach should consider. On the opposite ends of this debate are well-
known executive coaches like Marshall Goldsmith and psychiatrist Steven
Berglas, an author who also acts as a management consultant and executive
coach. It's useful to view their opposing ideas as bookends in a debate that
raises several important questions: What is coaching? How does the context of coaching influence its outcome? What are these contexts? How does

coaching differ from therapy? And how important to the coaching process are a client's past, a client's feelings, influences on a client's perceptions and behaviors, and motivations, past and present? The sharp differences between Goldsmith's and Berglas's views allow us to map out a reasonable middle ground for coaches who seek neither exclusion of the client's perspective nor psychotherapeutic specialization.

THE COACH AS DIRECTOR

In a profile of Goldsmith in *The New Yorker*, we learn that Goldsmith "tells his clients that he doesn't care about their past, doesn't care how they feel, doesn't care about their inner psyche—all he cares about is their future behavior. He provides them with a tightly structured program of things to do and a money-back guarantee that, if they do exactly what he tells them, they will get better" (MacFarquhar 2002, p. 120). Goldsmith's metaphor of the outcome of coaching as "getting better" evokes a medical model of treatment in which the doctor diagnoses the illness and prescribes the proper treatment. This approach represents one bookend, emphasizing coaching as prescription and the coach as the director.

Other elements of Goldsmith's approach are described as follows:

Goldsmith has turned against the notion of feedback in favor of a concept he calls "feedforward." "How many of us have wasted much of our lives impressing our spouse, partner, or significant other with our near-photographic memory of their previous sins, which we document and share to help them improve?" he says. "Dysfunctional! Say, 'I can't change the past—all I can say is I'm sorry for what I did wrong.' Ask for suggestions for the future. Don't promise to do everything they suggest—leadership is not a popularity contest. But follow up on a regular basis, and you know what's going to happen? You will get better." (p. 115)

What is the ultimate aim of coaching? According to this profile, it is not about changing behavior:

Coaching, [Goldsmith] had recently realized, was not, ultimately, about changing his client's behavior so much as changing perceptions of the client's behavior. He had observed that his clients had to change a hundred percent to get ten percent credit, partly be-cause people could be ungenerous, but mostly because they simply didn't notice. And in leadership, as he liked to say, it doesn't matter what you say—only what they hear. (p. 120)

Taken the wrong way, this could imply that real change is less impor-tant than impression management. Should clients really not worry about their own behavior and its consequences and effects on others but instead only about how they are perceived?

Finally, according to *The New Yorker* profile, Goldsmith's approach to coaching is pragmatic and antipsychological: "Goldsmith . . . has no patience for the psychological approach. 'My attitude is, it's easier to get unf---ed up than it is to understand why you are f---ed up, so why don't you just get un-f---ed up?' he says" (p. 120). This approach suggests that clients don't need insight; they just need direction (the right "tightly structured program of things to do"). And while it is certainly true that clients cannot change the past, it is equally true that they cannot escape it.

As portrayed in *The New Yorker* profile, Goldsmith represents one approach to coaching—the coach who disregards the client's past, his psy-chological state, and apparently his perspective, as indicated in this quota-tion from the article: "There was one guy I coached who spent hours on 'Marshall, you don't understand, let me explain why I have these issues, let me explain my mother, my father.' Whine, whine, whine. I tell clients, 'Here's a quarter—call someone who cares.' They don't need empathy. They need someone to look 'em in the eye and say, 'If you want to change, do this'" (p. 120). In this view, change is as easy as receiving the right direc-tion from a coach who can show clients the way. In the real world, argues Steven Berglas, things are more complex.

THE COACH AS PSYCHOTHERAPIST

In a *Harvard Business Review* essay, Berglas (2002) argues that "in an alarming number of situations, executive coaches who lack rigorous psy-chological training do more harm than good. By dint of their backgrounds and biases, they downplay or simply ignore deep-seated psychological problems they don't understand. When an executive's problems stem from undetected or ignored psychological difficulties, coaching can actually make a bad situation worse" (p. 87). Berglas exemplifies the opposite book-end from Goldsmith. He stresses a regimen of extensive psychological evaluation as a prelude to coaching and an in-depth coaching relationship that is in some ways difficult to distinguish from therapy. Berglas believes that today's popularity of executive coaching reflects a desire for quick fixes. The problem, he argues, is that these quick fixes often don't fix anything and may in fact do damage.

> *To achieve fast results, many popular executive coaches model their interventions after those used by sports coaches, employing techniques that reject out of hand any introspective process that can take time and cause "paralysis by analysis." The idea that an executive coach can help employees improve performance quickly is a great selling point to CEOs, who put the bottom line first. Yet that approach tends to gloss over any unconscious conflict the employee might have. This can have disastrous consequences for the company in the long term and can exacerbate the psychological damage to the person targeted for help. (pp. 88–89)*

In Berglas's view, every executive who is about to participate in coaching should first undergo a psychological evaluation to ensure that he or she is psychologically prepared for it and does not have any conditions that require more competent help than a coach who is not psychologically trained can provide. He cites several cases to support his position. One is a narcissistic manager, who Berglas concludes cannot benefit from coaching (and we concur). He also cites an executive who is driven by a fear of failure and another whose apparent assertiveness problem masked an inability to form intimate relationships with men. Clearly, these are cases where the clients would benefit more from therapy than from coaching. However, in our experience, the more common issues coaches face are leadership or life management issues, including difficulty balancing life and work, being insensitive to others, failing to delegate enough to empower and inspire subordinates, not being appreciative enough of others' contributions, and so on.

The most common issues can be handled through feedback, awareness building, skill building, goal setting, and discussion with a coach who is competent in managing the dialogue. In our opinion, Berglas's solution—having every candidate for coaching psychologically screened—is impractical and expensive. It also sends the signal that coaching is a psychological process and the people receiving coaching may have psychological problems. In many company and country cultures, this conclusion would automatically kill a coaching program because of the stigma attached to anyone who needs psychological help. This attitude is slowly changing as executive coaching is becoming more common throughout the world, but in many cultures it would still raise eyebrows if executives were known to be seeing a psychiatrist, and many executives would decline the opportunity to receive coaching if they knew it involved a psychological assessment.

Nonetheless, Berglas raises three cautionary red flags. First, in their zeal to create change programs for clients, coaches may fail to see warning signs of deeper psychological problems that may exist. Second, coaches may grasp that there are deeper psychological problems but lack the skill or credentials to deal with them and the integrity to withdraw from the assignment. Third, coaches may believe that these issues are irrelevant and focus on changing behavior without regard to any underlying dysfunctions. Berglas calls this the trap of treating the symptoms rather than the disorder, much like a doctor treating an internal injury by applying a Band-Aid. In all three cases, coaches may do more harm than good.

We believe that coaches do not have to be licensed psychologists, but they should be trained and certified in coaching (even if they are employees of a company and only coach internally). They must know the ethical and professional boundaries of coaching and adhere to a code of ethics that prohibits them from delving into matters they are not trained to deal with. They must know the warning signs when deeper psychological issues exist and be able to refer their clients to competent professionals. And they must beware of becoming arrogant, trying to supply all the answers, or dispensing advice in homespun homilies or clever turns of phrase and assume that this passes for wisdom.

The danger implicit in therapists acting as coaches is that they may not be able to separate coaching from therapy—in their own minds as well as the minds of their clients—and we have worked with many organizations where even the hint that coaching is therapy would doom the coaching program. As Berglas warns, however, problems may arise when coaches act as directors and ignore their clients' past, feelings, motivations, and beliefs. Like it or not, we are psychological creatures. Our brains are hardwired with powerful emotional as well as cognitive responses to stimuli, and our behavior is shaped to a significant extent by our personal and cultural history and experiences as well as our hopes, dreams, fears, and goals. Coaches who are either unaware of or have no patience with their clients' psychologies risk ignoring a substantial amount of the context of people's lives that affects how responsive they will be to coaching and what they can reasonably—and permanently—change.

There is danger, too, in assuming that coaching is all about giving clients the right program for them to follow. What if you're wrong? What if you have ignored (or simply been unaware of) an important but hidden constraint on their ability to effect this program? What if an unintended consequence of this program is that it exacerbates a psychological condition you did not or could not see? When you presume to know exactly what your clients should do to become better (however *better* is defined), you place an awful burden on yourself. You had better be right! If human beings were simple creatures, this might work. You might be able to diagnose the problem precisely, give clients the right corrective program, and send them on their way. But we humans are not simple creatures, so this approach is fraught with peril. Furthermore, it places the responsibility for change and growth on you, the coach, rather than on the client. When it's over, all clients can say is, "Thank God I had such a wise coach." They may not have learned anything other than how to follow directions. We believe that a more satisfying conclusion for clients is for them to realize that they have found most of the answers themselves and that their coach was a helpful guide.

COACHING VERSUS THERAPY

The contrast between Marshall Goldsmith's approach and Steven Berglas's concerns about coaches who lack rigorous psychological training raises some significant questions: What is the difference between coaching and therapy? Do good therapists make good coaches, and vice versa? These have been topics of considerable interest in past decades as more psychologists and others have joined the ranks of executive coaches. In an essay focused on the differences between coaching and therapy, Vicki Hart, John Blattner, and Staci Leipsic (2001) observed that in therapy "the focus is often on interpersonal health and an identifiable issue, such as acute depression or relational discord, that interferes with the client's level of functioning and current psychodynamic or psychosocial adjustment. The focus is typically retrospective, dealing with unconscious issues and repair of damage from earlier experiences. . . . It may even involve medication, adjunct therapies, and coordination of services" (p. 230). The most rigorous forms of psychological therapy are psychiatric treatment (which often involves medication) and various forms of psychological counseling, including cognitive-behavioral therapy, Gesalt therapy, group therapy, and so on. All are performed by highly trained, licensed professionals whose goal is to help patients deal with chronic and traumatic psychological problems and illnesses. Coaching should be conducted by highly trained, licensed professionals, too, but the lamentable fact is that anyone can hang out a shingle as a coach (and a lot of unqualified people do).

In contrast, one literature review of executive coaching defines the practice this way:

> *Executive coaching appears in the workplace with the intention of improving the executive's interpersonal skills and ultimately his or her workplace performance. It is more issue focused than therapy is and occurs in a broader array of contexts—including face-to-face sessions, meetings with other people, observation sessions, over the telephone, and by e-mail—and in a variety of locations away from work. (Kampa-Kokesch and Anderson 2001, p. 210)*

The symbolic trappings of therapy as opposed to coaching convey some of the critical distinctions. In therapy, clients, still often called *patients*, typically visit the therapist's office, where credentials are prominently displayed and other elements of the setting convey the authoritative role of the therapist in providing treatment. A therapeutic relationship begins with the requisite medical insurance paperwork being completed. The relationship is a therapeutic one, heavily modeled on the doctor/patient relationship of medical practice. In coaching, the coach typically comes to the client's office, where the client's home turf conveys quite a different locus of power. The relationship is a business relationship. Subsequent sessions may be conducted by telephone, by e-mail, or in some informal location. There is no insurance benefit; fees are typically negotiated with the company. Sometimes coaches are paid by the client, not unlike students making tuition payments for continuing education.

Coaching is intended to improve skills and ultimately workplace performance. As Kampa-Kokesch and Anderson noted, it is more issue focused than therapy, and it includes more types of interventions. Furthermore, coaching is typically more finite. A coaching program should last a specified amount of time and should be focused on specific work-related goals (such as improving an executive's ability to work with a board). A coaching contract, or action plan, is typically formulated quite early in the relationship, often by the end of the first or second meeting. This plan serves as the measure against which to assess progress. Therapy is usually not bounded by time, and its goals are less defined. Both coaching and therapy may touch on all aspects of a person's life. In coaching, however, life issues may be relevant but are usually not central; in therapy, life issues are central but business issues may be relevant. Coaching is usually more pragmatic and practical in its application. In coaching, the focal point is the person's performance; in therapy, the focal point is the person.

These are some of the differences. There are also similarities. Both involve trust-based relationships and are intended to help clients build their skills and capabilities. Both rely on feedback, assessment, and observation of clients. Both use dialogue as a primary tool. As part of dialogue, the coach or therapist must listen well, know how to ask insightful questions, know when and how to offer suggestions or advice, and know how to synthesize key points in the dialogue and identify or create memorable insights. Finally, though Marshall Goldsmith might disagree with us, both depend on insights from various parts of clients' lives (including the past) to help them better understand themselves, their patterns of behavior, their options, and their roadblocks. In therapy, questions about the past might include "When was the first time you remember feeling this way? How did you get along with your older sister? How would you describe your parents' relationship?" In coaching, questions about the past are typically different: "How have you handled this kind of situation before? What have been your toughest management challenges? Who were your mentors early in your career, and what did you learn from them?" In both coaching and therapy, these kinds of questions are intended to develop a context, to understand the environment and circumstances in which the person works and lives, decides what is important and what's not, and makes decisions that affect not only his or her life but the lives and work of others with whom the person associates.

Coaching is about change, and it's impossible, as Lester Tobias (1996) observes, to foster change unless you get at the root causes of problems and consider the context in which the person works: "To achieve lasting and fundamental change, people need to alter their perspectives, to see things in a new light, or to overcome internal resistances that may be unrecognized and habitual. Therefore, the [coach] needs to help the person get to root causes, whether the apparent problem is organizational or one of personal style" (p. 88). If coaching and therapy occupy opposite ends of a continuum, it's in the middle of that continuum that distinctions become blurry. Ultimately, maintaining distinctions between them is the fundamental ethical obligation for the coaching practitioner. The coach must be unhesitant about where to draw the line between coaching and therapy and must exercise appropriate tact and persuasiveness to direct a client to therapy, particularly in situations where the surfacing of issues in coaching pushes the client into dangerous psychological territory. A clearer distinction between coaching and therapy lies in the very different contexts that bring one person into therapy and another into coaching.

THE CONTEXTS OF COACHING

Clients' openness and willingness to explore their attitudes, perspectives, behaviors, decisions, alternatives, and operational effectiveness are shaped by the context in which coaching occurs. The most important element of the coaching context is the client's perspective, which includes the client's situation, the organizational context, the urgency of the need, the client's psychological readiness, the client's view of and respect for the coach, and the client's expectations.

The Client's Situation

Our research on coaching effectiveness told us repeatedly that coaches don't pay enough attention to the most important contextual element of coaching—the client's situation. It's not that coaches don't understand objectively what makes up the client's situation; it's that they don't fully appreciate and don't fully probe the subjective meanings the client attaches to that situation or the nuances of the organizational environment in which the client works, including the political, social, and cultural environment of the executive's organization. From an organizational standpoint, some cultures not only support personal and professional development (including coaching), they practically demand it. Other cultures pay lip service to development, even if they invest in it. Some treat coaching, and other forms of professional development, as just that—development, particularly at key transition points in an executive's career. Some can conceive of coaching only as a form of remediation, a last-ditch effort to save someone the company has invested too much in to lose. Still others do not invest the resources required to develop executives and almost openly disdain coaching. Clearly, the more supportive the organization is, the more likely it is that clients will be open to and accepting of coaching help.

From an individual standpoint, clients bring all sorts of predispositions and presuppositions to coaching, even in the most supportive business environments. Most coaches collect basic information about the client's background, such as level of education, years with the company, employment history, interests, family, and so forth. These form the safe territory for introductory conversation. On deeper levels, though, the client's situation has to do with understanding the person the client becomes at work and how the work environment tends to construct that person. It includes understanding how factors such as gender, age, race, social class, ethnicity, nationality, and position define the client and the client's experiences at work.

For instance, clients who are transitioning into executive positions of increasing responsibility have to manage the persona they must take on—either because the client assumes such a persona is called for or because the organization has expectations about who and what this new executive must be. Relationships with former peers who are now subordinates must be renegotiated. Former friendships can become strained as the new executive holds power that the old colleague does not. As much as there is a sense of achievement in these kinds of career shifts, there is just as often a sense of loss. Too frequently, new executives discover these issues only in hindsight and only after costly mistakes have been made. Coaching executives through such a transition phase means a heavy emphasis for both parties on understanding the context: helping clients distinguish pressures that are self-imposed from those that are imposed from without in order to evaluate those pressures and find the self who is both personally authentic and publicly effective.

THE ORGANIZATIONAL CONTEXT

Since one of the key factors that distinguishes coaching from therapy is that coaching is a business relationship, coaches must understand the business or organizational context in which their clients work. This involves knowing about the business itself: its history, current issues and problems, key people and their expectations, and the nature of their relationship with the client. In "Business-Linked Executive Development: Coaching Senior Executives," Thomas Saporito (1996) argues that coaches need to investigate three areas before the coaching relationship begins: 1) the "organizational imperatives" that shape the expectations for the executive, 2) the "success factors" that define what the client must do to fulfill these expectations, and 3) the "personal qualities and behaviors" that will be required to achieve these success factors (pp. 96–103). Some of this information can be obtained by reviewing the organization's website, annual reports, and other documents; some will come from interviews with human resource managers and those more directly involved in working with the client.

It is also important to understand the dynamics of power in the organization: who has it, how it is shared (or not), how power is gained or lost, and how it is exercised to accomplish the organization's work. Terry has written extensively about this subject in his book *The Elements of Power* (2011). In the chapter on power in organizations, he observes, "Five forces modulate the distribution of power in organizations: the formal authority structure of the organization, the prevailing leadership paradigm, the environment in which the organization operates, the informal working processes of the organization, and the ambitions and allegiances of individual members" (218). To truly appreciate the context in which an executive operates, it is imperative to understand how much power he or she has, where that power comes from, and how the executive is or should be using it to lead and influence others effectively.

Understanding the client in the context of the organization makes it possible to frame the coaching engagement more broadly than simply as a one-on-one relationship between coach and client. Lester Tobias (1996) observes that

> *when coaching is done in isolation, the absence of organizational context will inevitably limit the coach's perspectives on the presenting problem. Furthermore, it may also limit the coach's options regarding interventions. . . . It is essential for the coach to keep in mind that relevant others may not only be potentially part of the solution, but that they are usually directly or indirectly part of the problem. However maladaptive an individual's behavior may be, it never occurs in a vacuum, even though the more outrageous the behavior is, the more people will attribute it to the individual's personality.* (pp. 87–95)

Coaching may very well include other members of the organization so that issues such as unnecessary bureaucratic obstacles, unrealistic expectations, scapegoating, and other tensions that occur within relationships can be addressed. But such problems cannot be named, let alone addressed, unless the coach understands the larger organizational context in which the client works.

The Urgency of the Need

One of the most important psychological contexts is the client's sense of urgency and the threat of consequences or the benefits of success. That sense of urgency may arise from intrinsic needs or dissatisfactions or from extrinsic fears (of consequences) or hopes (for success). Psychological research suggests that intrinsic motives are more powerful and longer lasting, but extrinsic drivers can also be powerful. In any case, it's important for executive coaches to understand what motivates the client and whether the client feels that the need for coaching is urgent.

The Client's Psychological Readiness

We said earlier that the successful outcome of coaching depends in part on the client's openness and willingness to explore. While environmental factors certainly affect a person's openness, the most important factors are psychological. How mature is the client? In this case, *maturity* refers to the person's self-acceptance, willingness to admit mistakes, and openness to feedback. Each of us builds a self-concept, which Freud referred to as the *ego*, through which we define who we are. In less-mature people, that ego can be fragile and tends to be defended heavily. That's why some people won't admit that they are wrong or have made a mistake—to them, admitting error is an assault on their ego construct. Maturity tends to soften the edges as people develop a more realistic view of themselves and come to accept their foibles and weaknesses as part of their total being. With maturity come grace and forgiveness—toward oneself as well as others.

Central to this concept of maturity is the willingness to be vulnerable and imperfect, to acknowledge that one can improve, which leads to an awareness and acceptance of the need to change. Many executives never reach this point. They fear appearing imperfect, so they blame failures on others or on circumstances beyond their control and never admit to themselves or others that they need help or could do better and would benefit from coaching. These executives remind us of the observation attributed to Benjamin Franklin: "He that won't be counseled can't be helped."

Another aspect of maturity is *resilience*—the ability to rebound, pick oneself up, and march on despite adversity, roadblocks, criticism, and failure. In a study of resilience, Diane Coutu (2002) defines it as "the skill and the capacity to be robust under conditions of enormous stress and change" (p. 52). Resilient people share three characteristics: "an ability to face reality as it is, not as one thinks or wishes it should be; deeply rooted beliefs, sometimes reinforced by well-articulated values, that sustain a conviction that life has meaning; and the capacity to improvise with whatever is at hand, in particular to call on resources within oneself in unique and creative ways" (p. 48). Resilience is important because coaching may require clients to hold the mirror and see aspects of themselves they don't like. They need the ability to rebound from those experiences in order to make progress and stick with the program of change and improvement they have embarked upon. This may all sound familiar. It's what authors Reuven Bar-On, Daniel Goleman, and others have referred to as *emotional intelligence*. An emotionally intelligent adult is emotionally self-aware; is able to manage his or her own emotions, read others' emotions, and use emotion productively; and is good at handling relationships. These psychological resources make emotionally intelligent executives better candidates than others for coaching because they are more open, more responsive to feedback, more motivated to change, more willing to admit their weaknesses, and more willing to accept responsibility for themselves and their behavior. Clearly, executives who lack these psychological resources are not good coaching candidates. No matter how much quality coaching they receive, they are unlikely to change.

The Client's View of and Respect for the Coach

An element of context that coaches often overlook—but clients never do—is the client's view of and respect for the coach. Early in a coaching relationship, clients may grant their coaches the benefit of the doubt, but they remain wary and will decide within the first few meetings whether this coach deserves their trust and whether they find the coach credible and helpful. For a productive coaching relationship to be established, as further explained in the text box "Building Coaching Relationships" on pages 19–20, the coach must earn trust and demonstrate credibility.

The Client's Expectations

Finally, an important element of context is the client's expectations. Clients will define for themselves what is useful in the coaching relationship and what they find helpful about the dialogue. They enter into a coaching relationship with a set of expectations, which may or may not be realistic or clearly articulated. Their expectations are often based on their previous coaching experiences at work (both as coaches and clients), but may also be informed by their experiences as students, athletes, and children. They know how they learn best, how they respond to feedback in its various forms, what they are willing to try, and what is most helpful to them. The best way for coaches to discover their clients' expectations, of course, is to ask them.

It should be obvious how these elements of the context of coaching affect the dialogue between the coach and the client. They govern, among other things, the client's willingness to be open, honest, and candid with the coach; to disclose his feelings; to trust the coach with confidential information; to explore uncomfortable areas; to open new avenues of possibility; and to experiment with new perspectives, ways of thinking, and behaviors. We've been focusing on the elements of the context that relate to clients and their environment and perspective, but there are also important contextual elements from the coach's perspective.

BUILDING COACHING RELATIONSHIPS

Good coaching relationships are made, not born. You build them by establishing trust with people who want you to coach them. That trust usually consists of confidence, caring, and acceptance:

• Clients must have confidence in your coaching—that you know what you're talking about, that you are credible and experienced, that your guidance will be accurate and helpful, and that your coaching will help them.

• Clients must believe that you care about them—that you have their best interests at heart, that you care about them as human beings, and that your desire to help them is sincere.

• Clients must have confidence that you will not judge them—that you accept them for who they are.

You build confidence by being knowledgeable and resourceful, by walking your talk, and by being genuine. Ironically, admitting that you don't know something and admitting when you're wrong build credibility because they show that you're human and fallible. Pretending that you know everything, on the other hand, destroys credibility and confidence.

You show caring by being available, by taking an active interest in how clients are doing, by offering to help rather than waiting to be asked. Of course, you must maintain confidences, refrain from judgment or evaluation except in the spirit of being helpful, and follow through with the people you're coaching over a long period. Otherwise, your "caring" will seem transactional and superficial. You accept clients and suspend judgment by monitoring carefully the tendency to judge, which may operate in other domains of your life, in order to convey what Carl Rogers called "unconditional positive regard." No matter how poor people's performance, you as their coach nonetheless regard them positively as human beings. Suspending judgment is difficult because many people, especially in management positions, are trained to be judgmental. But if you can't set judgment aside during coaching, you won't be an effective coach. Interestingly, our research on coaching effectiveness indicates that many coaches do not suspend judgment or demonstrate the degree of caring that inspires trust.

• Forty percent of clients say that their coaches are occasionally judgmental.

• Thirty-one percent of clients say that their coach is impatient and hurries to finish the coaching.

• Twenty-five percent say that their coach does not always recognize either excellent performance or superior effort, even if it fails.

Effective coaching requires the right attitude about coaching and the right temperament. If people trust you, if they feel that you have their best interests at heart, if they find you credible, and if you take the time to be helpful to them, then you are more likely to develop an effective coaching relationship.

The Coach's Relationship with the Client

If the coach has an existing relationship with the client, then the dialogue will be informed by the nature of that relationship and the history of interactions between the two people. As a dialogue unfolds, it creates its own interactional history—a record, in each person's memory if not in written form, of the ideas, insights, discussions, disagreements, and developments that have occurred since the dialogue began. Even if the coach and client have not previously had a coaching relationship, if they have known and worked with each other in any capacity, the dialogue will be affected by what each person knows about the other and what has transpired between them. That history can help or hinder the coaching process, so it's worth thinking about what impact the existing relationship might have.

The Coach's Experience as a Coach

The coach also brings to the dialogue her experience as a coach and the history of all previous coaching experiences—the memories of former and other current clients, reflections on what worked and what didn't, and a perspective on how to approach coaching problems and challenges. A coach's experience creates a kind of expert system for her, which she draws upon when she coaches any client. The richer and deeper her experience, the more likely she is to have seen similar issues before, and she will remember how she helped previous clients with those issues. New coaches have to rely more on their instincts, education, and training; more experienced coaches rely on their internal expert system. This expert system is a useful shortcut, but it can also be a straitjacket if it forces you to see all similar problems the same way or assume that a new client's problems are identical to what you've seen dozens of times before. Our brain forms new neural pathways when we encounter new problems and develop new solutions. When we see similar problems, we are channeled toward similar solutions. If those solutions work, the neural pathways that channeled us toward them are reinforced and strengthened. This phenomenon has been called *hardening of the categories*, and it's why older, more experienced professionals are typically less creative than their younger, less experienced counterparts. Older professionals have more robust expert systems, but they tend to be less adept at trying new things or seeing problems from a completely different perspective.

So a coach's experience creates a great deal of the context in which she coaches. If she's careful, she uses her experience to make informed assumptions about each new client and new set of issues or challenges, but she also tests those assumptions and remains open to forming new opinions, exploring new avenues, and finding new solutions to problems that, within each client's unique context, are generally new to the client.

The Coach's Mandate as a Coach

If the coach has been hired or asked to provide coaching by someone other than the client, then the coach will have an assignment—along with some preconceptions about the nature of the problem and expectations regarding the desired outcomes of the coaching. For instance, the context could be that the client is part of a high-potential program in the company, and the coaching is being provided to help the client assess his skills and build them in areas that will help prepare him for his next assignment. Or the context could be that the client manages a division of the company and is in danger of derailing because she drives people relentlessly and is insensitive to their needs. She may not be aware that she's at risk of derailment, but it would not be unusual for the human resources director who arranged for coaching to tell her coach of the risk—but not want the client to be aware of it.

In our own coaching experiences, few circumstances make us more uncomfortable than having a mandate from a company that the client is not fully aware of. However, for various reasons, companies sometimes find it necessary to arrange for coaching without being totally candid with the client about the reasons for it or the consequences to the client if the coaching doesn't help. We have been in situations where we wished there had been more candor and where, frankly, the company's unwillingness to be candid was a symptom of an underlying systemic issue in the organization. But resolving a company's systemic issues is generally not feasible. If you can be helpful to clients, even though the company is not being candid with them, then you are still performing a useful service, however uncomfortable you might be with the context in which the coaching is taking place.

The Coach's Expertise

If the coach is an expert in the subject being discussed with the client, it is impossible not to bring that expert perspective into the dialogue In fact, some coaches are appointed on the basis of their experience and expertise in particular business areas or specific levels of management as well as their requisite coaching skills. This is not to say that the coach should start dispensing advice—merely that having an expert perspective will affect how the coach listens, interprets information, frames questions, and provides help. In our capacity as coaching providers, we have had a number of cases in which the client company has specified that the coach must, for instance, be someone with broad experience in manufacturing processes, or consumer retail operations, or regional sales force management. Those kinds of requirements are one reason why we do not believe that executive coaches must be licensed psychologists (as Steven Berglas insists). It would be extraordinarily rare to find a practicing psychologist who also has decades of experience in consumer retail operations.

The Coach's Objectivity

Finally, an important element of the context is the coach's degree of objectivity. Coaches who can avoid projecting themselves into the situation are generally better coaches because they can remain objective enough to recognize what is happening in the dialogue and steer it in a productive direction. Coaches who lose that objectivity often become too immersed in the content of the dialogue to recognize when it's becoming unproductive or is heading in the wrong direction.

Good coaches remain acutely aware of the context all the time. They take care to understand the departure point and establish the right context at the beginning of the coaching process. They try to understand how the context affects the client's openness and willingness to explore. They also use the context to help shape the dialogue as coaching continues. Even bad coaches are aware of the context, but they are often incapable of managing it or using it to their and the client's advantage. Instead, the context can become an impediment ("The culture doesn't support the kinds of changes he needs to make") or an excuse for lackluster results ("She wasn't willing to listen to feedback").

Beyond knowing and using the context effectively, coaches must be skilled at guiding and shaping the dialogue. As we said earlier, the two primary factors that determine whether executive coaching will be effective are the client's openness and willingness to explore and the coach's skillfulness in guiding the dialogue. The next chapter is the first of several that explore the special nature of the coaching dialogue.

2

Negotiating Expectations

Have a kickoff meeting with each person to be coached to get a common understanding of needs and expectations.

Try to determine the aspirations of the people you are coaching so that you can tailor your coaching to fit in with their goals.

Review each team member's goals for development and develop a game plan to get there. We've had discussions, but neither party committed to a real plan.

SUGGESTIONS TO COACHES FROM THE "COACHING EFFECTIVENESS SURVEY," KORN/FERRY INTERNATIONAL

I n the introduction, we described the two-minds model, which illustrates the differences in perspectives between coaches and clients. When these perspectives are not aligned, coaches risk providing the wrong kind of coaching on the wrong issues at the wrong time and never building the kind of trust and confidence essential in a coaching relationship. When, as a coach, you negotiate expectations for the engagement, you are trying to understand the client's perspective and share your own so that you develop a mutual understanding of the coaching process, the client's needs, and the desired outcomes. As our opening quotations suggest, coaches need to spend more time exploring what clients expect and reaching agreement on processes and outcomes. In chapter 1, we discussed the contexts of coaching. In effect, setting expectations means applying multiple contexts and establishing the conditions in which the coaching will occur.

Throughout the book, we focus on the mindset of the coach, but this is a good place to raise some cautionary flags about the mindset of the client. While many clients will welcome the coach's guidance and appreciate the vote of confidence that the organization's investment in the coaching signifies, coaching is not something that appears risk free to many clients. For some, coaching may suggest failure to succeed on one's own or may even conjure up memories of visits to the principal's office. For others, developing intimacy with a coach as a thought partner or trusted advisor will take time and will come only as the client gains confidence that the coach can reliably contribute to both process and context. The client's mindset is not a static thing; it will change as the relationship matures. Coaches who adapt successfully to new clients take time at the outset to explore the client's frame of mind about coaching. They monitor and adjust to changes throughout the engagement.

The two-minds model that we discussed in the introduction nicely illustrates the differences in perspective between coach and client, but in the real world even this seemingly complicated model is too simplistic because it ignores the organizational context in which coaching generally occurs. In large, sophisticated companies with well-established systems and procedures for developing people, the organization itself may have expectations about coaching that influence and even specify elements of the coaching process, such as when and how coaching will be conducted, how coaching fits in with the overall human development process, and how coaching effectiveness will be measured. Expectation setting, therefore, can involve not only the coach and the client but others in the organization who have a stake in the coaching process and its outcomes. Sometimes the goals and outcomes of coaching are syndicated with the client's manager, the relevant human resources manager, and members of a leadership development task force or development group that oversees leadership development in the company. When CEOs are being coached, the stakeholder group may include the board of directors.

Negotiating expectations means bringing the coach's and client's expectations into alignment within the organizational context in which the coaching is occurring. This is fundamental to our concept of adaptive coaching—starting where the client is and continuously adapting to his or her needs or preferences. While this may sound complicated, in practice it's a simple matter of knowing how to ask the right questions and taking the time to do so.

Expectation setting, which should occur at the very beginning of the coaching process, is an activity that we often refer to as *contracting*. The word *contracting* makes this part of the process seem very formal, but it doesn't need to be. Contracting can be as simple as saying, "What kind of help would you like?" The purpose is to reach a mutual understanding of what will most benefit the client and to ensure that you understand the client's needs and expectations from the coaching process. If you clarify the client's expectations about the kind of coaching you are going to provide, then you can be reasonably certain that you are being most helpful to him or her. If you aren't explicit about the agreement, then you run the very real risk of doing the wrong kind of coaching, which will frustrate both of you.

THE ELEMENTS OF THE CONTRACT

Some coaches prefer formal, written contracts or agreements with their clients. We tend to be more informal in our approach to coaching, but it isn't a bad idea to write down what you've agreed to and then send your statement to the client—or ask the client to write down the agreements and send them to you. Coaching is a jointly constructed journey, and mutually agreeing to the expectations up front is a reasonable and collaborative way to ensure that everyone involved clearly understands how the process will work. Furthermore, it's best to be explicit about these matters to reduce the risk that differing, unspoken assumptions on anyone's part will later derail the process or destroy trust.

Clearly, coaching contracts can include anything coaches and clients wish to include. The next several pages identify a range of issues and questions that should be addressed and resolved early in the relationship, whether they are explicitly named in the coaching contract or discussed in an initial meeting. What is the coaching about? Is its purpose performance improvement, leadership development, skill building, career development, life coaching, or problem resolution? In many cases, clients will be asking for coaching and should have a clear sense of why they want help. Sometimes, however, their organization decides they need coaching, either to resolve problems or develop their skills. In this case, determining the purpose of the coaching may be tricky, especially if the clients don't know why the coach is there, haven't asked for help, or are unclear or resentful about the fact that "help has arrived."

Goals

What are the goals of the coaching? We are referring here to the intended outcomes of the coaching. If the coaching succeeds, what will that mean? What will be different or better? The more specific you can be about the outcomes, the more focused the coaching is likely to be. Sometimes the goals may not really be clear until the coaching process has begun and the client has discovered enough to know what the desired outcomes should be. In some of our coaching engagements, the goals have been negotiated, in effect, among the coach, the client, the client's manager, and the relevant HR manager. When organizations hire external coaches, they frequently insist on accountability for the process, and they often have ideas about how the clients should change. The coaching is therefore goal driven not only from the client's perspective but also from the organization's perspective, and the coaching will not be deemed successful unless the organization feels that its goals have been accomplished. The coach's job becomes one of balancing organizational expectations with the client's needs and preferences.

Type of Coaching

What kind of coaching does the client want (directive or nondirective)? What would be most helpful to the client: advice, counsel, teaching, feedback, a sounding board? It's often good to ask simple questions about coaching preference, such as "How can I be most helpful to you?" or "What kind of coaching has worked best for you in the past?" Clients typically have very individual preferences—no matter what the coach wants to do or what the organization prefers. Only the client can really determine what works for him or her, and frequently this must be discovered through trial and error (and ongoing process checking) as the coaching begins—hence another meaning for our term *adaptive coaching*: adapting occurs in situ as both coach and client discover what works best.

Client Reservations

What reservations, if any, does the client have about engaging in coaching? Is the client a reluctant participant, perhaps simply carrying out an order from above or maintaining skepticism about what the coaching can achieve? If the client is receiving coaching to remedy performance problems, does she agree that these are the problems that need to be solved? Does the client feel she is being treated fairly by the organization or singled out? Does the client suspect that there may be a hidden agenda within the organization, such as the coaching being a screen for a planned termination? Has the client had prior experiences with coaching that were unsatisfactory? If the client has previously participated in psychological counseling, does he understand the difference between that and coaching?

Focus

What will be the focus of the coaching (tasks or skills the client needs to learn or broader career, program, or even life matters)? Again, this may not be clear at the beginning, and the client's expectations may change as you go. Often coaching begins with a specific task focus and moves into other areas as the dialogue advances and coach and client discover more about the real issues and needs.

Meeting Frequency

When and how often should meetings occur? Does the client want programmatic or circumstantial coaching? How frequently? How regularly? There may be some real-world constraints on what is possible because of work schedules, conflicts, sudden crises, and so on. Our experience is that this changes, too, as the process evolves. Generally, clients need more time at the beginning of the coaching process and less time later.

Meeting Location

Where should the meetings occur? This seems like an innocuous question, but the answer has potentially large ramifications. Do the topics being discussed require privacy? Should others in the organization know that the client has a coach? Does the intended location offer the right resources? The right atmosphere? Does coaching via telephone or e-mail convey the appropriate level of gravity? Does it allow the coach to observe the client— to know the client sufficiently—and to interact at the necessary level of intensity?

Other People

Who else might be involved? Who else should the coach talk to or get information from? Besides the client, are there any key stakeholders in this process? People who should know about or participate in the coaching? People whose feedback is crucial? Are these sources of information accept-able to the client? Are the sources reliable?

Commitments

What commitments are both coach and client expected to keep? For example, are both committed to being on time? To completing the process? To doing the homework (if there is any)? To being forthright and candid with one another? To saying when something isn't working? To maintaining confidences? To being accountable to any third parties that are involved?

Confidentiality

To what extent is the coaching confidential? Should anyone other than the coach and client be privy to the coaching process, discoveries, and outcomes? These questions are not as simple as they may appear. In our coaching, we generally argue that the goals and outcomes of the coaching process, along with the personal development plan, should not be confidential because of the need for accountability and reporting back to the sponsoring organization. However, any personal information or discussions that arise must be kept in confidence. Furthermore, if we promise confidentiality to anyone, we keep it. Generally, we do confidential interviews with people the client works with, for instance. We promise confidentiality so that people will be candid with us, but this means we can't share what we learn from them except in an aggregate sense (summarizing to the client, for instance, what we learned from all the confidential interviews).

Measurement and Accountability

How will you measure success? To what degree are the coach and client accountable for the outcomes? What are the organization's expectations? What does the client expect? To whom, ultimately, are coach and client ac-countable? The measurement part of the process is often neglected because it is difficult to measure progress—although it is easier in a coaching situation than it is in therapy. If 360-degree surveys, employee satisfaction or climate surveys, or other instruments are used, then pre- and post-testing can be an effective means of measuring progress. It is important to measure behavioral change (as observed by people the client works with) and achievement of the coaching objectives, as well. It is critical to determine the measures up front. Why? This helps establish accountability for results; it is a motivator (clients want to succeed); it sets a clear path forward, with clear change expectations; it provides a focus for both the client and the coach; and it helps the coach gauge progress.

Information Gathering

How will the coach gather information? With 360-degree assessments? Through psychological assessments? Using performance data? From interviews with people the client works with? By observing the client during performances? Through reviews of the client's work?

Information Sharing

What will the client agree to share with the coach (e.g., previous performance reviews, employee or customer satisfaction survey reports, 360-degree survey results)? Coaches typically have a preferred set of diagnostic tools like the ones mentioned that help them understand the client, diagnose the client's needs, assess the client's performance, and perform reality checks on the client's perceptions. Clearly, the client needs to understand what the coach would prefer to use, but this must also be negotiated. The client may be averse to certain types of assessment or may already have completed some of these assessments. Or the organization may prefer to use its own assessments and provide data rather than have the data gathered again. Part of the adaptive process is knowing what the client and the organization expect and then agreeing on tools that will give coaches what they need and will be acceptable to the client and the organization.

Client Preparation

What should the client do to prepare for coaching? What should the client bring to the sessions? The coach may have some ideas about what clients can or should do, such as reviewing their previous performance reviews, 360-degree surveys, or other assessment reports; thinking about what they want to get out of the coaching and writing their goals; preparing a personal vision statement; and so on. However, coaches should also ask their clients, "What would help you prepare for this coaching?" Some clients like to write out a list of questions for the coach.

Coach Preparation

What will the coach do to prepare, and what will the coach bring to the sessions? The coach should share what she normally does and how she prepares and should make sure that the client is comfortable with her methods.

Communication Outside the Coaching Relationship

Will the coach's role extend beyond the one-on-one relationship with the client? Sometimes coaches are able to uncover organizational problems that undermine the client's effectiveness. A coaching engagement may carry the expectation that the coach will convey these perceptions to the leadership group. Or a coach may feel compelled to communicate a view of problems that are beyond the capacity of the client to address. These issues are not obvious at the outset, but if they crop up, the coach's actions should be carefully negotiated with the client so as not to jeopardize confidentiality, place the client at risk, or undermine trust.

Work Between Sessions

Will the client be expected to do anything between meetings with the coach? Typically, yes. Often the coach gives the client some "homework," such as keeping a log, writing a summary, developing a presentation, working with others in the organization to identify problem behaviors, trying out new behaviors, and so on. Good coaches have a repertoire of exercises and self-development tools that clients can use in the areas they need to work on. The expectation of doing homework between meetings should be established early. We have found that very few clients resist doing these kinds of exercises unless they seem juvenile, irrelevant, or pointless. The right self-discovery or skill-building exercises, some of which we will describe later are engaging to most people because they help them learn more about themselves.

Process Checks

How and when should you do process checks along the way? We will talk further about process checks, but we want to mention here that they are "time-outs" from the coaching content in order to reflect on the coaching process. You don't have to schedule process checks formally, but it's important to remind clients that they should be thinking about whether the process is working for them or not, and they have an obligation to tell the coach if the coach is doing something that is not working.

Ending the Coaching Relationship

When will the coaching relationship end? It's a good idea to consider how long the coaching relationship might last. You can always cut it short or extend it, depending on how the process is going, but it's good early on to think about how to wrap up the coaching and move on. For one thing, this gives clients an expectation of closure (this is not an open-ended process; I have goals to meet by a finite time in the future).

You may not be able to answer all the questions we've just raised in an opening discussion with clients, but they are all relevant and should be addressed at some point as early as possible in the coaching process. Clearly, it's okay to revisit decisions you have made as both of you learn more about each other and as the client's expectations evolve and his needs become clearer.

AN EXAMPLE OF NEGOTIATING EXPECTATIONS

The coaching dialogue that follows allows you to see how the process of negotiating expectations works in practice. The dialogue includes some poor responses from the coach and explains in brackets why these responses are ineffective, followed by a better response. Also included are some annotations about the coaching dialogue that illustrate good coaching practices. In this example, the coach and the client work for the same company but do not work together. The coach is a midlevel manager in the engineering design group, and the client is a young engineer who works in the field with customers. The client has recently become a team leader and aspires to manage large projects but lacks management experience. The client is part of the company's high-potential program and has been encouraged to seek coaching as part of a broader development program.

Coach   I understand you wanted some coaching on managing projects.

Client   No, well, I do, yeah, but I'm not a project manager yet. I've just been made a team leader in our implementations group, and I've never managed people or projects before. Or teams. I mean, a lot of it seems intuitively obvious, but in the spirit of "I don't know what I don't know," I wanted to get some help. It's important that I do this right, and I already see some problems I'm not sure how to handle.

Some wrong coach responses:

Coach   Well, here are my rules of thumb on management. First . . . [Here, the coach is jumping in to solve the problem far too early. Besides, just listing best practices is one of the least effective ways to help people grow.]

Coach   What would you like to know about managing teams and projects? [A good question, but it comes too early in the process. There are still many basic expectations to set before delving into content.]

Coach   What problems are you seeing? [Same issue as above. It's too early to go this deep on the problems. Neither the coach nor the client knows enough yet to get into content discussions. The two of them need to figure out how they are going to work together first.]

A right coach response:

Coach   Okay. Well, before we talk about your new role and the problems you're seeing, let's figure out how I can be most helpful to you. Have you had coaching before? [It's usually helpful to know if the client has had coaching and what his or her experiences were. What worked well? What didn't?]

Client Not formally. My manager's always been available to answer questions, and she's clear about what she expects and how she thinks you're doing, but I'm not sure whether that's coaching or just a normal part of management.

Coach How about in previous jobs?

Client Yeah, actually, the first supervisor I had in the company was a good coach. He spent a lot of time showing me how things were done, and we talked a lot about what I wanted to do in my career, what kinds of challenges I should look for, that sort of thing.

Coach And that was useful?

Client Yes.

Coach How so?

Client Well, several ways. I appreciated learning what I needed to do to succeed. Having somebody who's been there lay it out for me was very helpful. I didn't always do things the way he suggested, but I appreciated his perspective. I also liked the fact that he was willing to help me out careerwise. We didn't just talk about how to get the immediate job done. We spent a lot of time talking about my options in the company, where I needed to work, who else I needed to work for, what other things I needed to do, you know.

Coach So you like coaching that focuses on a broader range of issues, not just how to solve a particular technical problem.

Client Yeah.

Coach And you'd like the benefit of a coach's experience in areas where you're developing.

Client That's right.

A misstep on the coach's part:

Coach Okay, then let's get started. [Don't close this discussion too quickly. It's better to keep probing and ensure that you've touched all the bases.]

The right next step:

Coach What else would be helpful to you?

Client I'd like you to give me feedback whenever you can.

Coach	I'd be happy to do that, but we don't work together, so the opportunities for me to observe you are likely to be limited. Would you be willing to share your performance reviews with me?
Client	Sure.
Coach	And any other feedback you get?
Client	Yeah, but, look, I also want to know what you think. One of the reasons I asked for you as a coach is because you're so good at what I need.
Coach	Fair enough, and I want to help you, but we need to be realistic about how much time I can devote to the coaching. Observing you leading your team is something I can do now and then but not regularly.
Client	All right. That's fair.
Coach	Maybe I could also talk to your manager from time to time and get her perspective. Would that be all right?
Client	Yeah. We'd just have to let her know what we're doing.
Coach	(nodding) I'll be happy to talk to her about it. Who else could give me some insights on how you're doing?
Client	The people I'm managing, for sure. And the other team leaders.
Coach	What about customers?
Client	Yeah, the ones I work with most of the time. They would have a good perspective, maybe not so much on team leadership but certainly on how we're serving them.
Coach	I'd like to be able to talk to all those people now and then and get their insights.
Client	Sure.
Coach	Confidentially, of course. If what they tell me is in confidence, they are more likely to be completely candid, which is what we want, right?
Client	Absolutely. But then how will I know how I'm doing and if I should be doing anything differently?
Coach	I'll summarize what I hear and offer suggestions, if that would be helpful.
Client	Yeah, great.
Coach	As we get going, I would like you to notify anyone else I might talk to that I might call them to ask for their observations of you.

You should tell them that it's okay to talk to me and that they should be candid.

Client Okay.

Coach What else would be helpful? [Again, the "What else?" question is very powerful.]

Client I guess I'd like your ideas on how to be an effective team leader.

Coach You sound a bit hesitant about that. [Listen carefully for subtleties in speech or nonverbal expressions indicating that the speaker means something other than what he or she is saying.]

Client No, I *really* do want your ideas. It's just that I don't feel like I need to start at square one. You know, I've worked with some really good managers. I've seen what they do. I think, for the most part, I have a sense of what I should be doing.

Coach That's right. You said much of it seemed intuitively obvious.

Client Right. I think it is, but I'd like to be able to ask for help when something happens that I'm not sure how to handle.

Coach Okay.

Client And I'd like to do some periodic checkups, just talk about how things are going, what issues I'm seeing, how I'm handling them, that sort of thing.

Coach Okay. Like everybody else around here, my time is limited, but I could meet with you once a month or so. Would that work?

Client That would be great. And if I have problems in the meantime, I could call you.

Coach Feel free to call anytime. Just leave a voicemail if I'm not in my office and I'll get back to you. So let's check calendars. Wednesdays or Fridays are probably best for me.

Client How about Friday afternoons? They're usually lighter.

Coach I have a standing meeting at 2:00 every Friday, but I could meet with you at 3:30 or 4:00. How about the first Friday of every month at 4:00?

Client I'll put it on my calendar.

Coach Why don't we meet in your office? That way, I can see your operation and get a better sense of your people and the things you're working on. [Nailing down the logistics is important because it makes the process more concrete and real.]

Client That sounds good.

Coach There are a few more things we might want to touch on before we get started. I usually find it helpful to begin with the end in mind, so as we get our feet on the ground here, it would be useful to set some goals.

Client Makes sense.

Coach Yeah, and it's good project management, by the way. So let's try to reach a point where we can agree on what you're trying to accomplish, and let's set a time frame for achieving those goals. Does that work for you? [The coach makes a small but important teaching point. Often, one of the best ways to teach is to model the principle and then explicitly point it out.]

Client Yeah. Do you have any idea what those goals should be?

Coach [Option 1] Well, you said you wanted to be a better team leader. Clearly, that's your number one goal. [It's far too early to know this. The real issues may be quite different. Besides, the coach should not cite the goals. That's taking the monkey off the client's back. One key principle of effective coaching is to enable the client to do most of the work.]

Coach [Option 2] Not at this point. I suspect that we'll figure that out as we go. However, it would be useful for you to reflect on that. Maybe you could come to our next meeting with some initial thoughts on your goals for this coaching.

Client Okay. I have a few ideas already, but I'd like to give it more thought.

Coach Great. You might also think about how we'll measure progress and success. What will it look and feel like when we've succeeded? What will that mean? And how will we measure it?

Client Makes sense.

Coach Do you have any other questions or concerns at this point?

Client Will the work we do together be confidential, too, or do you have to let my manager know what we're doing?

Coach You know, I think it would be best for you to share your development plan with her, once we've figured it out, and what the outcomes of the coaching will be when we're finished, but I'm under no obligation to report anything to anybody. So as far as I'm concerned, whatever we talk about is confidential. Does that work for you?

Client Yeah.

Coach By the way, it's important to me that this coaching be useful for you, so I'll be asking you from time to time whether what I'm doing is helpful. If it's not, I'd rather know sooner than later so I can change what I'm doing. This coaching is for your benefit, so you should be vocal about what's working for you and what isn't.

Client Okay.

Coach Great. Well, let me ask you to do one other thing before next time. Would you mind writing up what we talked about this morning and sending it to me in an e-mail?

Client No, not at all.

Coach It would help ensure that we're on the same page. If I think you've left anything out or if I think of anything else, I'll add it and send the message back to you. Let's go back and forth until we both agree on how we want this process to work. That way we're likely to get started on the right foot.

Client I really appreciate it. Thanks for agreeing to help me out.

Coach My pleasure. I'll see you in two weeks. In the meantime, call me if you have any questions.

In the rush to get to solutions, the initial phase of coaching often gets slighted. The client's perception that much of project management is "intuitively obvious" is an indication that the client wants to get on with solving his problem, and it is seductively easy for the coach to follow the client's wishes and jump too quickly to the heart of an ill-defined set of issues. This example illustrates how, by putting on the brakes, the coach is able to help the client clarify his needs and expectations while the coach begins to learn how to work with this particular client. The example also shows the collaborative nature of coaching, as coach and client construct a shared set of expectations ranging from high-level needs to logistics. The coach begins modeling a deliberative style of problem solving that pushes the client to break a big, amorphous problem into more tangible, well-defined specifics.

It's unlikely that the client would walk away from this session feeling that he had wasted his time, even though almost none of the discussion focused on his opening request to get some coaching on project management.

At the beginning of this chapter, we cited comments from clients indicating that they wanted their coaches to do more explicit expectation setting at the beginning of the coaching process. Our research on coaching indicates that this is a significant need. One of the items that clients respond to on the Coaching Effectiveness Survey reads, "At the beginning of coaching, he/she is good at clarifying my expectations and making the coaching process explicit." Of thirty-three items in this part of the survey, clients ranked this as the second lowest. The coaches who took this survey as a self-assessment also ranked this item very low. They recognized that they could be considerably more effective at negotiating expectations.

As you negotiate expectations with clients, they may tell you what they think their issues are and what they need from the coaching—and they may be right. However, in our experience, clients' real needs are almost never apparent at the beginning of the coaching process. Uncovering their real needs requires some exploration, and the tool we use to help us learn what clients really need is the *needs compass*, which we describe in the next chapter.

3

The Needs Compass

Use all interactions to observe people and to think about ways to help them improve their skills and behavior.

Be more open-minded with the people you are coaching (and their ideas). Try to broaden the perspective, take a step back, and take time to reflect.

Ask your coachees more where they see improvement potential by themselves. Match their point of view with your observations and work out an individual development plan with defined tasks, milestones, and feedback loops together with the coachees.
SUGGESTIONS TO COACHES FROM THE "COACHING EFFECTIVENESS SURVEY," KORN/FERRY INTERNATIONAL

How do coaches know what their clients really need? Clients typically begin the coaching process with a sense of what they need from the coaching. They will often say, "Here's why I need coaching," or, "This is the problem I'm dealing with," or, "Here is where I need to be more skilled." However, in our experience, the presenting problem is rarely the real one. As insightful as people might be about themselves, they frequently don't understand what they need, can't acknowledge it to themselves, or can't verbalize it to the coach. Clients tend to present their problems in ways that give them a safe psychological distance. They may oversimplify the problem; they may objectify the problem; they may rationalize the problem; or they may avoid or deny the problem altogether. They may disguise the problem they present until they develop trust in the coaching relationship, or they may misunderstand the problem or even distance themselves from it psychologically.

While the client may not understand the problem, coaches cannot afford to be wrong about their clients' needs. If you work on the wrong problems, you can't help the client. Therefore, it's essential for coaches to identify accurately what is really going on. This chapter is the first of two devoted to this crucial issue. Here we introduce a model for a systematic exploration of information sources about the client—what we call the *needs compass*. Chapter 4 shows how to use these sources of information in the coaching dialogue to discover the client's real needs.

THE NEEDS COMPASS

If you study maps of the Americas from the sixteenth through the eighteenth centuries, what you see is an effort to chart the discoveries of European explorers along with their inferences about what they hadn't yet explored. For about a hundred years, California appears as an island on many of the maps, apparently because the early explorers traveled up inside the Baja peninsula and assumed it continued all the way to the northern Pacific. Sometimes, mapmakers' superstitions and desires show up on the old maps. A 1655 map by French mapmaker Pierre Du Val shows the location of a fabled city of gold and locates Japan just northwest of California. The first widely disseminated map of the world, Abraham Ortelius's 1570 masterpiece, depicts various sea monsters in the Pacific. A 1750 map of what is now the northeastern United States has an elaborate cartouche that shows Native American people supplying raw materials to slaves, who ascend upward to deliver finished goods to the local gentry, who in turn offer the products to a royal figure seated on a throne. As exploration continued, the maps reflected an emerging awareness of how to match the map to the territory. South America, for example, changes from something that looks like a potato to something that represents its actual contours.

We developed our metaphor of the needs compass because we found that the process of discovering and mapping the client's psychological terrain is similar to the journey of exploration reflected in old maps. Facts gradually replace inferences and assumptions, and the more varied the sources of information, the fuller and more accurate the picture becomes. Only the most naïve cartographer, however, would believe that a map is ever a fully accurate representation of a territory. Even today, there are places on the globe that are represented by best guesses on maps. The proportion of the known to the unknown, however, has dramatically increased, making the domain of inference relatively small and the inferences increasingly reliable. The needs compass offers a visual tool for helping coaches remember the four primary domains of information about clients' needs: the coach's observations, the client's perceptions, others' observations, and work products and performance metrics. These four sources of information are like the four poles on a compass, as shown in figure 3. To build a map of the client's needs, the coach must investigate all four poles of this compass.

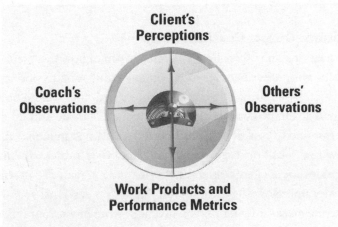

Figure 3: The Needs Compass

THE WEST POLE: THE COACH'S OBSERVATIONS

Your observations are your source of firsthand knowledge about the client. You need to see the client in action, and two sources of observation are available to you: observations of the client on the job and observations of the client during coaching sessions.

Observations on the Job

What to look for depends to some extent on the coaching content, but it's hard to imagine a coaching engagement that cannot be enriched by observing the client at work. You can observe clients to ascertain their needs or to monitor progress and behavioral change. People do tend to be on their best behavior when they're being observed, but you can still learn a lot by watching them perform. Note what your clients do that is effective or ineffective, that positively or negatively affects others, that demonstrates good or poor leadership or management, and so on. Note how they respond to challenges, stress, surprises, problems, and opportunities. Note how they use their time, how they prioritize, and how they make decisions. Note how they influence others, how they use authority, and how they communicate. It's helpful to keep an observation log, noting specifics so you can remind clients of events or incidents later. You should be as unobtrusive as possible (or your presence will seriously skew what you are observing).

Observations During Coaching Sessions

Your relationship with a client is a microcosm of how the client builds relationships with other people, so it's often illuminating to observe how clients relate to you during all your encounters with them. Note how they behave toward you. Be curious about what your clients do and do not do, how they respond to you, how they attempt to control or influence the situation, how they position themselves, and how they present themselves. These are clues about clients' operating styles and interaction patterns with others. Every impression is meaningful. After your sessions, spend some time reflecting on the interaction you just had; write down your reflections in the observation log. Look for themes or patterns indicating what your client needs. Develop a format that allows you to distinguish your observations from the inferences, hypotheses, or judgments you draw from them.

Coaching from Observations

One powerful coaching technique is to make your in-session observations transparent. Clients are often unaware of their behaviors and the impact of those behaviors on others, so a primary coaching technique is to observe and discuss their behaviors during sessions. This can have a powerful effect on clients because most of the people they interact with will not point out their behaviors in real time. In the following example, the coach observes how the client is behaving during the dialogue with the coach.

Coach   Something I keep hearing as I talk to people who work with you is that you have a strong need for control.

Client	I've heard that before. It used to be true, but I've worked on that a lot. I would say that I'm almost too much the other way now.
Coach	You feel like you've relinquished too much control?
Client	Sometimes, yes. Look, I really don't think this is an issue, so why don't we move on.
Coach	Before we do, I have an observation. You're trying to control me right now.
Client	No, I'm not. I just don't think this is important enough to waste time on it.
Coach	Well, it feels to me like you're being controlling. Maybe this is what the other people experience when they work with you, too. It has the feeling of "my way or the highway."

In addition to confronting clients for negative behaviors, you can observe and point out positive behaviors. In the following example, the client has historically had trouble recognizing and rewarding employees.

Client	This has been very helpful. I appreciate the time you've taken to help me.
Coach	No problem. By the way, you just showed me some appreciation.
Client	(a little surprised) I guess I did. It wasn't intentional.
Coach	(laughing) Maybe not, but it seemed effortless. Sometimes, all it takes is a little verbal pat on the back. Appreciation doesn't have to be expensive or time consuming.
Client	You're right. I just don't think to do it.
Coach	But you did now. Why?
Client	(reflecting) I don't know. You've been helpful to me. It just seemed like the right thing to say.
Coach	I think your instincts were good. Now let's apply that to the people in your department. When would a simple "thank you" be the right thing to say?

Beyond the coaching impact, observing clients during sessions enables you to better understand your clients' real needs. You observe with your eyes and your ears, and you look and listen for clues that indicate what the client's real needs are. For further information, beyond observation, see the text box "Transference and Countertransference" on pages 47–48.

THE NORTH POLE: THE CLIENT'S PERCEPTIONS

At the north pole of the needs compass are the client's perceptions. Early mapmakers conceived of four rivers flowing from the North Pole as a way to explain the existence of the oceans. Common sense dictated that the formation of the world flowed down from the top. They were wrong, of course, but the exercise in imagination was nevertheless revealing about what was on their minds. Similarly, the client's perceptions are important not so much for the truths they reveal, but for showing how clients think about themselves and how they present themselves to others: how they construct and communicate their self-image, where they are proud and where they are tentative, where they feel comfortable and where they don't, what they value, how they make and communicate decisions, what façade they've created and who they present it to.

The paradox is that these self-reports are rarely consistent with what others think about the client. Their value lies in helping coach and client develop a baseline for the changes to follow. Coaching is about managing human change, and the only person who can execute change is the client. It's essential, therefore, for coaches to know and clients to articulate their self-perceptions. As a coach, you note those self-perceptions and then return to them later—either to remind clients what they said and how they perceived themselves or to show how far they've come in their self-perceptions: "Sam, we've been working together now for eight months, and I just want to remind you what you said about your leadership skills when we began working together . . ."

Gathering Baseline Data from the Client

Areas of concern for most coaching engagements are typically centered around four topics: leadership, management, interpersonal skills, and teaming. What follows are the kinds of questions coaches can ask to solicit a client's baseline perception of herself. Note that you wouldn't use all of these questions in sequence. This is not intended as a formula but rather as a list of possible questions. Some questions are redundant in order to suggest different wording. The ones you use will depend on the nature and purpose of the coaching.

___

TRANSFERENCE AND COUNTERTRANSFERENCE

The coach's observations are obviously important, but they are only one source of information, and they are not fully objective. Thus, smart coaches do not rely on their own observations alone. Coaches have to beware of their need to shape the client in their own image, so to speak. Even the most detached observer still constructs a subjective view of the client. This perspective is influenced by many things: your worldview; your values; your gender, class, race, and cultural background; your experiences and personal history; your hopes and ambitions; and your unmet needs—all of which contribute inevitably to a psychological phenomenon called countertransference.

To understand countertransference, you have to start with transference. One of the most cogent explanations comes from a mystery novel, *Privileged Information*, by clinical psychologist Steven White (1999). In the following scene, White's main character, Alan Gregory, also a clinical psychologist, explains transference to his attorney, who is representing Gregory in a malpractice case.

> Transference is a component of virtually all human relationships. It's the process of reacting to or responding to someone in a current relationship as if that person had important traits, motivations, behaviors, et cetera, of an important someone from the past. It's often based on purely unconscious motivations, or can be stimulated by traits that the current person may have in common with the important person from the past. The "as if" part is crucial. Transference is an "as if" experience; it's not real, but it feels real to the one experiencing it. (p. 238)

Clients in therapy and in coaching relationships can transfer the feelings and perceptions that White describes to their therapist or coach.

Conversely, therapists and coaches can, and often do, transfer their feelings, attitudes, and perceptions onto their clients through the process known as countertransference. For instance, a coach working with a much younger man or woman may come to think of the client as a son, daughter, niece, nephew, or other family member, and begin acting accordingly toward the client. These thoughts may be entirely unconscious, but they can affect the way the coach relates to, thinks about, and helps the client. Members of the various helping professions learn to cultivate a degree of therapeutic distance from their clients so they can discern these phenomena when they happen and mitigate their effects.

In therapy, it would not be unusual for clients to think of an older therapist as a parent and to start acting out parental fantasies with the therapist. The therapist, aware of the transference, uses it to help the client gain insights. But using transference is very tricky and requires a great deal of training. It's best for coaches to be aware of their own feelings of countertransference, if such feelings occur, and try to set them aside and remain objective. The chapters in part 3 that focus on coaching women and minorities, coaching cross-culturally, and coaching crossgenerationally are designed, among other things, to give coaches the insights they need into these special populations to lessen the possibility of transference or countertransference and to enable coaches to relate to these clients on their own terms.

Psychologist Rachel Harris told us that one of the major ethical challenges in coaching (besides knowing therapeutic limits) is not using clients to meet your own ego needs. According to Harris, "This is probably the biggest way countertransference gets acted out, and these two issues are related. I want to feel like I'm the greatest coach ever, so I'm going to help you resolve all your psychological issues. Or I'm going to make you think that you need me to succeed. Or I'm going to make you emotionally dependent upon me so I can be a hero and rescue you." To avoid confusing your own needs with the client's needs, you must be aware of the countertransference that inevitably occurs in a helping relationship and guard against its effects.

Focusing on Leadership

♦ How would you describe yourself as a leader? What kind of leader are you?

♦ What do you think you do well as a leader? What don't you do well? What would you see as your developmental needs at this point?

♦ If you were to list your strengths in one column and your weaknesses in another, what would you say? [This is a good exercise to ask clients to do during a first meeting.]

♦ I'd like you to think of ten words that best describe you as a leader. Write them down and then rank them. Put the ones that are most descriptive and most relevant at the top.

♦ How would your direct reports describe you as a leader? What would they say you do well and not so well?

♦ What feedback have you received on your leadership? [After the client's initial response ask, "What else?" Keep asking "What else?" until the well is dry. This question is most useful for determining what the client remembers and what is most prominent. We tend to remember longest the events and comments that had the greatest impact on us, so asking people to recall feedback is like asking, "What feedback had the greatest impact on you?" Note whether the first memories of feedback are positive or negative and whether they reflect strengths or weaknesses. If they are negative, then the client may have experienced an emotionally potent failure, been stung by some criticism, felt the criticism was especially accurate, or has heard the feedback more than once and is troubled by it.]

♦ How have you changed as a leader in the past two years? [This is an excellent question that helps uncover the client's perceptions of her growth and development. You should follow it up with: "How haven't you changed?"]

Focusing on Management

♦ How would you describe yourself as a manager? What kind of manager are you?

♦ What are your strengths as a manager? What do you do exceptionally well?

Have you ever been recognized for your management? If so, what was the recognition for?

♦ What are your weaknesses as a manager? What do you tend to neglect or not do well?

♦ What are the top three ways you could improve your management skills?

♦ What would your direct reports say that you should do more of as a manager? What would they say you should do less of? [This type of question is particularly helpful in bridging the gap between the client's perceptions and the perceptions of others. Questions like this push the client into the mindset of direct reports and are often surprisingly difficult for many clients to answer.]

Focusing on Interpersonal Skills

♦ How would you assess your interpersonal skills? What do you do well with other people and what don't you do well?

♦ How comfortable are you in meetings where you do not know many of the attendees? How do you typically handle these situations?

♦ How comfortable are you in social situations where you don't know many people? How do you typically handle these situations?

♦ How sensitive are you to what other people need or want? How empathetic are you? Do you always know what's going on with other people? How they are feeling?

♦ Do you have a good sense of what motivates other people? Your direct reports, for instance? Give me some examples.

♦ How skilled are you at handling conflict? When conflict occurs, what do you typically do?

♦ How influential are you in situations where you have no authority? How do you typically try to influence others? What works for you and what doesn't?

♦ Would you describe yourself as a people person? Why or why not? How well do you get along with people? Which kinds of people do you get along with best and worst?

♦ How well do you communicate with others? What are your favorite forms of communication? Least favorite? In what ways do you communicate well? In what ways do you communicate poorly?

Focusing on Teaming

♦ How would you describe the management team that you are part of? In what ways does this team function well and in what ways poorly?

♦ What role do you play on this team? Formally or informally?

♦ How would you describe yourself as a management team member? How would others describe you?

♦ What overt or covert conflicts exist on this team? Where are the disagreements or tensions? What role do you play in perpetuating or resolving these conflicts?

♦ Regardless of how effective you are now, what are the top three things you could do differently to be a more effective management team member?

Collecting Client Observations Through a Performance Log

Finally, because you will have only limited opportunities to observe clients during performance events, a useful strategy is to ask them to "observe" themselves by being aware of how they are performing. A "performance log" enables the client to keep track of opportunities to enact new behaviors and to record what happened during those instances. The performance log is a useful tool for clients to record when they've done something well or poorly. For instance, you may have a client who is working on controlling anger. You would ask the client to record in the performance log every instance when she became angry: what triggered it, times when the triggering event was there but she was able to control her anger and how she was able to do that, how she felt about the new behavior, and what she could observe about its effects on others. Performance logs are best if used to help clients focus on very specific problems and the new behaviors they are trying to implement, such as becoming more comfortable making client calls, giving recognition, reprimanding employees constructively, or handling particularly difficult people. Performance logs are great tools for helping clients make self-observations on a continuous basis, but they have to be used with clients who need to increase their awareness of behavior or practice skills. Furthermore, you have to be sure your client has sufficient motivation to use the log faithfully. Often, very senior people have the best of intentions but are in actuality too busy for this kind of assignment or might consider it too menial.

THE EAST POLE: OTHERS' OBSERVATIONS

Conventional wisdom in coaching recognizes the value of information from those who work with the client, and it distinguishes two sources of information: data from 360-degree assessments and interview data. Although the case can be made for using one or the other source of information, we argue that they need to be used together for the data to be truly meaningful.

Data from Self-Only and Multi-Rater Assessments

To determine the perspective of others, a plethora of options are available. Assessments can be self-only or multi-rater; they can measure behaviors, competencies, skills, knowledge, abilities, and motivation needed for success in particular roles and business cultures. They can identify strengths and gaps relative to a desired state and propose specific developmental steps to maximize performance. Numerous assessment instruments are available commercially. Korn/Ferry's proprietary assessment tools include the Survey of Influence Effectiveness, Decision Styles®, Voices® 360, Choices Architect®, Learning From Experience™ , Coaching Effectiveness Survey, Behavioral Interviews and Skills Interviews, and viaEdge (a self-only instrument that measures learning agility).

Self-only assessments are useful indicators of a client's self-perceptions but generally do not accurately reflect how others view the client, so multi-rater or 360-degree assessments are helpful tools for creating a holistic picture of the client's behaviors, operating style, and coaching needs. In the past two decades, 360-degree feedback has become much more widespread and accepted. Many multi-rater assessments have achieved impressive levels of validity and reliability, and the use of standard instruments over time helps an organization achieve a consistent picture of performance norms among various groups of employees. However, 360-degree feedback is still not a commonly used tool in some cultures (many Asian and Eastern European countries, for instance) and is sometimes viewed with suspicion. The client's organization must have a culture geared toward professional development in a feedback-rich environment, in which people are expected to be accountable for their performance, listen to their stakeholders, and learn from their successes as well as their mistakes. Otherwise, individuals will not take the process seriously or will sugarcoat their responses because they do not believe that their reports are anonymous or are convinced that the instrument is really being used for evaluative purposes. Some professional services firms, such as McKinsey & Company, and some large, mature firms, such as GE, have feedback-rich environments in which 360-degree assessments are commonplace and accepted.

Where you can use it, 360-degree feedback offers a number of insights for coaching. First, it enables you to compare clients' views of themselves with others' views of them along a number of dimensions. The better survey instruments calibrate the differences in scores so you know which ones are significantly different, which are meaningfully different, and which are not statistically different. The better instruments also provide narrative feedback, so you have qualitative as well as quantitative data.

Second, 360-degree instruments show the patterns revealed in the highest- and lowest-rated skills or traits. Often, these groupings of highest- and lowest-rated skills yield broader insights into the client's needs. Bill W. is an example. On his leadership evaluation, he was rated highest on these behaviors:

- **Giving recognition:** recognizing others for their contributions and celebrating people's accomplishments

- **Acting with integrity:** telling the truth at all times and maintaining the highest ethical standards

- **Encouraging contribution:** actively soliciting others' ideas and using them appropriately to improve results

- **Showing respect toward others:** treating people with respect, regardless of their role or level in the organization

- **Setting high professional standards:** setting high quality and performance standards and helping others achieve them

Bill W. was rated lowest on the following behaviors:

- **Removing barriers:** removing the obstacles and barriers that prevent others from taking action or achieving better results

- **Taking risks:** being willing to take calculated risks and accepting responsibility for the outcomes

- **Being candid with others:** always being honest and straightforward with others, delivering bad news when necessary

- **Challenging others' thinking:** actively challenging assumptions, opinions, and traditions, and encouraging others to seek better solutions

These patterns of highs and lows revealed a person who worked hard at being professional and building harmony but who lacked an entrepreneurial edge. His desire to create a harmonious, respectful working environment overcame his willingness to be hard-nosed and assertive when necessary and blunted his effectiveness as a leader. To help him see this, his coach gave him a simple metaphor to keep in mind. He said, "Bill, you're working so hard at being a 'good boy' that the 'bad boy' in you can never get out. The bad boy takes risks, removes obstacles, is candid with others, and challenges them to think outside the box. The good boy, careful and respectful, engages others and builds a following. You need both—but you also need to know when each side of yourself should dominate at which times."

Third, 360-degree feedback is most useful when it helps clients see significant disparities between their own view of themselves and how others view them. Self-ratings that are significantly lower than others' average ratings can signal self-confidence issues or limiting self-perceptions (e.g., when clients think they are not good at something, they don't try it). Conversely, self-ratings that are significantly higher than others' average ratings can reveal arrogance and egotism, on the one hand, or deceptively inflated views of one's skills, on the other. Clients who rate themselves too low relative to others may not act with enough boldness or take enough risks; clients who rate themselves too high may not know when to seek help from others and may not be sufficiently aware of their limitations or skill-building needs.

Interviews with Respondents

In our experience, 360-degree feedback is useful but not sufficient as a tool for understanding clients' needs. It provides a panoramic view. Its results are sometimes dramatic enough to grab a client's attention. It can point the coach in the right direction, but rarely is it sufficient to permit a complete and accurate diagnosis. Instead, such instruments yield hypotheses to be tested through your interviews with others, your own observations, and your dialogues with the client. The east pole of the needs compass is best understood as the combination of 360-degree feedback with observations from people with whom the client works. These observations represent the human environment. In many cases, co-workers have observed the client far more than the coach has, so they have the deepest and longest-lasting impressions. They are likely to have seen the client at her best and worst. They will know the norms of the client's behavior, as well as her extremes. Furthermore, they are likely to be around later in the coaching process and can offer feedback on progress (or lack thereof). They are the behavioral witnesses to the coaching's success or failure. This means that it is crucial to select the right "others" to talk to.

You need to talk to a number of people in different roles relative to the client, just as with a 360-degree survey. Talk to the client's direct reports (who know what this person is like as a boss), to his peers, to his boss or other senior people, and perhaps to his customers or clients. (Some coaches may even ask to speak to the client's family members, although there are potentially serious unintended consequences to doing that, so we avoid it unless the family is part of the issue and volunteers to provide a perspective.) The point is to see clients from a variety of perspectives. Why? Because many people behave differently toward different stakeholders in their lives. The view from those who work for them (direct reports) may differ from the view of those whose needs they serve (customers). Some leaders treat their bosses and peers well but are dismissive or patronizing toward their staff. Others are conscientious and caring team leaders who don't communicate well to their boss and aren't effective collaborators with peers. You can't really understand a client's needs until you see that person from multiple perspectives, because then you learn how he handles different people at different levels in different situations.

The interviews with others need to be confidential, which means that what the respondents tell you will remain with you. You will not repeat it or share it with the client. Respondents will be more inclined to be open and candid if they know that what they tell you will not go anywhere else. We tell the respondents we are interviewing that we are coaching this person and that she has given us permission to talk confidentially with people she works with. We say that it's important for us to learn where the client has strengths and where she has developmental needs. If they have completed a 360-degree assessment on the client and we have a copy of their responses, we let them know that and say that we may ask them some questions based on their responses to the survey. We are especially interested in why they made the narrative comments they did and why they rated the client low on the lowest-rated skill areas and high on the highest-rated skill areas. We emphasize that the information they provide will not be repeated; however, it will be aggregated with all the other confidential interviews and in that form will be shared as a profile with the client. If people ask if they can see the aggregate profile, we decline because it is confidential between the coach and the client. We don't tell them who else is being interviewed, but at the end of each interview, we do ask them who else they think we should talk to.

The trickiest part of getting observations from others is assuring them that your intentions are honorable and that the information they give you will be used with integrity. It helps them to know that this is part of a developmental process, not an evaluative process, and that the client is being helped, not hurt, by the coaching. It helps them to know that the client is not "in trouble," "going to lose his job," or anything of the sort. It's helpful if the coaching is being done as part of normal executive, leadership, or management development or is otherwise part of a normal development program in the company. It helps, frankly, if the coach is from outside the company, because people may be less forthcoming when the interviewer is from inside the company or, heaven forbid, is the client's boss. In those instances, people are likely to "toe the line" and "play good."

One of the most important characteristics of coaches conducting confidential interviews with people who work with the client is curiosity. You have to continually push for more information, more examples, more detail. What is this person like? How does he make decisions? How does she prioritize? What are her strengths, and how does she use them? What are his weaknesses, and how do they affect him and others? What are the implications of the way this person operates? How has he grown in the past two years? Where will her skills need to be in the next two years? What does this person say he needs, and what does he really need? What would be most helpful to this person?

Curiosity drives a coach to drill deeper, learn more, ask more questions, and form a more complete picture of the client. The following list offers specific kinds of questions and responses that help elicit more information and help coaches assess the validity of what they are hearing.

♦ Can you give me an example of that?

♦ What else was going on when you saw that behavior?

♦ What else did you observe?

♦ Please explain.

♦ Tell me more.

♦ Have you seen that any other time?

♦ What was the effect on the team?

♦ How did you feel about that?

Even with the most systematic use of 360-degree feedback and carefully chosen interviewees, coaches must maintain a degree of skepticism about what they are hearing. You must be suspicious of information from sources that are too far outside the "norm" of everything else you are hearing from respondents. Reports that are too positive or too negative generally indicate that the respondent is not being candid, has a grudge, or feels protective of the client. Reports that are too general indicate that the respondent does not know the client as well as he needs to for the information to be of much use. In rare instances, the client may pressure respondents to give him or her a good report. If you sense that people are not really being forthcoming, you may need to talk to someone who no longer reports to or is no longer under the influence of the client.

Finally, as Lester Tobias (1996) says, "Because the problem is usually described as 'in' the person," these interviews usually provide "a good opportunity to point out the systemic nature of most individual problems or at least to emphasize that amelioration of the problem may necessarily involve the individual's manager or other relevant people in the organization" (p. 88). The others whose observations you get are people who are part of the system in which the client operates. Not only are they sources of information, but they may be part of the problem and part of the solution. So it's important to view their information in the context of an interconnected whole in which the client plays a part. The combination of 360-degree feedback with interview data is powerful. One final way to use these two sources of information together is to know how the person you are interviewing responded to the 360-degree feedback assessment. Obtaining the individual feedback report before the interview helps you structure the interview and cross-check what you are hearing. When you have these two data sources working together, you have successfully navigated the east pole of the needs compass.

It should be clear from the foregoing discussion that the key to successfully navigating the east pole is integrating the various perspectives about the client that you glean from others. In 2008, our global coaching practice identified a pattern of requests from client companies related to the integration of findings from multiple assessment sources. We discovered that meeting these requests was complicated. It involved certification in a number of instruments, a global network of coaches to deliver in many business centers, and a set of resources who are skilled practitioners as well as technical writers with strong detail orientation. We developed a new training approach so that our coaches could skillfully weave a variety of client-owned and third-party assessments. A best practice in this space is not only to use an online 360 and online self-assessment but also to include a verbal 360 with key stakeholders. Coaches then have to bring it all together by identifying common threads among the assessment and interview results, exploring and resolving disparities, and creating a compelling development story. The infrastructure required to do this well includes not only an integrated platform to take the assessment but also writing specialists to ensure the reports are clean, accurate, and consistent. Integrated assessment reports can provide tremendous value to clients, their stakeholders, and the broader talent management organization.

THE SOUTH POLE: WORK PRODUCTS AND PERFORMANCE METRICS

Ultimately, the goal of executive coaching is improved work performance, so an important measure of success and indicator of need is how the client has been performing. The south pole of the needs compass covers the client's work products and performance metrics. Businesses usually have an abundance of performance data on their employees, but these are the guiding questions for using that data for coaching engagements:

♦ What are the organization's expectations of the client? What does he produce, create, or manage?

♦ How is the client's business performance measured? What metrics or standards indicate how well the client is performing?

♦ Looking as far back as relevant, what do these measures indicate about the client's need for improvement?

This last question is the key, of course. The client may not be producing work products quickly enough or with high enough quality, and that may indicate a coaching need. In some cases, the business metrics are simple enough but the needs may be more complex. Terry coached a business unit president, for instance, whose unit was the lowest performing of eight business units in a company. The unit's costs were too high for the revenue it produced, and it had been losing market share for several years. Market conditions contributed to some of the unit's problems, but as Terry and the client examined the situation in more depth, it became apparent that the client's leadership style was largely to blame for the unit's decline. He was not visible enough with his frontline employees and was not spending enough time with key customers. In this case, the outcomes of the coaching were readily measurable as the unit's fortunes improved.

Beyond metrics such as top-line revenue, bottom-line profit, market share growth, and so on, business metrics can also include the kind of data revealed in climate, employee, or pulse surveys, on the one hand, and in customer surveys, on the other. Internal surveys, which go by different names, reveal how employees feel about the organization and various aspects of their employment (morale, the work environment, compensation, fairness, challenge, and so on). These kinds of surveys are good indicators of the effectiveness of the organization's leadership. Customer surveys reveal how the organization and its people and products are being perceived in the marketplace. Whenever we coach for a company that has these kinds of surveys available, we jump at the chance to use them because they reveal a tremendous amount about how the company's leaders and managers are working, how employees or customers feel about the company, and where our coaching clients may have needs.

As our discussion in this chapter suggests, there are numerous sources of information for coaches about what a client needs. The needs compass we have described is a simple framework for remembering the four major sources of information. Experienced coaches invariably use all four sources, but we have seen many less-experienced coaches who rely too much on their own observations alone, or on the clients' perceptions as the principal source, or on quantitative tools without regard for the illuminating effects of others' observations of the client. In our experience, coaches need to consider all four sources of information. None is complete or accurate by itself. Even with information from all four sources, however, you may still not understand clients' real needs.

Dealing with surface behaviors is almost never effective. Imagine a client coming to you and saying, "I need coaching on how to be more of a people person. My staff says I'm too focused on tasks and not enough on people." If you accepted that and offered suggestions on how to be more of a people person, you might give the client a handful of tactics that would make him appear to be more of a people person, but his underlying operating style will not have changed. As time wears on, he will gradually forget or stop using the tactics you gave him, and it will become business as usual. We have seen this happen countless times. The only way to really help this kind of client is to understand the underlying reasons why he focuses more on tasks than on people. Your sources of information may repeatedly tell you that he is insensitive, occasionally abrasive, and fails to encourage or recognize people, but those are symptoms, not causes, and treating the symptoms will not solve the problem. To solve the problem, you have to uncover the client's real needs, and that is the subject of the next chapter.

4

The Real Issues

Listen to all the facts before jumping in with suggestions.

Release your own agenda and take a genuine interest (shown through questioning) in the person you're coaching. Listen carefully and build the discussion to his or her needs.

Don't use the same approach with everyone. Alter it based on what works best for that person.

SUGGESTIONS TO COACHES FROM THE "COACHING EFFECTIVENESS SURVEY," KORN/FERRY INTERNATIONAL

Jan-Olof opened the coaching session and began the process of discovery that would help him understand his client's needs. Terry was supervising him as part of his coach certification and had received permission from the client to sit in on their discussion. Jan-Olof's client was Manuela F., a thirty-one-year-old software engineer who was considered a high-potential professional in her firm. In her high-potential program, Manuela was receiving coaching to assist in her ongoing development as a leader. After the preliminaries in their discussion, Jan-Olof asked about some of the feedback she had received from members of her program team.

Jan-Olof   As I spoke to members of your team, I heard the same thing several times—that you are a very hands-on leader.

Manuela   I think that's fair.

Jan-Olof   I did sense some frustration from people, however. They said you check every detail of their work and frequently stay well into the evening going over the work that was done that day.

Manuela   It's been frustrating for me, too, but the project is heating up. You know, we're only three months from launch, so I hope they're ready for it. If anything, we'll have to work harder.

Jan-Olof Why?

Manuela Because we have to get it right. Too much is at stake.

Jan-Olof So as you look ahead, you see even more late nights.

Manuela I don't see any way around it. I'm responsible for the quality of this work, and it has to be done right.

Jan-Olof I'm getting the sense that you don't delegate very well. Could you delegate some of the oversight you're doing?

Manuela Maybe. But if I have others review the coding, then I will just have to review the reviewers, right? So maybe I should just eliminate the middleman.

Jan-Olof You wouldn't trust others to be as good at reviewing as you are?

Manuela I have some great people working with me, but I have to keep the whole project in my mind. If I lost sight of what the programmers are doing, then I couldn't be sure that everything will come together at the end.

Jan-Olof Okay, well, let's talk more about delegation.

Terry Jan-Olof, let me interrupt here. Do you think you know what the real issue is?

Jan-Olof Yes, I think so.

Terry What is it?

Jan-Olof Manuela is checking every detail of the team's work instead of delegating that to others. She is frustrating the team and working many late nights herself. It's an unsustainable situation.

Terry So the fundamental problem is her unwillingness to delegate.

Jan-Olof Yes, I think so.

Terry Manuela, does that feel right to you? Is this the real problem?

Manuela No.

EXPLORING THE PROBLEM SPACE

In our experience as supervisors and coaches of other coaches, we have found that Jan-Olof's experience is not unusual. Many coaches jump too quickly from preliminary problem identification to solution. In his desire to be helpful, Jan-Olof is like a problem-seeking missile. As soon as he detects a problem, he hones in on it and tries to solve it. In doing so, he is making a rookie coach's mistake: treating effects rather than causes. Consider what Jan-Olof defined as Manuela's problem: she's checking every detail of the team's work, she's not delegating the responsibility for reviewing, she is frustrating the team, and she's working many late nights herself. These are *consequences* or *outcomes* of some underlying problem; they are not the problem itself. Until he understands the root causes, he cannot truly be helpful to her because, like physicians, coaches have to address the disease, not the symptoms.

It's useful to think of the problem solving we do in coaching as it is shown in figure 4. The left side of this figure is the *problem space*; the right side is the *solution space*. Before you can move to the solution space, you have to explore the problem thoroughly. Metaphorically, you need to *open up* the problem space until you have identified the core issues. Only then should you begin exploring the solution space. If you are impatient and leap to the solution space too quickly, as Jan-Olof did, you risk trying to solve the wrong problem or giving superficial advice for superficial issues, as Jan-Olof would have done had he said, "Here are some tips on delegating."

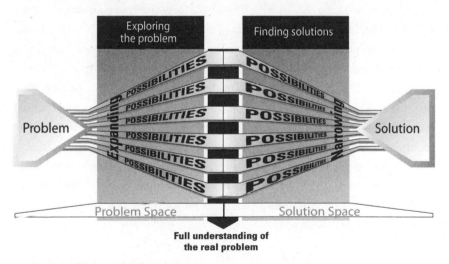

Figure 4: Problem and Solution Space

Clients' real needs emerge through a process of discovery. They are almost never evident from the *presenting problem*, which is what clients may say they need help with when they enter into a coaching relationship, or may come from the data coaches gather prior to coaching, although such data may be very suggestive. The real need is the root of the problem; it is the core issue that must be resolved or addressed for clients to change their behavior. Coaches and clients generally co-discover the real need by forming hypotheses about what the real need might be and then testing those hypotheses by looking for confirming or disconfirming information.

Physicians view symptoms as likely indicators of the underlying malaise. Then they seek confirmation of their diagnosis by interviewing the patient, ordering lab tests, and observing the patient over time. Eventually, the additional information they receive helps them pinpoint the real problem. Coaches view clients' behaviors as likely indicators of underlying problems, and they use the four poles of the needs compass to generate the additional data needed to confirm or disconfirm their hypotheses. Eventually, they arrive at the root cause that should be addressed. The difference between physicians and coaches is that physicians are experts and their patients generally are not, so physicians rely far more on their knowledge and expertise to discover underlying illnesses. Coaching, on the other hand, is a process of co-discovery in which both parties are experts in various ways. Coaching and medicine are alike, however, in that the core issue is a *cause*, not an *effect*. In coaching, you have not discovered the real need until you have identified the reason why clients behave the way they do.

Throughout the rest of this chapter, we will explore how coaches identify the real needs. The cases we examine will illustrate various coaching techniques, but we should note that experienced coaches do not rely on techniques. They rely on instincts formed by years of coaching experience and a good understanding of people and organizations. For every technique we illustrate, there are dozens of variations that different experienced coaches favor. It may be helpful to think of these techniques as tools in a toolbox. The best coaches possess many tools and know when to use them.

MANUELA'S REAL ISSUE

Let's return to the case that opened this chapter and see how Jan-Olof might have continued to explore the problem space to uncover the real issue.

Manuela I have some great people working with me, but I have to keep the whole project in my mind. If I lost sight of what the programmers are doing, then I couldn't be sure that everything will come together at the end.

Jan-Olof And, clearly, that's important.

Manuela Absolutely.

Jan-Olof Help me understand something. Are you particularly concerned about this project? Or do you approach every project this way? [Exploring context is a useful coaching tool. You need to know whether this event or behavior is unusual and, if so, why it is.]

Manuela (reflecting) No, I think it pretty much describes how I normally work. I'm probably more finicky about the details than most people.

Jan-Olof That's interesting. Why do you think that is? [He could speculate about why she's more finicky, but it's best to go to the source and ask the client.]

Manuela I don't know. I just have to make sure that everything is all right. Sometimes I double and even triple check things to be sure that nothing has been overlooked. I'm compulsive like that.

Jan-Olof Are you like that in other areas of your life?

Manuela My husband seems to think so. I drive him crazy sometimes. So I guess that's a fair statement.

Jan-Olof Have you always been that way? [Note that the coach does not ask more about her family life. Coaching is not therapy and, unless there seems to be some bearing on the problem at hand, the coach stays away from areas of the client's life that would be inappropriate to explore. However, trying to determine whether her work behavior has been longstanding is relevant.]

Manuela (pausing to reflect) No. I mean, it's hard to remember. I was always the one who dotted the i's and crossed the t's. You could count on me to get my homework done. You know, I don't know if this has anything to do with it, but I was really sick as a kid. I nearly died.

Jan-Olof I'm sorry to hear that. What happened?

Manuela I was riding in my aunt's car and we had an accident. Another car hit us broadside, and it broke my leg. I was in the hospital for a week, and then when I got home I got an infection and wound up back in the hospital, this time for almost a month. They said the infection almost killed me. I don't remember much of it.

Jan-Olof Sounds like a terrible experience. How old were you? [showing empathy]

Manuela Eight or nine. Eight, I think. (pause) I remember that it really scared me, not the almost dying part, which is hard for a kid to understand, but just the suddenness of it, you know. It was just so random. One day you're riding down the street on your way to the grocery store, and then something totally random happens and you nearly die in a hospital.

Jan-Olof Sounds like a tough lesson for an eight-year-old to learn. [showing empathy]

Manuela (nodding) I think it really shook me up. Afterward, I was always so careful. You know, always looking both ways before crossing a street. And when I was riding in a car, always checking the crossing streets ahead to see if a car was coming.

Jan-Olof Always dotting the i's and crossing the t's? [making the connection between her behavior following the accident and her behavior later in school and at work]

Manuela Right.

Jan-Olof Is that what you're doing when you check every detail of your team's work?

Manuela Yes, I think I'm just being cautious.

Jan-Olof Because you never know what could happen.

Manuela Right. I'm doing everything I can to control the situation.

Jan-Olof Even if you have to work late every night.

Manuela Yeah.

Jan-Olof And even if you continually frustrate your team.

Manuela It's a heavy price to pay, but I just feel so vulnerable. If I don't control every aspect of the situation, I feel like it could all come crashing down around me.

Jan-Olof I wonder if this is the key thing we need to work on—your need for control. As long as you feel vulnerable, you're going to behave in ways that protect yourself, no matter what the cost—to yourself and others.

Manuela I think you're right.

This case illustrates a number of fundamental techniques in coaching: empathizing, making connections between parts of the client's narrative (that the client may not see), holding up the mirror to clients, and exploring the context. Holding up the mirror to clients means helping them see themselves as others see them. When Jan-Olof says, "Even if you have to work late every night," he is holding up the mirror, showing his client the consequences of the unconscious choice she is making. In Manuela's case, her feelings of vulnerability and consequent obsessive need for control are the core issue. Through the coach's skilled questioning, she arrived at that insight herself, and awareness is the first step toward change. When you explore the context, you ask these kinds of questions:

♦ Is X true in every part of your life? [If not, then what is different about this part of your life?]

♦ Do you do X in every case? Do you always respond this way? [If not, then what is different about this situation?]

♦ Has X always been true for you? [If not, when was it not true and what's different between then and now?]

This last question is especially powerful. Another coach, Karen, worked with Simon T., whose presenting problem was an incapacitating fear of public speaking. As she explored this issue more deeply, Karen asked, "Is this true for you in every situation where you talk to large groups of people? Are there any circumstances in which this is not true?" As he thought about this, Simon realized that he was not fearful when he addressed his church and community groups. He taught Sunday school and periodically addressed the congregation. He was also a community advocate and frequently talked to various groups about civic and community issues. Karen then asked him what was different about those groups that made him less fearful. Simon realized in their further dialogue that he felt passionately about the issues he spoke about with his church and community groups—and that was not the case at work. One of the issues Simon and Karen later dealt with was why he felt no passion for his work. Had Karen merely given him tips on controlling stress and public speaking, she would have failed as a coach, because she would not have been addressing the real issue.

NICOLA'S TEAM LEADERSHIP

Sometimes you have to triangulate to discover the client's real needs. In ethnographic research, anthropologists refer to the process of cross-referencing at least three versions of the same story or experience as *triangulation*. By triangulating multiple points of view, you get closer to the truth of things because the anomalies can be identified and potentially eliminated. We are using the term in much the same way: to describe how coaches use the four poles of the needs compass to find patterns or themes that indicate what help clients need. Nicola R. is a case in point. She was a newly promoted senior executive in an insurance firm and received some executive coaching as part of her transition process. In her new role, she was responsible for the Asia-Pacific field sales force. In her previous roles, she had inherited intact teams that were already well functioning, but in her new role she had to build strong teams over a large geographic area with people who had not already gelled as teams. It was a challenge she had not faced before, and she told the coach that she thought that would be one of her biggest challenges. So team building was one of her presenting problems; however, team building is a broad skill area and her needs were still not clear.

Nicola's Leadership Assessment

To gather more information, the coach asked Nicola to complete one online 360-degree assessment and the Myers-Briggs Type Indicator® (MBTI) personality inventory. In addition, the coach wanted to gather qualitative information from key stakeholders and thus used a verbal 360-degree interview protocol to expand and drill down on the real needs.

The 360-degree instrument would provide some baseline data from others who worked with Nicola, the MBTI instrument would help her and the coach understand her operating style, and the verbal 360-degree interviews would further elaborate more specific leadership behaviors required for successful transition.

Nicola's Interpersonal Skills Assessment

The 360-degree instrument Nicola completed was Korn/Ferry International's *Survey of Influence Effectiveness* (SIE), an interpersonal skills survey that assesses how well people influence others. Nicola's SIE report revealed that she relies primarily on two tactics, logical persuasion and stating, to influence others. The influence tactics she uses far less frequently include appealing to values, socializing, alliance building, and consulting (asking others for their opinions). The skills portion of this survey yielded predictable results. She was rated highest on *asserting, persisting, behaving self-confidently, logical reasoning, finding creative alternatives, and negotiating;* she scored lowest on *showing genuine interest in others, building rapport and trust, having insight into what others value, being friendly and sociable with strangers, and sensitivity to others' feelings and needs.* Interestingly, in the "power sources" section, she rated herself significantly low on attraction, which is defined as "being open and approachable, available when others need you, and being able to make friends easily."

Nicola's profile suggested someone who is logical and driven but who lacks some basic social skills and sees herself as essentially isolated. A therapist might speculate about why that is the case, but her coach was principally interested in understanding what she really needed to function more effectively in her new role.

Another interesting piece was her MBTI profile, which showed that her preferred operating style is INTJ (Introversion, Intuition, Thinking, and Judging). We won't explain the entire MBTI construct here, but we will note that INTJs are the most independent of all the sixteen types. They tend to be very analytical, to behave confidently and forcefully, to make independent judgments, and to live in a conceptual world. Very task focused, they can easily overlook others and may keep important ideas and decisions to themselves far too long.

The final pieces of the puzzle came together when the coach completed the verbal 360-degree interview process. During these interviews the coach used a standard protocol with both quantitative and qualitative feedback about how well her sales team was currently performing. The protocol was customized to include questions that tie to the SIE and that use Korn/Ferry's Leadership Architect library of sixty-seven competencies. The coach used the popular *For Your Improvement* book published by Lominger International, a Korn/Ferry International company.

The coach found during this process that Nicola is seen by others as a skilled leader in the following competencies: "action oriented," "customer focused," "learns on the fly," and "problem solving"; she is viewed as being underskilled at "motivating others," "managing vision and purpose," and "building effective teams." Some of the qualitative feedback included the following comments:

> "Nicola is making decisions that her key leaders should be making. On the one hand, being that involved is good; but if she has time to operate at this level of detail it could cause confusion about what her leaders' jobs are and if they have real authority to make deci- sions or not."

> "You have to have a certain amount of intestinal fortitude to be on her team because she doesn't seem to appreciate what motivates and drives others. She could be more sensitive to feelings of subor- dinates . . . she is downright rude at times."

> "Nicola is one of the best leaders for this role; she has the intel- lectual horsepower to do it. However she could be more open to listening and not shut down the discussion too early. She could take more time to get to know her team members; she can invite others to truly own and then solve for the problems."

The emerging picture is that of an extremely bright producer who has been promoted based on the quality of her individual contributions but who lacks some fundamental skills in fostering a collaborative work envi- ronment. Most striking is her apparent insensitivity to how other people feel. She seems to lack emotional connectedness, which may explain her lack of skill in handling conflict. She may simply be unaware that con- flict is occurring or that emotional issues are derailing or could derail the group's effectiveness. This may not have mattered in her previous posi- tions, or her talents in other areas may have convinced people to overlook her lack of skill with people. However, in her new position, she will need to be much more perceptive about people and much better at building effective teams

Debriefing Nicola on Her Assessments
It goes without saying that the patterns revealed in these three data sources are consistent. They show an accomplished, strong-willed executive

and an independent thinker who has probably made significant intellectual contributions to her company but who lacks some key people skills. Given the demands of her new position, she is likely to hit a career-limiting wall unless she figures out how to be more sensitive to people and to work with them in a way that fulfills their needs. At least, those were our coach's hypotheses after reviewing the data and meeting with Nicola. During that meeting, he added his own observations and got Nicola's perspective. Here is a part of the dialogue that occurred after the coach and Nicola had reviewed the findings:

Coach So what do you conclude from the feedback?

Nicola It's pretty consistent with what I've heard before. But there were a few surprises.

Coach Like what?

Nicola Like the comment that I was rude.

Coach You don't recall ever acting that way?

Nicola (shaking her head) I guess I don't know what that means. I do my job. I'm good at it. I don't mean to ruffle anyone's feathers while I'm doing it, but there's only so much time to observe the niceties.

Coach You seem like you're very task focused. [a synthesizing observation]

Nicola I am.

Coach (pausing; observing; letting her think about it) [Sometimes the best coaching technique is silence; while clients are thinking, they are working, and it's best not to disturb them.]

Nicola I keep hearing that so-and-so had a birthday, or Marcia got married last week and why didn't I congratulate her. Nobody tells me about these things, so it's hard to stay on top of all the social events.

Coach They probably don't think you're interested.

Nicola Well, I am and I'm not. I've got a family. I care about these things, but work is work. When you come to work, you leave that stuff at home.

Coach Do you notice when someone at work isn't acting normally? [This is really the crucial question: Does she have any degree of social awareness?]

Nicola What do you mean?

Coach   Oh, when someone seems subdued or preoccupied? When someone who's normally a hard worker seems distracted? Or when two people are sharp with each other?

Nicola   Not normally. Oh, sometimes, sure. But . . .

Coach   But what?

Nicola   I just ignore it. They need to get over whatever's bothering them and get on with their work.

Coach   So I'm hearing that you do notice when people are out of sorts or moody, but you choose to ignore it. [reflecting back what he's heard as a way of reinforcing the conclusion she's reached]

Nicola   Usually, yes. Well, not usually. Most of the time. I just don't want to deal with it.

Coach   You know, some of the comments on your feedback describe you as being insensitive to others and needing to take more time to acknowledge them and understand what motivates and inspires them.

Nicola   (frustrated) Okay, but how important is that, really?

Coach   It seems important to the people who responded to your assessment. (pause) Let me ask you this. We agree that in your new position it's going to be crucial for you to build effective, smoothly functioning teams, right? [responding to her question about how important this issue is]

Nicola   (nodding)

Coach   Well, teams are about people. Are you going to be able to build effective teams by ignoring the people in them and focusing only on the tasks? [Implication questions like this one are powerful challenging tools.]

Nicola   No, clearly not.

Coach   Then learning to become more sensitive to people is a critical issue for you.

Nicola   (frustrated) So it would seem.

Coach   Well, let me put it this way. If you aren't able to improve your people skills and build high-performing teams, will you succeed in your new job? [a follow-up implication question]

Nicola   No.

Coach (pausing, noting her hesitation) What?

Nicola I just don't know how to do that. I've never been a "people person," whatever that means, and I'm too old to become someone I'm not.

Coach I think in anyone's dictionary this would be called a dilemma, and you seem frustrated by it. [showing empathy] I don't know that you need to become a people person or that you should even try to be someone you're not. That would be inauthentic and is not sustainable or satisfying in the long run. [challenging her assumption that she has to become someone she isn't]

Nicola Absolutely not.

Coach Maybe you just need to exercise some muscles that have been dormant a long time.

Nicola What do you mean?

Coach You said yourself that you notice when people are moody or out of sorts. You ignore it, so you aren't using what I'll call your "sensitivity muscle." But clearly you have this muscle or you wouldn't notice in the first place. Maybe being sensitive to others is more of a choice than a skill. Would it be useful to work on that?

Nicola Yes.

Nicola, it turned out, was virtually a poster child for the professional person with highly developed cognitive intelligence and relatively low emotional intelligence. In his book *Emotional Intelligence*, Daniel Goleman (1995) (whose book, by the way, along with his subsequent books on emotional intelligence, should be required reading for all coaches) describes a number of people like Nicola. Her need is not a seminar on team building, which would not address her real issues. Her real need is to build better people skills, which for her will mean developing greater awareness of others, becoming more politically aware, building bonds with others, learning how to foster cooperation and collaboration, and becoming more emotionally aware herself. In short, she needs to be more emotionally intelligent, and this is something she can learn, although it won't be easy for her.

What we have tried to illustrate with this case is how a coach triangulates from multiple sources of data to understand a client's real needs.

Inexperienced coaches tend to focus on surface issues. In this case, an inexperienced coach might have concluded that Nicola needed instruction on team building (maybe by attending a class on it) and that she needed to become a better listener. One can imagine such coaches saying to Nicola, "Here are some tips on better listening." But these are surface issues and do not address the fundamental problem, which is that Nicola is choosing to be insensitive to people.

Nicola's case illustrates several important points about finding the real needs. First, having multiple data points is essential. As you triangulate from different perspectives, themes and patterns emerge. You hypothesize from these patterns and themes. Then you look at other data points to see if your hypothesis is confirmed or not. Throughout the process, you seek those crucial moments of insight that enable you to glimpse what the real problem might be. In Nicola's case, one such moment occurred when the coach heard the following during the verbal 360-degree interviews: "Nicola is one of the best leaders for this role; she has the intellectual horsepower to do it. However she could be more open to listening and not shut down the discussion too early."

This comment told the coach that Nicola is highly intelligent and capable and that other people's needs are low on her radar screen. He hasn't asked her about this comment yet, but he will remember it and use it at the appropriate time to help her become more aware of other people's needs. Some of his coaching help may come down to advice, such as suggesting that before she ends meetings she ask if there are any other issues. However, Nicola is unlikely to achieve real growth until she learns to be more sensitive to others' feelings and needs—and more aware of her own.

JOHN W. NEEDS MORE BALANCE

John W.'s presenting problem was that he needed more balance in his life. He was working too many weekends and evenings, and it was starting to affect his family. He worked the long hours, he said, because he loved what he was doing. Now and then, he had tried to cut back on his work hours and stay home more, but inevitably a crisis occurred that kept him at the office, or a new project started that required his guiding hand, or an important customer would be in town, and so forth. He sought a coach to help him figure out how to achieve more work-life balance.

The feedback from a 360-degree survey showed that John was well respected by his boss, peers, and direct reports. He was known as a dependable, hard-working, high performer. Everyone—from his boss to his mother—had told him to slow down and spend more time at home. People worried about John burning out, but it never seemed to happen. He had heard all the advice and was aware of the potential consequences if he didn't slow down, but nothing had moved him to change. Knowing this, his coach's opening question conveyed some genuine puzzlement:

Coach Why are you coming to me now? [A great question to ask: What's different? Why now? What has made this coaching more urgent for you?]

John I don't understand.

Coach Well, people have been telling you for years that you should slow down and spend more time at home, but you haven't done that. I doubt that you need to hear that advice again. Has something changed?

John You mean, has my wife threatened to leave me, or something like that?

Coach (nodding) Something like that.

John No. I just can't keep this up.

Coach All evidence to the contrary. You seem to have incredible energy and a real love for what you're doing. [Confronting clients like this is a valuable coaching technique, especially when they say something that seems self-deceiving or contrary to reality.]

John I do, but I'm worried about sustaining this pace and realizing one day that I've missed out on a lot because I've been so focused on my work.

Coach You want to smell the roses before they're gone.

John That's right.

Coach I'm curious about something. It sounds like a lot of people have advised you to slow down and find more work-life balance, but you haven't heeded their advice. Why not? [first why]

John Well, I've tried to, but then something happens at work and I'm pulled back in.

Coach	Why are you pulled back in? [second why]
John	In a lot of cases, I'm the best person to handle the problem, and it's my area. I'm responsible.
Coach	Is someone else pulling you back in or are you doing it yourself?
John	Usually it's me.
Coach	And you're pulling yourself back in because you are the best person to handle all of these problems? Are you the only person who can handle them?
John	No, certainly not. We have a very capable group.
Coach	So you are choosing to handle them yourself even though you have other capable people who could do it. Why? [third why]
John	That's the million-dollar question.
Coach	I don't have that much in my wallet, but I'd still like to know the answer.
John	Why do I choose to do it myself? (reflecting) I guess because I want the outcome to be perfect.
Coach	Why? [fourth why]
John	I have very high standards. I want everything leaving my unit to be top-notch.
Coach	And you can't trust the people in your unit to do top-notch work?
John	No, that's not fair. They do a great job.
Coach	So you choose to do the work yourself, even though it takes you away from your home and family, not because only you can make it perfect, but for some other reason.
John	Yes.
Coach	What? [fifth why, in a different form]
John	(pausing to reflect) I don't know. I think it just boils down to the fact that I like the work. I never get tired of it. You know? I like the action.
Coach	Sounds really satisfying.
John	It is.
Coach	Then what's the problem? [sixth why, another form of the question]
John	I don't know. When I really think about it, I don't have a problem. I'm doing fine. Everyone else keeps telling me I have to slow down.

Coach	So it sounds like the real issue is figuring out how to help other people in your life understand and accept your choices.
John	I think you're right.
Coach	Before we move on, let me just test one thing. You said earlier that you were worried about waking up one day and realizing that you had missed a lot. What are you afraid of missing?
John	You know, at this point, I'm not sure.
Coach	Would it be worth thinking about as we work together?
John	Yes, but at this point I'm clueless, frankly. I mean, yes, I'd like to spend more time with my wife and kids—not that I don't spend time with them now. My family isn't complaining. But I don't see every soccer game or go to every school event.
Coach	And that's okay?
John	It's okay with me. My wife enjoys that stuff, but I can only handle so much of it. And my kids don't seem to care one way or another.
Coach	You have good relationships with them?
John	Oh yeah. Great.
Coach	Okay, so what would be most helpful to you at this point? [This question is a great general question for coaches to ask. Use it often.]
John	I'd like to spend more time talking through my priorities and then figure out how to help everybody be okay with that. Or what to do about it if they're not.

This work with John illustrates another coaching technique for surfacing the real needs—the technique of the *five whys*. Its origins are in the quality assurance movement, and we've heard it hails from Japan, but that may be apocryphal. The point of the technique is to keep asking why until you arrive at the root cause. Children, with their boundless curiosity, seem to use this technique naturally, as anyone with a two-year-old at home knows. *Why, Mommy? Because. But why? Because I told you so. Why?* And so on, until Mommy is forced to admit that she doesn't know why. Being as curious as a two-year-old about why clients behave as they do is one of a good coach's greatest gifts. Boundless curiosity helps both coaches and clients drill down until they reach bedrock. Table 1 summarizes the techniques we have discussed in this chapter that help coaches surface their clients' real needs.

TECHNIQUE	QUESTIONS OR STATEMENTS
Exploring Context	Is this true in every part of your life? If not, what's different? Has this always been true? If not, why not?
Questioning	Why do you think that is?
Empathizing	That sounds frustrating. You seem troubled by that. You look pleased.
Makeing Connections and Synthesizing	You are always dotting the i's and crossing the t's.
The Five Why's	Why? Why? Why? Why? Why?
Trusting Silence	After asking a great question, wait at least 15 secdonds for the client to respoind before speaking again.
Reflecting and Paraphrasing	You said yourself that you notice when people are moody or out of sorts.
Identifying Contractions	All evidence to the contrary. You seem to have incredible energy and a real love for what you are doing.
Returning Later to Issues	Earlier, you mentioned [topic]. Tell me more about that.

Table 1: Coaching Techniques for Discovering Client's Real Needs

THE TEN RED FLAGS

Now and then coaches encounter the kinds of needs that cannot and should not be dealt with through coaching. When the behavioral problems are serious enough, only trained therapists or psychologists should be involved. But this begs the question: How can coaches who are not trained psychologists recognize when serious psychological problems are present? They may not know it when they see it. The answer, we believe, is that coaches should learn how to recognize problem behaviors so they know when to refer clients to a therapist. The worst case, as Steven Berglas (2002) rightly argues in "The Very Real Dangers of Executive Coaching," is for unqualified coaches to either ignore serious psychological problems or try to handle them without having the proper training. To help coaches recognize referable behaviors, we suggest they look for the following ten behavioral red flags. Our red flags are based on our experiences as coaches but also on the American Psychiatric Association's (1994) *Diagnostic and Statistical Manual of Mental Disorders*, Edition [DSM-IV], the bible for clinical diagnosis of psychological problems.

1. The client has low affect (i.e., does not demonstrate emotional highs or lows); the person's expressive range is very narrow; he seems to be chronically depressed, is profoundly unhappy, or has a sense of hopelessness. May indicate depression.

2. The client is excessively dependent on others, is incapacitated without the constant approval of others, fears being rejected by others, fears being abandoned, and has low self-regard. May indicate a dependent personality.

3. The client's life is very chaotic; she cannot seem to get it under control. Or the client has extreme emotional highs and lows, is moody and unpredictable. May indicate bipolar disorder.

4. The client has a pattern of unstable relationships with others; behaves impulsively; and alternates unpredictably between feelings of boredom, anxiety, anger, and depression. May indicate borderline personality disorder.

5. The client's beliefs are not consistent with reality, such as hearing voices or seeing things that aren't there. May indicate schizophrenia.

6. The client does not trust others, is reluctant to confide because the information could be used against him, or is unreasonably suspicious of others' motives or actions. May indicate paranoia.

7. The client is persistently angry or aggressive and shows no concern for the welfare of others. May indicate antisocial personality.

8. The client expresses thoughts about suicide or has other self-destructive impulses or behaviors. Suggests suicidal tendencies.

9. The client is very egocentric and seems to care about no one but herself, displaying grandiose self-importance. In addition, this person may be clever, articulate, and extremely manipulative. May indicate narcissism or psychopathic personality.

10. The client says to you something like, "You are the only person who cares about me." There are similar or other inappropriate expressions of love toward or interest in you. Or there are frequent comparisons of you with someone else in the client's life toward whom he has a strong positive or negative reaction. May indicate transference.

These kinds of behaviors indicate the potential for serious psychological problems and are not within the purview of coaching. Only certified mental health professionals and physicians should handle them. Having said that, we should add that in our many years of coaching, we have not experienced these kinds of problems with any regularity except for depression and narcissism, the latter of which can cause a client to be uncoachable, as we describe in the coachability chart that appears in the following section.

COACHABILITY

As we are assessing clients' real needs, we should also assess how coachable they are. The plain fact is that not everyone can be coached, and both the coach and the client should know that up front. A number of factors affect a client's coachability, including the following:

- The client's ego strength (sense of self, pride, and humility versus arrogance)

- The client's feelings of vulnerability—the more vulnerable the person feels, the greater the ego defenses are likely to become and the less coachable he or she may be

- Openness to feedback (the client's willingness to hear and accept messages that disconfirm his self-image)

- The client's self-assessment of need, along with a sense of urgency; also, extrinsic indicators of the need for change—such as poor performance numbers, the results of 360-degree feedback, observations from others

- The client's perception of the value of the process and the likely outcomes

- The client's trust in the coach

- The client's experience with coaching (favorable, neutral, or unfavorable)

- The client's awareness of the need for change

- The client's fear of consequences if she does not seek and accept help; the executive's excitement about the positive outcomes if she does change; in short, risk versus reward

- The client's responsiveness to extrinsic pressure (from boss, peers or subordinates, the environment)

- Finally, the presence or absence of serious psychological problems

These factors combine in complex ways to determine how willingly a client enters into a coaching relationship and how motivated the client is to change. Helping clients change is the principal purpose of coaching, so it's important to know at the outset of coaching how coachable a client is. To help coaches assess coachability, we have developed a framework that includes seven levels of coachability—from C0 (not appropriate for coaching) to C6 (highly coachable). Our scale reflects the degree of difficulty in coaching a particular client. The lower the number, the less coachable the client is likely to be. Table 4 describes each of these coachability levels, the behaviors normally observed, and the requirements for change (which can help coaches determine the right approach to the client).

Coaches should make a coachability determination early in the coaching process. Clients who seek coaching are generally more coachable because they are more motivated to seek help and feel a more urgent need to change. When clients have not sought coaching, however, a low degree of coachability can hamstring the process to the point of making it worthless. So coachability is no trivial matter. We also advocate that coaches share their coachability determination with their clients (except for C0), especially if the coachability is C1, C2, or C3. If you don't think a client is coachable, it is best to be transparent about that and discuss it with the client. If the client disagrees with your assessment, then you have a fruitful area for dialogue. If the client agrees, then you may both want to consider whether the likely outcomes of coaching are worth the investment of time and energy.

We have known coaches who view low coachability as a challenge, but we've also noted how frustrated they are by the lack of progress. Coaching is about helping people change, and if they don't want to change, don't like the message, or don't believe they need to change, then trying to force them to endure coaching is a bit like trying to push cooked spaghetti across a table—and keep each piece in a straight line. You are unlikely to succeed, and the process and result are likely to be messy.

The application of our coachability model is wide ranging. The coach, the client, the human resources partner, and the sponsoring manager each benefit from using it to indicate how likely it is that the client is going to demonstrate noticeable behavioral change.

Coaches

Coaches can use the coachability scale in a number of ways and at multiple points in time. An initial assessment of coachability is important to establish early in the coaching process. As mentioned earlier, some organizations systematically include coachability in their established coaching process. All stakeholders, including the client, are prepared for and expected

Coachability Level	Behavioral Descriptors	Observed Behaviors	Requirements for Change
C0 (not coachable at present)	Identified psychological or medical problem, such as depression, borderline personality disorder, obsessive-compulsive disorder, chronic substance abuse, and schizophrenia. Dysfunctional behavior resists typical coaching. Normal functioning is impaired beyond the scope of a coaching intervention.	Stressful life events have recently occurred. Is inattentive or easily distracted. Anger is poorly managed or inappropriately expressed. Appointments are missed or canceled. Decisions are avoided or made too quickly. Typical activity level is lowered or inconsistent. Has very little affect (emotional range is narrow). Direct reports express a high level of dissatisfaction with behavior and leadership.	Needs help from a trained clinician; coaching is not the appropriate relationship for the change needed. Coaching may need to be revisited at a later time or when more normal functioning is restored.
C1 (extremely low coachability)	Narcissistic personality. Is strongly independent; may have an arrogant/overbearing manner; sees no need to change; will not admit to serious weak-nesses or areas for improvement; feels invulnerable. May be antagonistic or hostile toward the coaching process and the coach; may lobby against the coaching program, labeling it wasteful and unnecessary.	Exhibits impatience; is easily frustrated. Works alone. Doesn't invite feedback or participation. Doesn't listen or respond empathically to others. Shows up late for appointments. Closed to new learning and shows no interest in change or new experiences. Interrupts during conversations. Expresses a strong need to be right. Direct reports express detachment, complacency, hopelessness, or low expectation of change. Turnover may be higher than expected.	Is often unresponsive, even to the strongest threats or potential consequences; may leave the organization and blame others rather than "submit" to change; may change only in response to a significant, dislocation life or work event (divorce, death of a loved one, loss of a job, failure to be promoted, etc.) May need more time and effort to engage in coaching than most organizations are willing to give. May accept consultation from an "expert."

Table 2: Coachability

Coachability Level	Behavioral Descriptors	Observed Behaviors	Requirements for Change
C2 (very low coachability)	Resists or deflects feedback; uses defenses to deal with reported "flaws," weaknesses, or development needs; for example, explains away issues or offers rationale for negative perceptions. May behave indifferently toward the coaching process, but puts no effort into creating or executing an action plan. Tends to be negative toward the coaching process, saying that it is not helpful.	Demonstrates a lack of self-knowledge in interactions with others. Uses a variety of defenses to avoid change. May behave as though feedback is criticism. May act in an indirect way rather than onfront an issue openly. Reports express fearfulness and lack of two-way communication. During coaching, may try to dominate the discussion or other-wise seek to deflect the focus away from feedback and coaching needs.	Needs strong extrinsic motivation (rewards or threats), typically not from the coach. Must be faced with the consequences of inaction or lack of commitment. The coach must be extremely candid; must have development plan closely linked to performance measures, and progress should be tracked by coach and boss, with frequent periodic reviews.
C3 (fair coachability)	Is complacent and unmotivated to change; feels that personal performance and business results are fine. Considers this coaching process another fad (it will pass). May pay lip service to change but is not really committed to it and will make only token efforts to execute the action plan.	Behavior is geared toward maintaining the status quo. Comfortable behaviors are repeated. Unable to identify any needed areas of change. Behavior is consistent, but low risk. Reports express lack of challenge or creativity. May acknowledge some change needs but has no sense of urgency. May accept coach's suggestions but show no real commitment to change.	Typically, must be shocked out of complacency through the implica-tions of not changing; best motivator is an alteration of the conditions that led to complacency; may respond to authority. Can be deceptive with coach by appearing to agree to change but with no real commitment; individual feedback comments are often more powerful than feedback scores.

Table 2: Coachability (continued)

Coachability Level	Behavioral Descriptors	Observed Behaviors	Requirements for Change
C4 (good coachability)	Prior to the assessment, saw no need for change. Accepts some feedback; did not initially see the value of the 360-degree process but acknowledges that it gave an accurate picture; may not be certain how to proceed to learn effectively. Demonstrates some resistance to the coaching process, but has a growing awareness of the need for change; urgency depends on the implications of not changing.	Demonstrates adequate performance. Behavior is consistent, but there is more potential. Demonstrates adequate to good problem-solving and interpersonal skills. Responds to logical and factual presentations, but behavior may lack consideration of emotional input.	Will respond to strong feedback and assertive but helpful coach; walk carefully through the 360-degree results and build buttoned-up development plan; tie coaching process concretely to performance metrics and monitor closely. Needs to see concrete benefits of change and is likely to support the process and stick with it if early results demonstrate those benefits.
C5 (very good coachability)	Accepts feedback and shows an earnest desire to improve; sees the value of the 360-degree process; is busy but feels that self-development is important and will find a way; initially may not be enthusiastic about coaching but becomes committed as the benefits become clear.	Demonstrates talent. May lack work-life balance in behavior. Demonstrates competitive behavior. Work skills are solid, with specific needs for improvement evident. May have behaviors that promote a sense of unavailability. Reports express satisfaction, but may have more potential than is demonstrated currently.	Will be intrinsically motivated once the picture is clear; coach should primarily use questions to help discover acceptable trade-offs. Change may be inadvertently derailed by day-to-day business, so monitor and provide continous feedback and reinforcement.

Table 2: Coachability (continued)

Coachability Level	Behavioral Descriptors	Observed Behaviors	Requirements for Change
C6 (excellent coachability)	Has an intrinsic need to grow; has been a lifelong learner; personal history shows evidence of self-directed learning; strong achievement motivation. Sees 360-degree feedback as intrinsically valuable and seeks it beyond the coaching program; is widely read and can cite favorite books on leadership, development, and related areas. Is often modest and has a realistic sense of self.	Demonstrates high potential in behavior. Demonstrated skills are above average with many strengths. Expresses need for new challenges and learning. Places a high value on performance and growth. Challenges others and holds high expectations for achievement. Keeps schedules and commitments. May not readily exhibit the effects of stress. May have difficulty understanding and motivating those who are different in style. Reports express respect for leadership, feel challenged and want even more.	Is likely to be self-directed, so monitor loosely; act as a sounding board, provide resources and ideas; ask clients to share other feedback he or she is receiving; inquire about client's next steps and ongoing development plans. Usually responds best to a facilitative approach.

Table 2: Coachability (continued)

to discuss the client's coachability. Regardless of the coachability level, the initial conversation should be between the client and the coach. They need to agree upon and rehearse how the message will be shared with others in order to maintain trust and eliminate the possibility of backchannel communication with human resources or the sponsor. If the client's coachability is low, this conversation is especially important.

It is also important to recognize that coachability is not always a static measure; rather, it is dynamic and can change quickly based on the business environment (coachability can be rated low, for instance, when a senior executive is on point to lead an acquisition and she is not available for coaching or cannot commit to development) and many other factors. Coachability is not intended to be predictive, nor is it psychometrically validated; rather, it is one indicator, among others, that can inspire conversation and dialogue about the client's commitment to development and whether coaching is the best way to achieve the desired outcome. In fact, our coaches frequently report that conversations about coachability, especially when an executive is C3 or C4, can lead to much stronger commitment and a transformative coaching experience for all stakeholders. Similarly, they report that some executives and stakeholders determine to postpone or cancel coaching until the time and personal commitment can be made, thus saving the company considerable money by using coaching at precisely the right time for precisely the right candidates.

Human Resources Partners and Sponsors

When talent review cycles are complete and a pool of high-performing or high-potential talent has been identified, it is rarely true that the entire population will receive funding for executive coaching. Coachability can be one criterion human resources or sponsors use to determine the best candidates for individual executive coaching. High coachability (C5 or C6) can be a prerequisite for receiving executive coaching. Moreover, if a coaching engagement begins with this requirement in place, the human resources partner and sponsor can include coachability as part of the coaching process and ask the coach to provide an independent assessment before the full financial investment is committed for the coaching engagement. Some people may react to this requirement as evaluative (only those who need it most receive coaching); however, many large organizations have used coachability as a screening tool to ensure that the right candidates are receiving the limited funding available for individual development.

Clients

Most leaders who are going to receive executive coaching have direct reports who will also benefit directly and indirectly from the coaching engagement. The coachability model is one tool that executives can introduce and use on a routine basis with their direct reports during performance management discussions and other coaching conversations. By introducing the model and using the language of coachability, managers can more effectively convey when they want to raise difficult issues such as commitment to learning and willingness to change. Indeed, the language of coachability is a vehicle for broader discussions of learning, performance, and career development.

We will close this chapter with a best-practice example of how coachability can enhance an organization's talent management process. One of our clients, a multinational company, asked us to include coachability in their programmatic coaching offering. They were expecting to have an audience of three thousand executives per year, the top ten percent of their talent. Some percentage of that top talent group would be eligible for executive coaching, and we were asked to include coachability as a standard feature so that the executives, human resources partners, and sponsors would come to expect the rating from the coach and would have a dialogue about continuing or discontinuing coaching if the rating were C3 or lower. The human resources partners and sponsors were also asked to use coachability to select the most coachable executives. However, we knew we could not realistically expect the screening process to be used consistently. Thus our coaches became accustomed to introducing coachability to all executives (and stakeholders), having a conversation about coachability with all stakeholders, and documenting coachability in our monthly reports to the talent management team, who owned the coaching program. The company has now used this practice effectively for nearly a decade, and we have seen coachability ratings steadily increasing as executives in the top talent pool have come to recognize the importance of being open to feedback, coaching, and development.

5

Adapting to Clients' Preferences

To be more effective as a coach, realize that each person has specific skill sets and tailor the coaching to each person's needs.

Know your audience. People are at different places in their lives. You should determine where they are and not use a cookie-cutter approach to coaching. For some people, the "rah-rah" approach is best, but others need personal reflection.

If appropriate, hold back your advice and focus on helping coachees find their own options and make their own plans.

SUGGESTIONS TO COACHES FROM THE "COACHING EFFECTIVENESS SURVEY," KORN/FERRY INTERNATIONAL

Megan Jones is a department manager for a large insurance company. She manages a group of two hundred people and has nine direct reports. Megan is fifty-seven and has been working in this industry for more than thirty years. She is considered one of the most knowledgeable people in the company in her functional area. When she coaches her direct reports, she usually observes them, gives them feedback on the specific things she's noticed, and offers advice based on her many years of experience. She feels that their careers and personal lives are their own business, so she confines her coaching to matters related to their performance. Megan is capable of coaching differently, but this is the approach she prefers. We would call her coaching style *directive, circumstantial,* and *specific* (DCS). She coaches the way a typical manager coaches subordinates.

In contrast, Rolf Petersen prefers a nondirective style. Like Megan, he is a department manager and is very experienced and knowledgeable in his industry. But when he coaches people, he prefers to ask what they think about their performance, what they conclude from the outcomes, and what they would like to do differently. He is considered a mentor by a number of younger people, and he mentors them regularly, about once every other month. He prefers to meet them for lunch or to talk casually after work, and he tries to help them think through a broad range of issues—from what assignments to seek and what training courses to take to how to think about their careers and, in some cases, how to resolve personal problems. Rolf believes that building their job skills won't be enough for them to succeed; they also need to mature as professionals, understand themselves better, and become leaders in their own right. Because he coaches people regularly and focuses on the whole person, not just the person's job skills, we would call his coaching style *nondirective, programmatic,* and *holistic* (NPH). He acts more like a counselor than a manager.

Both Megan's and Rolf 's approaches to coaching are appropriate for some clients and inappropriate for others—and indeed this is one of the major themes of this book. In coaching, one size does not fit all. Some clients want a wise elder to advise them; others want a more collegial coach who will listen to them and ask the right questions. Some want to benefit from other people's guidance; other clients want to bounce their ideas off someone who is a stimulating thought partner. Though at first glance these distinctions may appear superficial, they have profound implications for how coaches provide help, and if coaches are to be equally helpful to all their clients, they must be adaptive in their approach.

In the first chapter we introduced our coaching styles taxonomy, which has three dimensions: directive versus nondirective, programmatic versus circumstantial, and specific versus holistic. The first dimension—directive/nondirective—reflects **how** coaches prefer to give help. The second dimension reflects **when** coaches prefer to help—during regularly scheduled meetings that constitute a coaching program or circumstantially as needs arise. The third dimension reflects **what** coaches focus on during coaching—specific tasks, skills, or behaviors on the one hand, or the client's overall life and development on the other. Although most coaches are capable of operating on either side of these three dimensions, depending on the circumstances, we have found that coaches usually prefer to use one style of coaching. We have also found that the people being coached have their preferences. Naturally, they are most satisfied with the coaching they receive when they are coached the way they wish to be coached. These three dimensions of coaching form eight distinct coaching styles, on which we will elaborate in this chapter.

HOW YOU PREFER TO GIVE HELP: DIRECTIVE VERSUS NONDIRECTIVE

Fundamentally, the difference between directive and nondirective coaching, from the coach's perspective, is the difference between telling and asking. This difference reflects a perspective on helping that has to do as much with the coach's assumptions about how people learn as with the client's self-concept and individual needs. Directive coaches believe that they help best by teaching and advising; by sharing their knowledge, experience, and perspective; and by observing others perform and giving feedback and corrective suggestions. In this mode of helping, impetus for change begins with the coach, and the coach's perspective drives the interactions. Nondirective coaches believe that they help best by asking insightful questions and listening; by stimulating their clients to think, reflect, and explore; and by helping clients observe themselves and learn from their own experiences. In the nondirective mode of helping, the impetus for change remains centered in the client, and the client's perspective drives the interactions.

Most coaching involves some combination of both approaches, but coaches generally prefer one approach to the other. Coaches who prefer the directive style have probably internalized this style from their childhood experiences and have learned that this is the "right" way to help. Coaches who have difficulty engaging in anything but directive coaching usually have a need to impart their knowledge and experience to others as a way of attaining or exercising their expertise. Such coaches are confident in their perspective, believe they are accurate observers of others, and have the authority (moral or positional) to advise others. The underlying assumption about learning is that people need to be guided, motivated, or instructed via sources external to themselves and need to be protected from failure by having the right answer from the start. Directive coaches may also be exercising their authority as managers or may believe that the management function requires or expects managers to coach directively.

Directive Coaching

Directive coaching is seductive. Our memories are filled with larger-than-life figures, often from the sports arena, like Vince Lombardi, Don Shula, John Wooden, or Phil Jackson, who help people perform at their peak or lead their teams to victory. In the popular imagination, anyway, these gruff but wise masters of motivation enable us to do better than we ever thought we were capable of doing. They always seem to know what we need. They see things about us that we can't see. Their confidence inspires us. Their criticism may sting, but it also motivates us to get back on our feet and try even harder. When we grow up, we want to be like them. Their power and their wisdom draw us to them as our ideal models. Beyond its validation by popular culture and mass media, directive coaching may be preferred by many coaches because it satisfies a deep human need to be respected, to be valued for one's knowledge, to be seen as someone whose opinion counts. In short, directive coaching is a form of self-validation and a source of validation by others.

Directive coaches coach from their perspective. They have a viewpoint about us and our performance, and they tell us what that viewpoint is. They observe us performing and tell us what they think, good or bad, about how we're doing and what we could be doing differently. At best, they really are experts in their field. They know more than we do, and we benefit when they share their insights. Some directive coaches are managers or supervisors whose roles dictate that they give direction to those who work for them, and this is how they think they should coach, whether or not they always know what they're talking about. Thus, the fundamental characteristic of directive coaching is that it springs from within the coach. The coach's perspective drives the dialogue with the client. The "arrow of influence" goes essentially one way, from the coach to the client. The directive coach is sharing his knowledge, his perspective, his opinions, his observations. These are conveyed to the client in order to be helpful, but in a purely directive mode; the coach does not solicit the client's views or ask the client to reflect on her own. The flow of knowledge is one way. The coach is the source, and the client is the vessel for receiving the coach's perspective. Directive coaches may ask insightful questions and be good listeners, but their fundamental modus operandi is to direct us toward the path they think we need to take. If they are right, and we submit to their will, then we may perform better and profit from the experience.

This may sound one-sided—and it is—but we should remember that this is what some clients want. Directive coaching is a perfectly legitimate and appropriate way to coach in some circumstances, as we note in this chapter. Clearly, directive coaching can be powerful, and it has a place in human development. It is the most appropriate form of coaching when the coach is much more of an expert in the topic than the client is. You wouldn't want an expert coach to be teaching you how to operate a piece of heavy equipment and say, "How do you think this equipment works?" When the coach is more knowledgeable, the most efficient way to be helpful is to share the knowledge. Likewise, when the situation is hazardous or requires special handling of materials, directive coaching is more appropriate. No one wants novices experimenting in situations in which safety is an issue. Similarly, if there is one and only one way to do something, then directive coaching makes the most sense. Finally, when there is little time for coaching, then directive coaching may be the most efficient way for a coach to provide help.

As these situations suggest, directive coaching is sometimes the most appropriate way to coach, regardless of the coach's or the client's preferences. Telling people how to do something is simply less time consuming than leading them through a process in which they discover the answers for themselves. Directive coaching is appropriate when you are imparting knowledge, explaining how to do something, and showing a client how something works, or when you don't have time to do anything more than very quickly tell the client to do something. Obviously, directive coaching is also the right approach when clients ask for advice and when it is what clients want.

Nondirective Coaching

Coaches who prefer to work nondirectively have often had a significant experience in their childhood or young adulthood with a nondirective coach whose approach had a profound effect on them. As a consequence, they hold a more egalitarian view of themselves as members of society in which they have no special right or privilege to advise others. Or, they may resist telling others based in a belief that they can never fully understand the nuances of another person's situation and thus can never really provide trustworthy advice or instruction. At most, they can advance highly qualified suggestions or alternatives that the client must weigh independently to reach his or her decisions. This style of coaching can sometimes look as if the coach lacks the confidence to advise someone else, but the reality is usually quite the opposite: nondirective coaches must exercise considerable self-restraint against telling their clients what to do (particularly when they are reasonably sure they know), and they exercise great patience born of confidence in the people they are coaching that they will find the right path with the proper support and subtle guidance to evaluate alternatives for themselves. Thus, nondirective coaches have learned to help others by helping them to help themselves. Such coaches view themselves as managers or leaders more in the servant leadership mode.

Nondirective coaches don't have the glamour associated with directive coaches; in fact, by design they choose to work with subtlety and near invisibility as their influence fades into the choices they help their clients make. As a result we have fewer models of nondirective coaching embedded in our collective psyche. Nondirective coaches prefer to act as counselors and guides. If you prefer to be nondirective, you tend to ask rather than tell, and you facilitate coaching sessions by soliciting the client's perceptions and ideas, asking probing questions, listening, and counseling by helping clients to explore issues and generate their own solutions. Your fundamental orientation is bilateral. You try to ensure that clients accept ownership for the discovery, problem-solving, and skill-building processes.

Here's one example. When Susan was a freshman in college, she had one of those life-changing encounters with a teacher that characterizes the best in nondirective coaching. She was taking the requisite freshman English course and learned from the student grapevine even before the term began that her teacher was notorious for failing most of her students. So when Mrs. Blake called her up after class on the second day to discuss the diagnostic essay the class had written the day before, she was sure that her college career was about to end before it even began. Instead, Mrs. Blake told her that the essay revealed a level of preparation in writing far beyond that of anyone else in the class. What she wanted, Mrs. Blake said, was for Susan to decide for herself whether each writing assignment was sufficiently challenging, or whether she wanted to do something that would challenge her further.

Susan came up with her own assignments for the rest of the term. Far from giving her a free ride, though, Mrs. Blake was as tough, if not tougher, in her feedback (and her grades) as she was on the other students in the class. The lessons Susan learned, however, went way beyond becoming a better writer.

What Mrs. Blake did was issue an invitation to Susan to reconstruct school on her own terms: to set higher standards for herself than were the norm, to do work that was intrinsically interesting to her rather than take the easy way out just to get high grades, to define problems in her own way and to solve them in her own way, to develop the courage to work in the unknown. Although not obvious to Susan at the time, Mrs. Blake's invitation reflected a philosophy of teaching and a set of values about human development grounded in notions about individual freedom and self-actualization that ran counter to prevailing educational notions anchored in the behaviorism of grading and authority. Equally important, she touched Susan's life at what educators would call a "teachable moment"—a moment when Susan was willing to accept the challenge and to work without a net. Mrs. Blake was both resource and critic, the knowledgeable guide who helped along the way but didn't map out the journey beforehand.

The two primary skills of nondirective coaching are asking and listening; the basic orientation is one of holding back. The best nondirective coaches have an elegant repertoire of questions and know how to ask the right questions at the right time to evoke insight in the client. This is the real key to success in nondirective coaching. Questions that merely elicit facts are not particularly insightful. Insightful questions are those that provoke the client into questioning why something is the case or what the implications are of various courses of action, or that capture the imagination by getting the client to think of possibilities.

The best nondirective coaches are masters of nuance. They know how to listen with the heart as well as the head, with the eyes as well as the ears. They become so deeply engrossed in the client's narrative that they sense and explore the subtleties that less skilled coaches would miss, and this is where the real power of nondirective coaching comes into play. We can imagine that the client's narrative is like a city street. Coaches who stay on the surface may see some interesting shops along the way, but unless they go underground, to the subway system, they will not understand how things really work. Otherwise, the problem is this: clients already know what is on the street level. If the coach stays there, nothing insightful is likely to happen. Only by exploring the subterranean structure do you provoke greater insight, because clients generally don't go there themselves (although they know it exists).

Another aspect of nondirective coaching that is key is people's desire to be self-sufficient. Clients want to be fully functioning, effective people and they want to be treated that way. All of us want to be capable. For the most part, we want to discover things for ourselves. Our need for self-actualization demands that we exercise our intelligence and achieve on our own merit (rather than being pulled along by some "wiser" person). We think this is why 83 percent of clients we surveyed said they prefer coaches who ask questions rather than "being told what to do." Non-directive coaching appeals to most people's need for self-sufficiency and self-directed growth.

Clients' Perspectives on Directive and Nondirective Coaching

We have been exploring the philosophical and psychological underpinnings of directive and nondirective coaching from the coach's point of view. The client's perspective on these dimensions of coaching is equally revealing. In our research on coaching style preference, we asked clients what their coaches should do to be more effective. Some clients indicated a strong preference for directive coaching:

- Be more to the point and sometimes more directive.

- Be more specific and outspoken about what you want people to do.

- Take a more assertive and active role in the coaching process, looking for long-term coachee growth and development.

- Assume more leadership and make coaching more explicit.

- Give more positive feedback and provide direction.

- Be more forceful.

- Share experiences that have worked in helping the coach be more successful in his career to help encourage new ideas.

- Tell more experiences based on examples while coaching.

Overall, 43 percent of the thousands of clients we surveyed said that they preferred directive coaching. However, 83 percent of these clients said, "I prefer the coach to ask questions and help me explore the issues myself," while only 17 percent said, "I prefer the coach to tell me what he or she thinks I should do." This suggests that while some clients want an advisor or an expert coach to show them how to do things, most clients nonetheless still prefer that their coach use questions to stimulate them to think about the issues themselves. Indeed, the vast majority of the comments we received in our research indicated a preference for nondirective coaching methods:

- Ask for self-observation first. Then give your feedback.

- Empower the person with a procedural question to find the answer, assisting them, if needed, in finding it.

- Ask more open questions and make people think for themselves first.

- Take time to sit down with people, probe for the understanding of their behavior in a specific situation, and help them see different ways to act in that situation.

- Work on becoming more of a probing coach by becoming a "master of the question."

- Probe deeper into the individual to better understand how to help.

- Solicit the other person's perspective before offering opinions.

- Allow me to search and discover the best way to do things, instead of telling me what to do. Dominate less in discussions.

- Ask open and insightful questions that encourage me to explore my ideas further.

- Minimize lecture. Not many people are good at just listening.

- Allow the people being coached to make the final decision for what they need to do and take responsibility for their decisions.

The irony is that most coaches prefer to coach directively, but most clients prefer to receive help nondirectively. For coaches to move beyond their more "natural" preferences to be directive, they need to come to terms with the philosophical and psychological assumptions beneath the two approaches and try on those that undergird the nondirective approach. Directive and nondirective coaching are not merely different sets of techniques. They reflect very different paradigms about human agency and change, and they demand that coaches approach the task from very different places regarding themselves and others.

WHEN YOU PREFER TO GIVE HELP: PROGRAMMATIC VERSUS CIRCUMSTANTIAL

The second dimension of coaching style involves the frequency and regularity with which you prefer to coach. If you prefer the programmatic approach, you view coaching as an ongoing developmental activity. Programmatic coaches typically see themselves as mentors or long-term counselors. They want to take clients under their wing, so to speak, and guide them over a long period, much as a parent helps a child develop or a master guides the development of an apprentice. Programmatic coaching relationships can extend for months or years. Coach and client meet regularly, and there is a sense that the coach is strongly invested in the client's welfare, growth, and development over the long term. The coach takes the long view and creates a program for helping the client develop continuously. For programmatic coaching to work, both the coach and the client must make a long-term commitment to the process. In contrast, in circumstantial coaching, the coach provides help on the spot, often immediately after the coach observes the client doing something or when the client shows the coach one of her work products and says, "What do you think?" Circumstantial coaches are typically more spontaneous in their coaching. They coach when it occurs to them to coach, when an opportunity presents itself, or when someone asks for coaching or feedback. Circumstantial coaching tends to be much more short term and task focused and is consequently more tactical than strategic.

We've known many coaches like this. Ben James is one. A senior consultant for a major accounting firm, Ben frequently travels with younger consultants and uses travel time in airplanes and rental cars to coach them. His coaching isn't regular, but he rarely misses a chance to give younger consultants advice, give them feedback on something he saw them doing, or inquire about their interests and counsel them on their opportunities with the firm.

Like the differences between directive and nondirective coaching, those between programmatic and circumstantial coaching are more profound than they seem at first. Programmatic coaches commit to the long-term development of the person, so they tend to think long term—where the client needs to be in a year or two and how she is going to get there, how the person learns best, what kind of progress the person is making (or not), and so on. For clients to prefer this style, they must likewise have a long-term development perspective, which implies that they see themselves as developing continuously. They have a sense of their evolving possibility, and they want to be more than they are today. They also recognize that getting where they want to go will take time and a commitment to continuing evolution. They don't expect to get there overnight; in fact they may realize intuitively what developmental psychologists have discovered over time: that you can't skip stages to get to the end of the line fast, that in fact there is no end of the line. Development unfolds along a series of plateaus, with mastery at the next level possible only as a result of mastery at the previous level. Clients who prefer programmatic coaching expect to make a continuing investment in their own development—and they may be doing so outside of the coaching as well—with continuing education classes, self-directed study, and so on.

Clients asking for circumstantial coaching generally know what they want. For client and coach alike, there is a sense of short-term gratification working in circumstantial coaching. The goals are easily specified, often in concrete, behavioral terms, and the payoffs are generally crisper, cleaner, and more easily achievable. Circumstantial coaches are adept at reading the situation quickly, helping the client identify the needed behaviors, and providing the needed support and feedback as the client tries out new skills. Such coaching takes place as the need arises.

What makes programmatic coaching different is the presence of a program and, in the coach's mind, a model of development that informs that program. The coach, for instance, may subscribe to any of a number of models of adult development: stage, holistic or incremental, cognitive development, moral or character development, leadership, or behavioral models. But effective programmatic coaches maintain a coherent theoretical perspective that informs the development plan that drives the coaching, and they usually articulate that plan to engage the client's informed participation. Clients may not know precisely what they want when they ask for programmatic coaching. The payoffs may not be well defined or even understood at the beginning of the process. Developmental models help to establish a framework that makes sense to the client but also allows the coaching to unfold and the emphasis to change. With this kind of defining framework, programmatic coaching tends to be scheduled regularly over a sustained period of time, with even the busiest clients making a commitment to the discipline of regular meetings.

In our research on coaching style preference, we asked clients to answer the question, "What should your coach do to be a more effective coach?" A number of the suggestions we heard indicated a clear preference for more programmatic coaching.

- Ensure that coaching is part of an ongoing process of professional development.

- Set regularly scheduled meetings with the individual team members, and then hold them sacred!

- Establish a set schedule for coaching sessions.

- Set aside more specific time for coaching with the people he needs to coach.

- In my opinion it is important to view coaching more as a part of a long-term development process, instead of a way to solve specific performance problems.

- Do it in a more structured, intentional way—not just as needed for specific projects.

- Take a more assertive and active role in the coaching process, looking for long-term coachee growth and development.

- Focus more on long-term issues.

- Given exceptionally difficult time constraints for coach and myself traveling frequently, a monthly formal coaching meeting could be arranged.

- More strategic, less tactical.

- More long-term/structural approach to coaching.

- Chart out long-term coaching goals and benefits.

- I would love for the coaching to be constant and not necessarily when I have a problem. His advice has been so valuable and helpful that the more I get, the more confident I feel.

- Develop a professional development plan for all the team members and revisit the plan periodically to make sure the coach and team members are on the right track.

- Do coaching more regularly. Raise the bar for yourself and for others. Be more aware of your coaching role.

- Be more proactive in coaching. Coach on a regular basis, without being explicitly asked, and not only on technical skills.

- Create a long-term plan of action that goes through the following process:

  - *Highlight areas of improvement.*

  - *Highlight long-term goals—both personal and professional.*

  - *Create a specific plan of action to address the weaknesses and move toward the goals.*

  - *Create a structured mechanism to review the above.*

  - *Take a more strategic view of long-term growth needs of your team members.*

- *Review each team member's goals for development and develop a game plan to get there. We've had discussions, but neither party committed to a real plan.*

- *Agree to a coaching approach and schedule with the people to be coached by you. Try to stick to these commitments even in busy times.*

Some coaching clients also expressed a preference for circumstantial coaching. Here are a few of their suggestions to their coaches.

- I would like short talks between the regular sessions. Half a year is too long for feedback linked to specific observations.

- I would appreciate it if he can increase unrequested coaching/support for my job. I suppose that this can increase the level of professionalism in our daily work.

- He could concentrate the coaching more at moments when it is needed the most instead of at moments when there is sufficient time.

- Provide more frequent coaching such as casual, impromptu sessions to let the coachees know when they are doing a good job or also when they have made mistakes.

Only 19 percent of clients we surveyed prefer circumstantial coaching. They may feel that they don't need much coaching, just a little now and then and at the right moments. They may not have a good programmatic coaching relationship or may not feel the need for programmatic help. However, 81 percent of clients enjoy the sustained attention from a coach and would prefer to receive regular coaching from someone they trust. The research on coaching styles shows that an overwhelming majority of clients would rather be coached programmatically. The problem with circumstantial coaching, they say, is that it can be too infrequent, and it sometimes comes too late to be helpful.

The research also shows a notable disparity between how coaches view themselves and how they are viewed by the people they coach. When asked how they coached others, 77 percent of the coaches said they coach programmatically; however, only 56 percent of clients perceived that their coaches did programmatic coaching (and 81 percent said that's what they want). Nearly 81 percent of the coaches said that they coach others regularly, on an ongoing basis; but only 61 percent of clients said they receive regular coaching. We noted throughout our research that coaches frequently had very different perceptions of themselves and how they coached compared to the perceptions of those being coached.

WHAT YOU FOCUS ON WHEN COACHING: SPECIFIC VERSUS HOLISTIC

The last of the three dimensions of coaching style preference concerns what coaches focus on when they coach: tasks, skills, or issues (specific) or the whole person (holistic). Specific coaches tend to coach on one behavior or issue at a time and make it the only focus of their coaching. If this is your perspective, you tend to give specific feedback and coach only on the skills related to that feedback. You tend to be short-term focused, and your interest is to improve one skill or issue at a time.

Gordon Fulbright is such a coach. He's a district manager for a nationwide printing company, and he coaches sixteen people on an ongoing basis. He thinks one of his primary roles as a manager is to help people build their skills, so he regularly gives people new assignments and then works closely with them to ensure that they have the skills to succeed. When he thinks they need skill development, he takes the time to work with them, pairs them with more highly skilled people for a period, or sends them to skill-based training programs. He focuses on very specific development needs. Like most managers, he sometimes becomes aware of personal problems someone is having, and if those problems impact the person's work, he will get involved. Otherwise, he prefers to keep work and life separate and does not feel he has the right to "impose" himself on people. Nor is it his responsibility to solve their life problems. People sense that he is reluctant to get involved in their personal lives, so they don't ask him for advice or help in these areas unless it is to request time off for a doctor's appointment or some other urgent life need.

In contrast is Liddy McKay, who takes a more holistic approach to helping people. Holistic coaches like Liddy prefer to coach on broader issues of professional development. People who view coaching holistically believe that coaching serves the larger goal of total personal and professional growth, so they are more likely to focus on the long term and to view the whole person as their coaching domain. Liddy is a branch manager for a brand name merchandiser. She regularly coaches about twenty-five people in her territory, and she views her role as helping them in every way, so when one of her department heads needs help dealing with a family problem, Liddy offers her counsel; and when another of her people wants career counseling, Liddy provides it. Liddy doesn't impose herself on her direct reports or get involved where she hasn't been invited, but everyone knows that she is available to help them work through any issue.

Specific coaching tends to be more behavioral and, as the profile of Gordon Fulbright indicates, it remains bounded by the demands of the job. Specific coaching is more skill based and more tactical. Holistic coaching blurs the line between life at work and life outside work. The two are linked, in the coach's perspective, and they influence each other. As in programmatic coaching, the coach must have an espoused theory about professional life as an integrated part of the client's overall lifestyle. And the client must understand and accept the coach's philosophical position as something that has a ring of truth about it.

The danger of holistic coaching is that it can foster dependence on the coach and even manipulation. Philosophical positions taken in holistic coaching are not value neutral; they come with a certain set of expectations or assumptions about how life "ought" to be lived. Competent, experienced coaches are aware of these potential traps. They articulate their values and help clients consider those values self-consciously and take personal responsibility for making their own value decisions.

Despite these dangers, our research on coaching style preferences indicates that the overwhelming majority of clients (83 percent) prefer to receive holistic coaching. Only 17 percent prefer specific, skill-focused coaching. Most of the people who receive coaching want a coach to take a more holistic approach, yet in our research only 53 percent of clients said that their coach "takes a more strategic view of my long-term growth needs" and "focuses on all aspects of my development." Some of the clients who said they wanted more holistic coaching offered these suggestions to their coaches:

- Try to coach more on a general level than on individual technical skills.

- I would appreciate more attention to career options and guidance regarding the skills needed to remain competitive as the organization evolves.

- Don't just coach on business stuff. It is okay to coach personal stuff, such as family, stress, and attitude.

- Look at the total objective—not just the specific issue: How can the coaching improve my overall performance?

- Support career development and personal goals.

- Focus feedback not only on specific problems but also on overall effectiveness.

- Offer more comprehensive overview of performance development versus coaching on a specific area that needs improvement.

- Attempt to look at the broader picture.

- Don't separate personal topics.

- I would like to have more feedback, not only regarding the project but also regarding social skills and competencies.

- Coach not only on specific expertise areas but also in overall development.

- Try to develop the attitude and skills to coach people on their overall development. In my opinion you tend to focus on the here and now. You miss the opportunity to help people in a broader way with their development.

- Of course, some clients do prefer more focused coaching on specific skills or issues, and these were some of their comments to their coaches.

- Help to overcome one or two specific weaknesses.

- Make coaching more explicit by discussing short-term goals and actions.

- Have more frequent dialogue on what's working and what is not working.

- Schedule coaching on a regular basis, as a group, on various skills to be developed, such as computer review, selling skills, negotiations, and so on.

- Coach on more specific items or tasks.

- Occasionally focus more on specific coaching needs than the more general needs.

- Offer more time to discuss specific areas where improvement or change is needed to help obtain consideration for special projects.

- Keep coaching on a more direct point or points.

The lesson we draw from our research and the suggestions clients made to their coaches is that while different people prefer either end of the spectrum, specific or holistic, there is a similar mismatch between what coaches do and what clients want. At least half the time, clients want a more holistic coaching experience, while their coaches are providing specific, highly focused coaching. The obvious lesson is that coaches should be more aware of their clients' preferences and should adapt their coaching style and approach accordingly. However, coaches may very well be operating not just in their personal comfort zone but in their professional comfort zone by sticking to more specific coaching. Less obvious, though perhaps more difficult to resolve, is the implication that coaches need considerable education, training, skill, supervision, and certification to be able to offer the kind of holistic coaching that clients so often want.

THE COACHING STYLES TAXONOMY

These three dimensions of coaching style preference form the taxonomy of coaching styles shown in table 3. Following the table of coaching styles are suggestions for coaching the people who prefer each style.

DIRECTIVE

	SPECIFIC	HOLISTIC
PROGRAMMATIC	**DPS** These coaches are experts in their field who coach by instructing, giving feedback and demonstrating skills. Working from their knowledge and experience, they focus on specific skill-based issues, like performance skills. They coach on an ongoing basis over an extended period, and their goal is to build a broad but tactical set of skills or knowledge. These coaches often create development programs that lead clients through a sequence of learning steps over time.	**DPH** These coaches are committed to the long-term development of their clients. They take a directive approach because of their hierarchical position or superior knowledge base. They may, in fact, know better than their clients, but their goal is to help clients achieve equal status and effectiveness. They are prone to giving career advice and take a strong interest in their client's growth along many dimensions. They typically coach over an extended period and see their clients evolve significantly.
CIRCUMSTANTIAL	**DCS** These coaches are typically busy, coach only in response to a specific need, and focus on the isolated skill or task they think needs improvement. Because they generally have a hierarchical relationship with the people they coach, they favor a directive approach. Their experience and expertise often make them more knowledgeable than clients, so they tend to make performance observations, give feedback, and set expectations. These coaches expect to see short-term performance improvements.	**DCH** These coaches interact with clients only occasionally, and when they do, they are mainly concerned with the development of the whole person. Their guidance tends to come from a position of superior knowledge, expertise, or moral certitude though their advice is not necessarily spiritual in nature. They often coach by telling stories or relating experiences from their own lives and hold themselves up as examples to follow. Words of wisdom typically come from this type of coach.

Table 3: Coaching Styles Taxonomy

NONDIRECTIVE

	SPECIFIC	HOLISTIC
PROGRAMMATIC	**NPS** These coaches have a long-term interest in helping clients develop, and they focus on specific skill-based growth needs. They are often more highly skilled at tasks than clients are, but they prefer that clients work through the issues themselves. They see their goal as helping others help themselves, and they tend to refrain from giving advice or exercising authority. Oftentimes, they are team members or peers and may have a mutual coaching relationship with the clients.	**NPH** These coaches take a broad view of their coaching responsibility and strive, through a series of regular interventions, to help clients develop the full spectrum of their capabilities. They believe in self-development, so they are supportive and encouraging but generally refrain from telling clients what they should do. They are often not subject matter experts, and they may not be highly skilled in areas where clients want help. Their role is to guide others in self-discovery.
CIRCUMSTANTIAL	**NCS** These coaches often have a peer relationship with clients, and their preferred mode is to act as thought partners or sounding boards for their clients. They generally coach only when asked for coaching, and they focus entirely on specific skill-based needs. They may tell clients how they have done something previously, but they mainly coach by asking questions, listening, and thoughtfully responding to questions in order to help clients solve the problems themselves.	**NPH** These coaches serve as wise advisors. They are generally older and far more experienced than their clients, and they act as shepherds gently guiding in the right direction, posing questions that help clients discover the path for themselves. They are often exemplars: models of the way to live one's life or assume particular responsibilities. They coach infrequently, but because of their stature, their interventions are likely to be very impactful.

Table 3: Coaching Styles Taxonomy continued

DPS

For clients who prefer DPS coaches, do the following:

- Use the directive process.

- Based on your skills and knowledge of the subject matter area, create a long-term skill development plan for the clients. Be able to show them a sequence of stepwise improvements in performance and be able to demonstrate each skill along the way. Your credibility as a coach depends on your mastery of the skills.

- As these clients are looking for expert guidance and direction, be willing to tell them what to do, but confine your advice to the skills they need to improve.

- Model the skills and explain what you're doing as you do it.

- Give specific, concrete feedback after observing them trying to use a skill. If they've done well, then recognize their success and reinforce the things they did right. If they haven't, offer constructive suggestions and, once again, show them what skilled performance looks like.

- When they have mastered the skills, recognize them in public for their successes.

DPH

For clients who prefer parent coaches, do the following:

- Use the directive process.

- Based on your knowledge and experience, create a long-term development program for the clients. Your credibility as a coach depends on their view of you as a wise counselor and guide, so you must be a good role model in every respect. It won't be enough for you to be highly skilled in the areas in which they need development; you must show them the way in every aspect of professional life—from how to do a particular job to how to choose the right opportunities, from how to behave like a professional to how to lead and motivate others.

- These clients are looking for wise counsel, and they may view you as a mentor. Give them direction, but also find ways for them to grow independently and encourage them to find their own way. It probably won't be the path you took, so they must be encouraged to develop their own sense of direction.

- Give honest feedback but try to be encouraging always. And applaud every little success along the way.

NPS

For clients who prefer facilitator coaches, do the following:

- Use the nondirective process.

- Be sure to devote enough time to the contracting phase. Help them define what coaching they want, when they want it, and how they want to be coached. You may have ideas, but they must always feel in control of the process.

- Ask clients to articulate their long-term growth needs and the specific skills they want to improve. Offer suggestions but let them drive the process.

- Resist the temptation to give advice; instead, ask questions that will help clients identify their skill gaps and discover the right way (for them) to close those gaps.

- Prompt them to set a schedule for the coaching. They will probably want to be coached at intervals over a long period, so ask them to set a schedule that is comfortable for them and acceptable to you.

- Remember that you are, in essence, facilitating a process of self-discovery. So begin meetings by asking what progress they've made and end by asking what they want to achieve by the next meeting. Ask, ask, ask, ask—don't tell.

NPH

For clients who prefer counselor coaches, do the following:

- Use the nondirective process.

- Take a broad view of your coaching responsibilities. Clients who want counselor coaches are seeking self-improvement on many levels, so be prepared to deal not only with job-related problems but also with life and career concerns.

- Be totally supportive and encouraging, forgiving when clients err, and enthusiastic when they succeed. You should have an attitude of unconditional positive regard toward clients, and they must always feel that you're on their side.

- Be a resource to clients—help them find the teachers, models, and experts they need. You don't have to be a role model and expert in the field or a master of the skills they are learning.

- Use feedback and observations of their performance to help them learn how they appear to others, and don't be afraid to confront them on tough issues.

DCS

For clients who prefer manager coaches, do the following:

- Use the directive process.

- Take a strong lead in shaping the coaching agenda. Clients who prefer manager coaches expect a lot of direction. You should not be overbearing or too controlling, but you should lay out the plan and state the development goals as you see them.

- Find specific events when you can observe clients' performances. Tell them what you will be looking for and give constructive feedback immediately after the event. To help them calibrate their progress, tell them how much better they did than the last time you observed them (or say that you don't see any progress) and make concrete suggestions for improving performance from there.

- Tie clients' performances to the performance of the business, unit, section, or other group. Be sure they know how their performance impacts the whole.

- Do progress checks with clients periodically to ensure that they are receiving what they need. Modify your approach if they aren't.

DCH

For clients who prefer philosopher coaches, do the following:

- Use the directive process.

- Be willing to share your view of what's right and what's wrong. Clients who prefer philosopher coaches are looking for overall guidance and direction. They want a guru who can impart words of wisdom on a variety of subjects.

- Take a holistic view of the clients. Consider not only their job performance but every part of their lives. If you confine your coaching to narrow job concerns, you will not be satisfying their needs.

- Ask questions to stimulate their own thinking and to help them develop their own insights, but note that they will not be fully nourished unless you also tell them what you think. Use stories and anecdotes to illuminate your ideas and find pithy ways to summarize your points. Clients will want to know "the moral of the story." That's why they came to you.

NCS

For clients who prefer colleague coaches, do the following:

- Use the nondirective process.

- Act like a peer. Clients who prefer colleague coaches don't want a higher authority (even if you are one). They want a peer-like coach who can act as a thought partner or sounding board. They are not looking for wisdom; they want to talk to someone who shares their experiences and can see the problems from their perspective.

- Be sure that your contract with them is clear and not too ambitious. You should be available when they need you, but don't set a regular schedule or have a long-term plan.

- Show a lot of empathy. You must put yourself in their place as you are asking questions and helping them explore the issues. Show that you feel or have felt the same thing they are feeling.

- If appropriate, ask clients for help, too. Mutual coaching is often an excellent way for peers to help themselves develop their skills.

NCH

For clients who prefer mentor coaches, do the following:

- Use the nondirective process.

- Be interested in the people you are coaching and be dedicated to helping them grow as working professionals and human beings. Clients who prefer mentor coaches expect someone who is committed to them as individuals and to their long-term career development, and they are looking for guidance along many dimensions.

- Recognize that each person has to create his or her own path. Guide clients through questions, suggestions, and modeling of the self-discovery processes that you went through in your growth as a professional, but expect them to make their own way.

- Be a resource to your clients. Help them meet the right people and build their networks. Help them uncover the right opportunities for them, learn to exploit their strengths, and mitigate their weaknesses. When you spot something that would be helpful to them, be sure they know about it. Give advice now and then, but guide mainly by helping them see what's necessary and right for them.

In our research on coaching style preferences, we surveyed more than two hundred coaches and several thousand coaching clients. The results indicate interesting disparities between how coaches view themselves (see table 4), how clients view their coaches (see table 5), and how clients prefer to be coached (see table 6).

As table 4 shows, more than half of coaches view themselves as either DPH (22 percent) or NPH coaches (30 percent). An overwhelming majority of coaches say they prefer to be programmatic (77 percent) and holistic (68 percent) in their approach, while 58 percent believe they use nondirective coaching. The composite profile, then, of the average coach

	DIRECTIVE		NONDIRECTIVE	
	SPECIFIC	HOLISTIC	SPECIFIC	HOLISTIC
PROGRAMMATIC	DPS 10%	DPH 22%	NPS 14%	NPH 30%
CIRCUMSTANTIAL	DCS 3%	DCH 7%	NCS 4%	NCH 10%

Directive	42%	Nondirective	58%
Programmatic	77%	Circumstantial	23%
Specific	32%	Holistic	68%

Table 4: How Coaches View Themselves

	DIRECTIVE		NONDIRECTIVE	
	Specific	Holistic	Specific	Holistic
Programmatic	DPS 12%	DPH 15%	NPS 13%	NPH 16%
Circumstantial	DCS 9%	DCH 12%	NCS 10%	NCH 13%

Directive	48%	Nondirective	52%
Programmatic	56%	Circumstantial	44%
Specific	44%	Holistic	56%

Table 5: How Clients View Their Coaches

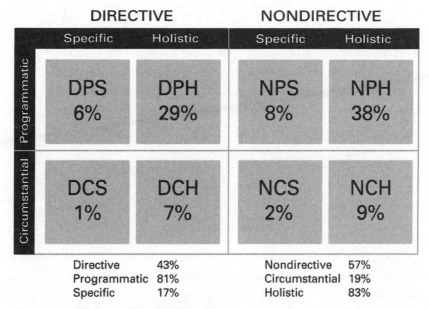

	DIRECTIVE		NONDIRECTIVE	
	Specific	Holistic	Specific	Holistic
Programmatic	DPS 6%	DPH 29%	NPS 8%	NPH 38%
Circumstantial	DCS 1%	DCH 7%	NCS 2%	NCH 9%

Directive	43%		Nondirective	57%
Programmatic	81%		Circumstantial	19%
Specific	17%		Holistic	83%

Table 6: How Clients Prefer to Be Coached

is one who is nondirective in approach, who takes a programmatic view of clients' development, and who focuses on the whole person. This profile is consistent with the composite view of coaches by clients themselves, although clients tend to see their coaches as slightly less nondirective (52 percent) and considerably less programmatic (56 percent) and holistic (56 percent). The vast majority of clients want to be coached programmatically and holistically. In fact, according to table 6, more than 80 percent of clients prefer programmatic coaching, and 83 percent prefer holistic coaching. Finally, more than half of clients prefer nondirective coaching. They want coaches who are thought partners and counselors rather than advisors and teachers. Most clients don't want to be told what to do; they want to figure it out for themselves through a coach's skillful questioning and listening. If we look at the composite view of clients, we see that 38 percent of the tens of thousands of clients we surveyed told us that they prefer coaching that is nondirective, programmatic, and holistic. However, in their view, only 16 percent of clients say their coaches coach this way. Clearly, there are some significant mismatches between how coaches prefer to coach and how clients prefer to be coached.

Of course, coaching is really not a numbers game. You can't coach by percentages. No matter what the aggregate numbers look like, coaching is always a personal and individual relationship—one coach and one client at a time. So we present these statistics to demonstrate that there are important differences between how coaches prefer to coach and how clients prefer to be coached. However, the key to effective coaching is to adapt your approach to each client's preferences.

ADAPTING TO CLIENTS' PREFERENCES

Although any coaching can be helpful, people benefit most from coaching when they get the type of coaching they prefer. If you are a directive coach, for example, but one of your clients responds best to a nondirective approach, then that's what you should use, regardless of your preference. A good time to discover what type of help a client prefers, obviously, is during the context-setting part of beginning a coaching relationship. At this point, you are explicitly asking what the client wants, and you should explore whether he wants to take a "tell" approach (directive) or an "ask" approach (nondirective); whether he would benefit from a series of scheduled coaching sessions (programmatic) or from occasional, on-the-spot coaching (circumstantial); and whether he wants to focus on particular job skills (specific) or broader career, personal, and professional topics (holistic).

As you work with someone over time, you will discover his preferences in any case. It will become clear to you and your client, for instance, that the two of you need to get together more or less frequently, that you need to focus on a particular key skill, or that he responds best and learns more when you ask him questions that help him discover the answers for himself. Coaches who are not paying attention to these factors, however, are usually less effective in the long run because they aren't providing what the client really needs. It probably does not occur to many coaches that they should adapt their style. We've known some who had the attitude that "I am who I am" and if people want help then "what they see is what they get." Like the guru in the cave at the top of the mountain, these coaches want supplicants to come to them for wisdom. They might benefit some people, but they don't have the kind of helpful attitude that is characteristic of the very best coaches.

The best coaches are like Carol Blum, a data management supervisor for the exploration group of a major oil company. Her preferred style of coaching is facilitator (nondirective-programmatic-specific). However, only a handful of the twenty people she coaches want that approach. Quite a few, like Julia Cortez, prefer directive coaching, so Carol meets with a group of them regularly and teaches them new skills, answers their questions about operational problems, and leads them through brainstorming and problem-solving sessions intended to help them learn more about data management.

Another group of employees, including Mike Girardi, prefers Carol to coach them in the mentor style. Mike likes her nondirective style, but he doesn't approach life programmatically himself, and he couldn't imagine having regularly scheduled meetings. So Carol meets with him whenever he asks for coaching or whenever she's reviewed one of his work products and has some suggestions. When they talk, she always asks how he's doing, how his plans are shaping up, and where he'd like to be in five years. Mike is self-directed on skill building, so that's not what he needs, but he appreciates Carol's willingness to talk to him about more holistic life issues. In her group of twenty, Carol has people with a wide range of coaching preferences. Some prefer a manager coach or a parent coach; others prefer a colleague coach or a counselor coach. What makes Carol so effective is that, as a coach, she is willing to be whatever kind of coach her clients need her to be.

A SELF-TEST ON COACHING STYLE PREFERENCES

How do you prefer to coach? To conclude this chapter, we include the following simple self-test to help you diagnose your preferred coaching style.

COACHING STYLE PREFERENCES SELF-ASSESSMENT

This is a forced-choice questionnaire. For each pair of statements, indicate which statement best describes how you prefer to coach by circling the corresponding letter in the right-hand column. Though some statements may seem close, force yourself to choose one or the other.

1	I prefer to observe the people I'm coaching, determine what help they need, and then offer suggestions, advice, and feedback.	D
	I prefer to act as a sounding board for the people I'm coaching, asking questions to help them think through their issues and needs and letting them discover the right answers for themselves.	N
2	I prefer to help my coaching clients build specific skills or deal with specific issues.	S
	I prefer to coach people more broadly on their overall development, including career choices and non-work-related issues.	H
3	I prefer to coach people on an ongoing basis—weekly, monthly, or quarterly—and to schedule coaching sessions regularly.	P
	I prefer to coach people only during periodic performance reviews or when the need arises.	C
4	I prefer to coach by sharing my knowledge, experience, and perspectives with the people I'm coaching and telling them what I think they need to know. In my coaching, I am most like a teacher.	D
	I prefer to coach by being a good listener and responding thoughtfully to what I hear. In my coaching, I am most like a counselor.	N
5	I prefer to coach people on every aspect of their personal and professional lives. I am comfortable discussing people's career plans and enjoy helping them think through their options.	H
	I prefer to coach people on particular performance problems or short-term skill development needs. I am less comfortable discussing people's career plans and don't see myself as a career counselor.	S
6	I prefer to coach only when something happens that indicates I need to do some coaching.	C
	I prefer to coach people regularly, as part of a comprehensive program for building their skills and improving their performance.	P
7	I usually give people feedback on their performance and tell them how I think they are doing, making suggestions as appropriate.	D
	I usually ask people how they think they are doing and use questions to help them explore their perceptions before I tell them what I think.	N

8	I am very comfortable discussing people's personal problems and offering my suggestions, where appropriate.	H
	I am not comfortable discussing people's personal problems and offering my suggestions.	S
9	I prefer to coach people only when they think they need help, which depends on the circumstances.	C
	I would rather meet with people I'm coaching routinely so we can work together continuously on their development plan.	P
10	I think that as a coach I should refrain from giving people advice. Instead, I should guide them through a process of self-discovery where they learn to solve their own problems and help themselves.	N
	I think that as a coach I should set the agenda for coaching sessions and give people the kind of help I think they need. That's what they expect from a coach	D
11	As a coach, I am most interested in how people develop over time. I try to help them think through where they want to be in a year or two and what it will take for them to get there.	P
	As a coach, I am most interested in helping people solve their immediate problems and learn what they need to learn to be more effective now. I think the long term takes care of itself.	C
12	As I coach, I am most intrigued by someone's overall development as a person, and that may include his or her spiritual and personal growth. I enjoy coaching on a wide range of issues that help the whole person.	H
	As I coach, I am most interested in helping people build their work skills and become more capable in areas directly related to their job.	S
13	I don't have, or would prefer not to have, a personal development plan that defines my developmental needs and indicates how I am going to get there.	C
	I have, or would prefer to have, a personal development plan.	P
14	I don't like it when people won't just speak up and tell me what they think I should do.	D
	I don't like people to give me advice.	N
15	I most admire coaches who are masters of particular tasks, skills, or disciplines.	S
	I most admire coaches whose whole approach to life and work is worth modeling.	H

To determine your coaching style preferences, enter the number of times you circled each letter in the spaces below. The letter in each pair that you circled most often indicates your preference in the three dimensions of coaching style.

D (Directive) _____

N (Nondirective) _____   Your preference _____

To determine your coaching style preferences, enter the number of times you circled each letter in the spaces below. The letter in each pair that you circled most often indicates your preference in the three dimensions of coaching style.

D (Directive)   _____

N (Nondirective)   _____   Your preference _____

P (Programmatic)   _____

C (Circumstantial)   _____   Your preference _____

S (Specific)   _____

H (Holistic)   _____   Your preference _____

PART

2

Practicing Adaptive Coaching

This part of the book focuses on the skills required to practice adaptive coaching. The six chapters here offer a number of annotated sample dialogues between coaches and clients, as well as questions coaches might ask to further the dialogue and help clients develop insight.

We begin in chapter 6 with a discussion of how coaches can best initiate coaching relationships and open each coaching session. Openings are obviously important because they create first impressions, can build (or destroy) trust, and establish the environment in which the coach and client will work together. Equally important are closings, which we discuss in chapter 11. We believe that effective coaching follows a clear pattern of opening, middle, and closing. To achieve satisfying results throughout a coaching relationship, coaches must manage their openings and closings skillfully.

Coaching of all kinds is done largely through discussions between the coach and the client. We refer to these discussions as the *coaching dialogue*, and in chapter 7 we describe how effective coaches manage the dialogue. The dialogue is a journey of discovery, and the context we spoke about in the first part of the book is the territory in which that journey takes place.

Knowing how to manage the dialogue and use it to provoke insight is one of a coach's most important skills. Because the dialogue is a process of discovery, it can lead to areas a coach is not prepared to address, such as serious psychological problems. When this happens, coaches must know how to stop the dialogue and refer clients to professionals who are competent to handle such problems. Responsible coaches know the ethical limits of their work with clients and do not violate those limits.

Chapters 8, 9, and 10 describe the core dialogue skills, including listening and asking questions; sharing your observations with clients, which includes giving feedback, reframing, and reflecting; and pushing clients (advising, teaching, and confronting), as well as pulling them (encouraging and doing process checks). We have used the push/pull metaphor to illuminate the dynamic nature of the coaching dialogue. Mastering the skills described in these chapters is crucial. Without them, coaches cannot sustain an effective dialogue with clients.

6

Initiating Coaching Sessions

Start coaching at the beginning of the process, not in the middle.

Get to know the person very well, i.e., personal goal setting, how the person becomes motivated best, in order to provide an adequate coaching method.

Keep a clear record of what has been discussed during previous meetings or coaching sessions to chart progress and to revisit specific issues from previous sessions.

SUGGESTIONS TO COACHES FROM THE "COACHING EFFECTIVENESS SURVEY," KORN/FERRY INTERNATIONAL

In our research on coaching, we explored how effective coaches were at negotiating expectations up front. We learned that "negotiating expectations" was the second-lowest rated coach behavior among the thirty-three behaviors we studied. Moreover, the coaches agreed. They rated themselves very low on this statement: "At the beginning of coaching, I always clarify everyone's expectations. The coaching process is always explicit." Consequently, a number of clients don't know what to expect, and the coaches don't always know what their clients want and need from coaching. Clearly, it's difficult to meet someone's needs if you don't know what they are, so this step is an important element of the first meeting.

Aristotle's notion that "well begun is halfway done" applies very much to coaching. The coaching relationship, begun at the first meeting of the coach and the client, must start well if real trust is to develop. Because of the fragile nature of trust, rarely are there opportunities to overcome a bad start. In this chapter, we are going to explore what it means to start well: how to initiate a coaching relationship, what you can do prior to the first session with a new client, how to conduct the first session, and how to open subsequent coaching sessions. Our experience as coaches suggests that everything you do in the early stages of coaching is critical to developing a successful coaching relationship.

INITIATING A COACHING RELATIONSHIP

Coaching can be initiated in a variety of ways. Sometimes, clients seek out a coach and ask for coaching. Generally, when they do so they have already thought about who would make the best coach for them, and they approach someone who, they believe, can help them. Other times, coaches are appointed for clients, perhaps by clients' managers or a human resources manager. Sometimes a coaching relationship evolves because one person has been helpful to another and the latter asks for coaching. Coaches can sometimes initiate a coaching relationship when the client has not explicitly asked for it. Although it's possible to simply ask someone if she wants coaching, sometimes it's better not to use the "C" word. Instead of saying, "Would you like coaching?" you might say:

♦ Would you like to spend a moment talking about how else you might have done that?

♦ Would it be helpful to think through your alternatives?

♦ I would be happy to spend some time talking through this issue if you would find that useful.

♦ Would you like some suggestions on how you might deal with this?

Some people don't like to think they are being coached but will welcome the help and respond favorably to these kinds of statements and questions. This works even with very senior executives if they find the potential coach credible. Oftentimes, coaching relationships evolve over time. You do some impromptu coaching for someone and she finds it helpful and later asks if you would be willing to provide more coaching. Such coaching relationships can evolve from nothing to a formal coaching program in a matter of weeks or months.

In some cases, a coaching relationship is assumed, generally in hierarchical organizations. The boss is presumed to be a coach for her subordinates. The team leader is expected to coach the members of his team. In assumptive coaching relationships like these, an authority relationship already exists that can predispose the coach to take a directive approach and predispose the coaching "clients" to accept coaching even if they have a negative or neutral relationship with the coach and don't find that person trustworthy, credible, or compatible. In our view, these are not true coaching relationships but are merely extensions of the supervisory relationship that exists, and the "coaching" is more likely to be direction setting from an authority figure. Managers and supervisors who truly want to act as coaches need to establish coaching relationships that are parallel to the authority relationships they already have. In other words, they may need to step outside their roles as managers to act as coaches. In our experience, some managers are capable of this but many aren't. Further, some clients cannot suspend the reality that their "coach" is still the person who evaluates, promotes, and rewards them in the other role as boss or manager.

Whatever the case may be, for a coaching relationship to form and be sustained, the client must believe that the coach is trustworthy, credible, and compatible—and that there are tangible outcomes to the coaching being provided or a reasonable expectation of such outcomes. Coaching is an intimate relationship between one person who seeks help and another who agrees to provide it. Figure 5 illustrates that without trust, credibility, and compatibility (or chemistry), it's unlikely that clients will agree to be coached or will derive anything from it if the coaching is forced upon them.

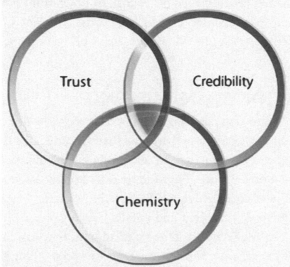

Figure 5: Components of Relationship Building

Trust and credibility are bedrock fundamentals, but even credible and trustworthy coaches can sometimes strike out with particular clients because of a lack of chemistry. Chemistry is one of those concepts that is difficult to define, although most people know what it means. We like some people and don't like others, often for reasons that are mysterious but may revolve around how much commonality we feel with them and how compatible their values, attitudes, and behaviors are with ours. As people are considering a coaching relationship with us, they invariably subject us to a "chemistry test" by asking themselves the kinds of questions shown in the text box "Checking for the Components of a Good Coaching Relationship" on pages 125–126.

The "fit" question applies to coaches as well. You may be asked to coach someone and decide, for whatever reason, that this is not someone you can coach or, frankly, want to coach. The chemistry may not be right for you. When this occurs, it is best to refer the client to someone else whose style and approach are better suited to that person. Compatibility works both ways.

However a coaching relationship is initiated, there will be a moment or a period in which both coach and client reflect on whether this is a relationship they want to enter into. Either may feel compelled to do so because of existing relationships or a sense of obligation, but the most fruitful coaching relationships are generally those in which both parties consent to participate and in which trust, credibility, and chemistry are mutually felt.

PREPARATION FOR COACHING

One could argue that coaching begins even before the first meeting of coach and client as the coach prepares for that meeting. This is especially true of external coaches who may be serving a new organization or a new person within an organization, but to some extent it's true of any coaching relationship. The context setting we discussed in chapter 1 begins before the first meeting with the client and entails learning about the organization and how it works, identifying the stakeholders of the coaching process and what they expect from the coaching, and understanding the climate for coaching and development in the organization. Finally, before the first meeting with the client, a coach may initiate data gathering through 360-degree surveys, psychometric assessments, and confidential interviewing of people who work with the client.

Prior to coaching, it's important for coaches, especially external coaches, to develop an understanding of the organization. How is the company

---

CHECKING FOR THE COMPONENTS OF A GOOD COACHING RELATIONSHIP

TRUST
- Are you honest and worthy of trust? Will you always tell me the truth?
- Do you keep your promises and commitments? Will you do what you say you will do and deliver what you promise?
- Will you be candid with me, even if it means giving me bad news?
- Will you treat me fairly?
- Will you look out for my interests? Will you do what's right for me?
- Will you avoid surprising me with problems or costs I hadn't counted on?
- Will you keep any secrets I tell you? Will you be discreet?
- Will you be there when I need you?

CREDIBILITY
- Are you a reputable coach? Have you helped other people successfully?
- Do you have the education, experience, and background I need?
- Do you know what you're talking about?
- Do you understand my needs, and have you helped others with similar needs?
- Do you speak confidently?
- Do your answers to my questions reveal deep knowledge of the subject?
- Do you ask knowledgeable and insightful questions of me?
- Have you worked in my industry or company before?

CHEMISTRY

- Do we have any commonalities? Do we share the same values, perspectives, or attitudes?
- Are you interested in my industry? Are we curious about the same things? Do we have insights to share with each other?
- Do you understand my operating style and preferences, and are you willing to adapt? Will you work with me the way I want? Will you communicate with me the way I like to communicate?
- Do you know what's important to me, what my priorities are?
- Do I enjoy working with you, not just because you're a nice person and we have some common personal interests, but because you add value to me?
- Do I like you? Would I enjoy being in your company?

---

organized? Who are the key people surrounding the coaching client? How does the organization work? What are its values and culture? In chapter 1, we argued that coaching does not occur in a vacuum. It's imperative for coaches to understand the environment in which the client operates and the values, perspectives, and expectations at work in the organization. We've worked in organizations, for instance, that are highly competitive, where individual accomplishment is most highly rewarded, where feedback is threatening, and where coaching tends to be a top-down activity associated with annual performance appraisals. We've worked in other organizations that are highly collaborative, where teamwork and cooperation are most highly rewarded; where feedback is encouraged and shared openly; and where coaching is valued, flows in all directions, and occurs almost spontaneously at many points throughout the year.

We have found, not surprisingly, that clients' receptivity to coaching depends to a large extent on the organization's climate and culture. We have also found that many organizations do not have a culture that is conducive to coaching. In our research on coaching, for instance, 37 percent of the respondents said that managers or team leaders in their organization are not expected to coach others regularly. Fifty-two percent of respondents reported that in their organization coaching is not used as a systematic tool to help people develop professionally. Seventy-two percent said that coaches in their organization are not recognized and rewarded for doing coaching. Finally, only 21 percent of respondents said that they receive coaching in conjunction with regular, formal evaluations of their performance. Although these numbers may not be surprising, it is nonetheless difficult to believe that more organizations do not take advantage of coaching as a primary tool for developing their people. In any case, it's important to know, before coaching in an organization, how coaching is perceived in that organization and how open clients are likely to be toward it.

Beyond understanding the organization, it's important to identify and negotiate expectations with the relevant stakeholders. The stakeholders include not only the person being coached but potentially a range of people including the client's direct reports, peers, and boss or other people higher in the organization. They could also include the relevant human resources manager and others responsible for talent development in the organization. An important reason for identifying and talking to these stakeholders is that they form the "ecosystem" within which the client operates. Not only can they be helpful in assessing the client's strengths and weaknesses (they are the "east" pole of the needs compass we discussed in chapter 3), they are a source of ongoing feedback and information during the coaching process. They can help reinforce behavioral changes the client is trying to make, and they can help evaluate progress. Where it is feasible to do so, involving these members of the client's ecosystem in the coaching process makes the client's development a more open and collaborative endeavor.

In most of the coaching we do, we interview the key members of the client's ecosystem during our initial information gathering and diagnosis of the client's real needs. We also suggest to clients that they be transparent with these people about what they are working on and what they are trying to accomplish. If they are willing to share their development goals and measures of success—which, together, constitute a large part of clients' personal development plans—then these people can participate in the development process by reinforcing positive changes, telling clients when they have backslid, and keeping the coach informed on progress. People in clients' ecosystems become part of their broader support network, and having such a network is obviously beneficial in human change programs (it's one of the fundamentals of group therapy, for instance, as well as twelve-step programs like Alcoholics Anonymous). Even if clients are not willing to be transparent about their coaching program with the people they work with, it's still important for coaches to know who those people are and to interview them confidentially prior to coaching.

CONDUCTING THE FIRST COACHING SESSION

The first meeting between a coach and a client is obviously very important. It can set the tone for everything that follows. For that matter, it may determine whether anything follows. In our view, the initial meeting should be an ambitious one. In the professional coaching we provide, that meeting can last from two to four hours, and the coach can achieve the following:

- Building rapport and trust
- Exploring the context of the coaching by learning more about the organization and the client's role
- Negotiating the expectations for the coaching relationship
- Discovering the client's self-perceptions and sense of needs
- Sharing feedback and observations gleaned from confidential interviews
- Exploring the client's real needs
- Agreeing on initial steps in the client's development plan

This approach to the first meeting may appear to be most appropriate if you are doing programmatic coaching. However, coaches using the circumstantial approach should also begin the process with a lengthy first meeting that accomplishes many of the same things.

Building Rapport and Trust

If you don't know the client well, you need to spend time becoming acquainted. It's best not to rush into the coaching until both people are comfortable with each other, and this requires a slow and sensitive approach in most cases. Typically, you would introduce yourself, ask the client to introduce herself, give some background information on yourself, and ask if the client has any questions about you.

Exploring Context and Negotiating Expectations

Generally, after getting acquainted, it's important to explain how the process will work, especially if the client has never had coaching before, if this coaching process will be different from what the client is accustomed to, or if you are coming in from outside the organization and the client has never worked with you before. In most cases, the client's chief concern is the degree of confidentiality of the process. In most of the coaching we do, the process is entirely confidential except that we prefer for the client's development plan to be shared with key stakeholders, so this is the expectation we express. Whatever the particular ground rules are, it's important to make them clear in the first meeting and ensure that the client understands and agrees with them. In chapter 2, we referred to this as negotiating expectations, or contracting. Essentially, you are trying to become aligned on the ground rules you both will follow during this coaching relationship.

Some coaches prefer to explore the contexts of coaching (see chapter 1) before they talk about how the process will work. It probably doesn't matter which comes first as long as the client is comfortable. In any case, when you explore the contexts, you are trying to understand both the client's organization and her role in it. Generally, context setting and contracting takes the form of casual conversation in which the coach asks a lot of questions and solicits questions from the client. Some of the questions you might ask are:

◆ Who are you? Tell me about yourself and your organization.

◆ What would you like to know about me?

◆ Why do you want coaching?

◆ Why now?

◆ How important is this coaching?

◆ What do you expect from the coaching?

◆ What would be the best outcome of this coaching for you?

◆ How do you want to work together? What works best for you?

◆ Have you had coaching before? How did that turn out?

Discovering the Client's Self-Perceptions

If the client has completed 360-degree assessments or psychometric surveys, or if the coach has observed the client beforehand or conducted confidential interviews with people who work with the client, then there is a temptation to share this feedback early in the first meeting. Clients will obviously know if they have completed an assessment and are often aware of the coach's other data-gathering activities. They will be curious about what the coach found. However, to avoid biasing their perceptions, it's best to defer sharing feedback and observations until after you have explored how they perceive themselves and what they think they need.

In chapter 3 we suggested the kinds of questions you might use to ask clients about their leadership, management, or interpersonal skills. Even before asking these questions, you might open by asking clients what they believe are their strengths and what are their weaknesses. We often ask some variation of these questions:

- What do you think you do well? What don't you do well?

- How would you describe yourself as an [executive assistant, engineer, designer, team leader, etc.]?

- What do you think are your developmental needs?

- What would you like to focus on?

The purpose of these questions is to get clients' high-level views of themselves, to force them to synthesize from their perceptions of themselves and the feedback they've gotten from others. It's often insightful to compare their own view of themselves with the views you glean from 360-degree surveys (e.g., *Survey of Influence Effectiveness, Voices® 360*), psychometric assessments (e.g., Myers-Briggs Type Indicator®, FIRO-B® assessment, California Psychological Inventory™), and confidential interviews.

Sharing Feedback and Observations

If you have gathered information on the client prior to the first meeting, then you need to share that information in some form. If the client has completed some assessments, then you should give her the feedback reports (if she doesn't have them already) and walk through them with her. It's important that you have read the reports already and developed a perspective on what you've discovered there. Clients can read it for themselves, but they are usually curious about what conclusions you have drawn from their reports. However, refrain from saying, "Here are your reports and here's what they mean." Instead, you might first ask what the client got from her report, what surprised her, what confirmed what she already knew, and so on. Note any significant findings, positive or negative, and inquire about them.

- Did you expect to be so highly rated in these areas?

- Were you surprised to receive lower scores in these areas?

- Why do you think people rated you high (or low) in this area?

- What does this profile suggest to you?

If the client has completed a 360-degree survey that includes narrative comments from respondents, then it is especially important to discuss all narrative comments. Look for patterns among the narrative comments that suggest key strengths or weaknesses.

- This is an interesting comment. What do you think it means?

- Why do you think someone would make this suggestion?

- When you read these comments, do you see any patterns? What about these three comments? They seem to suggest the same thing, don't they?

- Now that you've read all the comments, how would you summarize your feedback? What do people say are your strengths, and where do you have developmental needs?

Generally, it's best to ask clients to interpret the data and draw their own conclusions, although you should have your own perspective and share it with clients, especially if your interpretation of the reports differs from theirs. If you have done confidential interviews, you obviously cannot share the confidential information, but you should synthesize it and give clients an overview of the impressions you received. You might also ask clients how they are performing in their jobs and what their performance measurements indicate. Are they meeting or exceeding expectations or do they have a gap to close? Essentially, you are trying to close the loop on the four poles of the needs compass that we described in chapter 3, taking in all relevant information to help understand where the client is now and where she needs to be.

Exploring the Client's Real Needs

In the dialogue that follows the discussion of feedback, you synthesize initial impressions and begin to explore the client's real needs, as we discussed in chapter 4. In our experience, the real needs emerge over time and through a number of conversations. It's unlikely that clarity on the client's real needs will come during the initial meeting, although you will probably make some progress and perhaps substantial progress. Generally, identifying the real needs is like peeling an onion. You may peel some layers during the first meeting, but there will probably be more layers to go. To peel the remaining layers, you need to build more trust and stimulate more insight through the continuing dialogue and your ongoing observations of the client.

We have found it useful near the end of the first meeting to ask clients to summarize. We keep a running summary ourselves, so we can compare the client's views with our own. We ask clients to summarize the feedback, noting where people thought they were strong or weak, and to identify the two or three key things they need to work on. These are their developmental needs, and if clients list more than a handful of needs, we suggest they prioritize. People may want to improve in dozens of areas (we've seen this), but they won't be able to focus on more than two or three things at a time. Prioritizing forces them to decide what areas of development would have the greatest immediate impact on their work or their lives and results in the greatest degree of improvement. When clients list more than two or three developmental goals, we suggest that they take a phased approach and focus on less important areas only after mastering the more important ones.

Creating a Personal Development Plan

In the programmatic approach to coaching, this discussion of needs and goals leads naturally to the creation of a personal development plan. (In circumstantial coaching, you may simply agree on what to look out for as you observe the client performing.) One of the primary tools in programmatic coaching is a development plan, so creating one is an important outcome of the first meeting. If you don't know enough to complete the plan by the end of this meeting, then you should at least discuss how you will get it done. When clients prefer programmatic coaching—and 78 percent of them do—they expect you to help them develop through a systematic process.

However, 41 percent of the coaching clients we surveyed said that they do not have a plan for their professional development. They aren't sure what skills or knowledge they need to build and do not have a clear set of developmental goals. Moreover, 56 percent of clients report that the coaching they receive is often not focused on the right things and does not help them learn exactly what they should do differently to be more effective. These statistics indicate that a significant number of coaches are not helping their clients identify what they need to change and are not helping them find systematic ways to accomplish their goals.

Personal development plans can take many forms, but most identify three things: clients' goals based on their needs, the steps they have agreed to take to reach those goals, and how they will measure success. The steps they agree to take generally involve behavioral changes and are very concrete. In chapter 12 we discuss a human change process model that helps coaches lead clients through the difficult process of change, and we will defer further discussion of action steps until that chapter. The key, during this first meeting, is to end with some formal or informal sense of the path forward. If you are doing programmatic coaching, then that path should be articulated in a personal development plan that the client agrees to undertake.

OPENING SUBSEQUENT COACHING SESSIONS

In subsequent meetings, the opening is important but less crucial than in the first meeting. If all has gone well, trust will continue from the first meeting and will build steadily as the coach is being helpful. Nonetheless, the opening is a "warming up" period in which the coach reestablishes and builds upon the context, learns what's been happening, and continues to show (by asking questions) that the client's world, interests, and needs are the focus of this process. As you open subsequent sessions with clients, you can reestablish the dialogue by asking these kinds of questions:

♦ How are you?

♦ How are things at work? (at home, if relevant)

♦ What's happened since our last meeting?

♦ What progress have you made? Or failed to make? Why?

♦ How did you feel about our last meeting?

♦ Should we do anything differently this time?

♦ Is there anything we need to talk about today?

♦ What would you like to accomplish today?

♦ Where should we start?

Of course, you might want to do a number of other things early in subsequent meetings: discuss any "homework" you might have asked the client to do, share your observations of the client's performance, look at particular work products, and so on. However, opening the meeting with the kinds of questions listed here accomplishes several important coaching goals. First, it reminds the client that this change and development process is essentially his, not yours. You are a helper, but he is driving the changes. Second, it emphasizes that your perspective is less important than his perspective and that you are primarily interested in knowing about him. Third, opening this way lets you know what's on the client's mind and can help guide the dialogue in the right direction.

Initiating the coaching process can seem mundane if you perceive that the initial session serves primarily social purposes: introducing oneself, getting acquainted, asking context-setting questions, and so on. However, just as on the first day of school or the first day in a new job, openings create indelible impressions, and our research on coaching suggests that many coaches squander the best chance they have to create powerful coaching relationships. It doesn't have to be that way.

7

Managing the Dialogue

Ask probing or leading questions, exhibit patience, and voice dis-
agreements so that discussion can help facilitate the coaching process
further. Make certain you voice the thoughts you wish to express (don't
assume others are reading your mind).

Listen and let the client explain the problem/situation before offer-
ing a solution prematurely.

Avoid a lot of miscommunication by asking the right questions at
the right time.

SUGGESTIONS TO COACHES FROM THE "COACHING EFFECTIVENESS
SURVEY," KORN/FERRY INTERNATIONAL

The work of coaching is done largely through conversation. In fact, over the period of time a coach works with a client, there will be many conversations. Together, these conversations constitute the dialogue between the coach and the client. Coaches typically begin the process knowing very little about their clients; clients begin knowing a lot but may be unable to articulate their experience in insightful ways and may be blind to some aspects of themselves and their operating style that influence where they have been and where they are going. *Dialogue is a process of discovery*. It is intended to chart uncharted territory, to map what clients have done well and poorly, to explore what challenges they've faced and how they have responded to them, to find and remove roadblocks, to uncover possibilities, and to scout the territory ahead. Dialogue is an act of exploration to help clients determine what they must do to navigate the rest of their journey safely and successfully. What can make coaching so powerful is that clients don't have to take this journey alone. Their coach is a guide, a helper, a friendly ear and voice, an experienced navigator who can help handle the rough spots, identify dangers, and point out the important sights along the way. Coaches, then, are co-creators of their clients' journeys, and the primary tool they use is dialogue.

DAVID BOHM'S CONCEPT OF DIALOGUE

One commonly thinks of dialogue either as a conversation between two or more people or as the words spoken by characters in a work of fiction. The term acquired a more specialized meaning in the early 1990s when British physicist and philosopher David Bohm used it to describe a multifaceted process that helps groups of people explore their perceptions and assumptions and deepen communication and understanding. Bohm felt that many of the world's problems occurred because people talk at cross-purposes, don't examine their assumptions, are unaware of how their perceptions influence their thought processes, and try to prevail in conversations by imposing their "truth" on others. The result is a thoughtless form of communication that leads to misunderstanding and conflict.

In 1991, Bohm outlined his ideas on dialogue in a paper entitled "Dialogue: A Proposal" (coauthored by Donald Factor and Peter Garrett). First, the authors explain their use of the term and their purpose for proposing this new form of communication:

Dialogue, as we are choosing to use the word, is a way of exploring the roots of the many crises that face humanity today. It enables inquiry into, and understanding of, the sorts of processes that fragment and interfere with real communication between individuals, nations and even different parts of the same organization. (Bohm, Factor, and Garrett, 1991

According to the authors, "In dialogue, a group of people can explore the individual and collective presuppositions, ideas, beliefs, and feelings that subtly control their interactions" (ibid.). This enables them to communicate more clearly and explore ideas in an unbiased atmosphere that allows for more reflection—and therefore more insight. As Bohm explains:

Dialogue is a way of observing, collectively, how hidden values and intentions can control our behavior, and how unnoticed cultural differences can clash without our realizing what is occurring. It can therefore be seen as an arena in which collective learning takes place and out of which a sense of increased harmony, fellowship and creativity can arise. (ibid.)

The key to having a fruitful dialogue is removing the element of competition among the people conversing. As Bohm says, "In dialogue . . . nobody is trying to win" (1996, p. 7). Author Deborah Flick elaborates on this concept by distinguishing between the "Conventional Discussion Process," which she says is an artifact of the "debate culture" that exists today, and the process of dialogue, which she refers to as the "Understanding Process." In her book *From Debate to Dialogue,* Flick (1998) observes, "The framework of the debate culture is built with a host of interlocking, invisible assumptions about the way to discover 'the truth' and what is right, good, and of value, or not. These assumptions encourage and reinforce beliefs and behaviors that place a premium on being right, persuading others, winning, and finding 'The' answer" (pp. 3–4). What makes dialogue so difficult for most people is that we are trained from an early age to be right. In virtually all of our educational experiences, being right is rewarded and being wrong is punished. We are encouraged less to explore, listen, and be open to other perspectives than we are to have our own point of view or to discover the "truth." Consequently, we learn the mindset, habits, and interactional patterns of the debate culture—attitudes and behaviors that remain with us as we later try to coach others.

What makes dialogue difficult for most people is that it feels like you are giving something up. You have to suppress the urge to be right (and prove others wrong). You have to listen without reloading. You have to be willing to examine your assumptions and beliefs publicly and with an eye toward uncovering where they came from—no matter where that might lead or what it might expose. It can be a frightening experience, not one you can undertake with a steady hand and a calm heart if your ego depends on being right and you fear being vulnerable. However, if dialogue is not about being right, it's also not about being wrong. Rather, it's about suspending judgment and exploring ideas in an atmosphere in which exploration itself is both the journey and the outcome. Once people make the leap from a debate mindset to a dialogue mindset, they find that dialogue is liberating and mind expanding, not threatening. As Flick explains,

> *The Understanding Process invites us to surrender our assumptions, the building blocks of our opinions and perspectives. In a dialogue atmosphere that is accepting rather than faultfinding, ideas flow more easily and our willingness to explore them deeply and nondefensively is heightened. We are inspired to ask insightful, illuminating questions as our understanding deepens. (p. 17)*

Dialogue does not demand that we give up our own ideas while we listen to someone else we might disagree with. It merely asks that we suspend our judgment and explore those contrary ideas with an open mind. Flick adds, "A key to practicing the Understanding Process is the knowledge that understanding someone from their point of view does not necessarily mean agreeing with them. Nor does deeply understanding another perspective require we surrender our own beliefs and values" (p. 7).

One of the principal benefits of dialogue is that it fosters more open communication by removing the element of judgment. If I am participating in a dialogue, as Bohm defines it, I should be able to say what's on my mind without fearing that others are judging me, finding fault with my ideas, or forming adverse opinions about me. Of course, I have to trust that what I say will not be used against me later, so dialogue requires a degree of trust among the participants. Interestingly, trust is both a prerequisite and an outcome of dialogue. In his 1991 proposal, David Bohm describes how trust builds through the experience of dialogue.

> *As sensitivity and experience increase, a perception of shared meaning emerges in which people find that they are neither opposing one another, nor are they simply interacting. Increasing trust between members of the group—and trust in the process itself—leads to the expression of the sorts of thoughts and feelings that are usually kept hidden. There is no imposed consensus, nor is there any attempt to avoid conflict.*

Bohm's concept of dialogue applies to coaching in numerous ways. To show the parallels, here are the precepts and practices of dialogue:

- The purpose is to facilitate open communication.

- A key method is to examine perceptions and assumptions, to try to understand the basis for long-held beliefs and behaviors.

- The participants should be unbiased and open to exploration.

- One key goal is that it is not about debate, where there are winners and losers.

- In dialogue, everyone wins.

- Another goal is to understand how "hidden" values and intentions control behavior.

- There is no single right answer. There may be multiple "truths" from multiple perspectives.

- Two of the primary skills are asking and listening.

- Participants must learn to suspend judgment. Fault finding is anathema to the process.

- Participants do not necessarily have to agree with one another. The goal is not to reach consensus, though that may be an outcome.

- As trust grows, so does the participants' willingness to disclose thoughts and feelings that are usually hidden, which results in greater insight.

- A successful outcome is the emergence of shared meaning.

It should be apparent that these are also the precepts and best practices of coaching. Coaching is not about imposing one's will, perspectives, or ideas on another person. It's about helping clients explore, understand, develop insight, and change their attitudes and behaviors so they become better leaders, managers, colleagues, and contributors to the enterprise.

Dialogue is particularly relevant in coaching executives because, with rare exception, the coach will not have performed the client's job and cannot give direct, experience-based advice on how to handle the situations and challenges the client is facing. Sure, it would be great if every CEO could have Jack Welch as a coach (notwithstanding Welch's personal choices after retiring from GE), but the reality is that most of the people coaching CEOs have not been a CEO themselves. Furthermore, even if they have, they are unlikely to have been a CEO in their client's industry, in a business the size of the client's business, or in a business with the same challenges and problems their client is facing. Most executive coaches do have a background in business and a good understanding of general business issues, but they will have only a proximate understanding of the issues, challenges, problems, and opportunities each of their clients is facing. Besides, coaching is not about offering specific problem-related advice to struggling executives. It is about helping those executives grow and develop in their own ways. That's why the dialogue is a journey of discovery for both the coach and the client. The text box "The Benefits of Dialogue" further describes the value of dialogue.

THE BENEFITS OF DIALOGUE

- Dialogue engages clients much more than a one-way monologue does. It engages the other person's mind and makes him part of the solution building. The alternative, advice giving, is generally not as helpful, partly because it has a parent-child feel to it and partly because advice is frequently off target or irrelevant.
- Because dialogue is more engaging, clients tend to be more committed to the results. People are generally more committed to solutions they helped create.
- It is collaborative, so the outcomes are usually better. As the cliché says, "Two heads are better than one."
- It helps coaches avoid making damaging assumptions. More often than you might think, coaches make assumptions that are simply incorrect. They assume that they understand the problem, that they know what's best for clients, that there is one right way to solve the problem, and so on. Because it's collaborative, coaches

don't have to shoulder all the burden of being right. In dialogue, what's "right" is co-discovered, so the responsibility is shared.

- It enriches the problem-solving process by expanding the possibilities. Dialogue generally opens up more avenues because people view problems from different perspectives. So dialogue helps expand the solution space.
- It teaches clients how to think about their problems and challenges. Dialogue has the benefit of educating clients on what kinds of questions to ask themselves. In observing their coach guiding the dialogue, clients learn how to do it and become better able to help themselves—and others.

Coaching can be powerful—indeed, life changing—if the journey is interesting, the discoveries unexpected, and the insights actionable. Or the journey can be dull, uninspiring, and empty. The two primary factors that determine the difference between these two outcomes are the client's openness and willingness to explore and the coach's skillfulness in guiding the dialogue.

If dialogue is a journey, then context is the territory in which the journey takes place. It affects how the dialogue is shaped and what is possible. Good coaches remain acutely aware of the context all the time. They take care to understand the departure point and establish the right context at the beginning of the coaching process. They try to understand how the context affects the client's openness and willingness to explore. They also use the context to help shape the dialogue as coaching continues. So one of the ways to assess a coach is to observe how well she understands the context and uses it effectively. Even bad coaches are aware of the context, but they are often incapable of managing it or using it to their and the client's advantage. Instead, the context can become an impediment ("The culture doesn't support the kinds of changes he needs to make") or an excuse for lackluster results ("She wasn't willing to listen to feedback").

Beyond knowing and using the context effectively, coaches must be skilled at guiding and shaping the dialogue. As we said earlier, the two primary factors that determine whether coaching will be effective are the client's openness and willingness to explore and the coach's skillfulness in guiding the dialogue.

DIALOGUE SKILLS FOR COACHES

It would be difficult to argue with the proposition that the two most fundamental coaching skills are asking and listening. Being attentive to the client, *really* hearing what's being said, and being facile at asking insightful questions take coaches a long way. These fundamental skills, by themselves, would probably suffice in many coaching situations. However, to create a rich and insightful dialogue, coaches must also express empathy, give feedback, reflect on what they've heard, make generalizations, and advise or confront, among other things. Asking and listening are the foundation skills; the additional skills discussed next add depth, nuance, and character to the interaction between coach and client. A full set of dialogue skills includes the following:

Opening	Encouraging	Specifying
Listening	Giving feedback	Advising
Empathizing	Reflecting	Confronting
Questioning	Process checking	Reframing
Collaborating	Generalizing	Closing

In chapters 8 through 11, we will elaborate on these skills, noting in particular how they further the dialogue and how the most artful coaches use them.

MANAGING THE EBB AND FLOW OF THE DIALOGUE

In his *Journals* (1835–1862), Ralph Waldo Emerson said, "The art of conversation, or the qualification for a good companion, is a certain self-control, which now holds the subject, now lets it go, with a respect for the emergencies of the moment." He might have been talking about how you manage the ebb and flow of a coaching dialogue. The art in coaching is knowing when to "hold the subject" and when to let it go, when to push and when to pull, when to listen and when to disagree, when to continue exploring the problem space and when to move to the solution space.

Coaches who manage the ebb and flow of the dialogue artfully produce insight as well as a satisfying sense of pace throughout the conversation; those who cannot manage the dialogue artfully draw out parts of the conversation too long, cut other parts too short, and produce frustration rather than insight.

When you are coaching, you have to maintain a meta-level of awareness about the process, focusing not only on what the client is saying—engaging in the moment-by-moment flow of the dialogue—but on the larger journey being taken, knowing which paths the client feels comfortable going down, which ones are being avoided, and which ones the client doesn't see. To illustrate the art of the dialogue, we are going to follow part of a coaching session with Joe W., who became president of one of the divisions of a large manufacturing company last year. Joe is a strong operational manager with a record of successfully turning around financially troubled business units. In his current role, he has been able to cut costs and improve operations, but he has not been as effective at mobilizing people around a vision or motivating the people in his division. When he arrived, he replaced twelve of fourteen current executives with people he had worked with before. It's not clear that he knows how to build a unit from within. At the same time, he has not been as customer focused as people expected he would be. He is effective with customers when he meets with them, but he spends most of his time working on operational problems in the division and relatively little time in the field with customers.

As the coach began working with Joe, he asked Joe to take the *Myers-Briggs Type Indicator*® personality inventory and discovered that Joe is an ESTJ (Extraversion, Sensing, Thinking, Judging). According to Sandra Krebs Hirsh and Jean M. Kummerow (1998), "ESTJs are logical, analytical, decisive, and tough-minded, using concrete facts in systematic ways. They enjoy working with others well in advance to organize the details and operations to get the job done" (p. 13). Because they are so decisive and tough-minded, ESTJs like Joe are prone to make decisions quickly, perhaps without considering all the facts—or everyone's opinion—and pushing people to act before they are ready to. Indeed, as the coach interviewed people who worked with Joe, he heard a common refrain: that Joe is a "ready, fire, aim" type of manager. He asked Joe about this during one of their meetings.

Coach   Have you had a chance to read the MBTI® booklet I gave you?

Joe   Yes, I leafed through it last week. Interesting.

Coach   Did the description of ESTJs seem to fit you?

Joe   Yes. I was surprised, to tell you the truth. I've never put much stock in those things, but they nailed me. I guess I'm just not sure what to do with it. Okay. That's the way I am. So what?

Coach   Well, let's reflect on the implications of your style. One of the things I heard about you from some of the people I interviewed is that you're a "ready, fire, aim" type of leader. What does that imply? [Rather than deal head on with Joe's indifference to his MBTI profile, the coach adds another piece of data and asks the client to reflect on the implications. By doing so, the coach is an ally, not an adversary.]

Joe   That I make decisions too quickly. Without considering all the facts. But, you know, in our business you have to act quickly. You have to get to the core of a problem as quickly as possible and then solve the damn thing. You can't study things to death.

Coach   Help me understand that. [Here the coach is using the "Columbo" method, after television's Lt. Columbo, played by Peter Falk. The Columbo method means asking for clarification or asking a simple question, as though you didn't understand.]

Joe   What?

Coach   You said, "in our business." Which business? Manufacturing? Is this always true of manufacturing?

Joe   It is if you want an efficient operation, which is critical to making your margin.

Coach   Granted. So speed is of the essence in operational management?

Joe   Right.

Coach   And you said you need to solve problems quickly. That makes sense. How important is gathering the facts? [Using a question to challenge the client's interpretation of the "ready, fire, aim" description. Is it really about making decisions without having sufficient facts?]

Joe   Obviously, you can't make sound decisions without the facts. It's critical to have the right information before you make a decision.

Coach So what do people mean, then, when they say that you are a "ready, fire, aim" type of leader?

Joe I'm not sure.

Coach How do you make decisions? [This question represents a fundamental shift in the dialogue. The client is not progressing in his understanding, so the coach asks him to reflect on how he makes decisions. The point is to ground him in his experiences of decision making. Note, in the following statement, that he hasn't been self-conscious about this process previously. One of Joe's issues is that he acts unself-consciously and may be unaware of his impact on others.]

Joe I don't know. I haven't thought about it. (reflecting) I take in the information I need, you know, look at the numbers, listen to what people have to say, and so forth, and then make a decision.

Coach Right on the spot? Just like that? [confirming what he's hearing]

Joe Yes. The moment I know what needs to be done, I make the decision.

Coach And you announce it to others?

Joe Right.

Coach And stop taking in more information? Stop listening?

Joe Yes, I guess so.

Coach So, bear with me here. I'm trying to imagine what it's like to work with you. I come to you with information, and you're listening to me. Suddenly, you make your decision, tell me what it is, and further discussion is cut off. I'm cut off, even if I have more to say or feel that other facts, which I haven't given yet, are relevant. If I worked for you, is that how it would feel to me? [This is an important element in Joe's education. He is not naturally empathetic, so the coach forces him to see what the experience looks like to others.]

Joe I hadn't thought about it, but, yes, I suppose so.

Coach What does it feel like for you when you make a decision? [This question helps the client be more self-aware. It's a kind of introspection he may not have done before.]

Joe I don't know. I am considering the facts, sort of reformulating the problem or issue in my head as I'm taking in information, and

	then I suddenly see the solution. Like snapping your fingers. It's just suddenly there.
Coach	Then what?
Joe	Then I'm ready to move on. No, I see this now. I think I just literally stop listening at that point. I'm eager to move on, get this problem resolved, and deal with the next one.
Coach	(silent; listening) [This seems like an insightful moment for the client, so the coach remains silent. When the client is working, don't interfere.]
Joe	It's like a door slams shut. That's the only way to describe it.
Coach	How do you think the people working for you experience it? [Again, a question that calls for empathetic understanding of others—not Joe's strong suit.]
Joe	Like a door slamming shut. (pause) It must be frustrating as hell to work for me sometimes. [This bit of expressed empathy is a major victory in this dialogue.]
Coach	Do you ever go back and revisit a decision you've made? When more information becomes available?
Joe	Sure. All the time. You can't be right about everything. You have to understand. I'm not stubborn like that. I'm not afraid to admit when I'm wrong. If we need to revisit a decision, we do so.
Coach	That's good.
Joe	So I guess the "ready, fire, aim" comment is about being too impulsive in the first place. [Another major victory: Joe is labeling his own behavior, and naming it is an important step in changing the behavior.]
Coach	I'd say so.
Joe	All right. Good point. So I need to think more before making a decision. [The client has just articulated a change goal, which is a critical step in the dialogue, but the coach knows better than to leave it at that. The hard work is still ahead.]
Coach	Well, if the goal were to be less impulsive in your decision making, then reflecting more before making a decision is one way to do it. Would it be useful to explore more options?
Joe	Sure. Because as I think about it, I don't know how to slow down

my decision making, honestly. When the door slams shut, it slams shut. How do you change the way you think?

Coach Maybe you don't. Let's assume that door keeps slamming shut. Until now, what follows the door slamming shut is that you announce your decision and stop listening. Is that right?

Joe More or less. (pause) Yes, that's about it.

Coach So let's focus on that moment. What else could you do? [Exploring options is a useful device in dialogue. We've moved from the problem space to the solution space, but only temporarily, as we will see.]

Joe I guess I could just keep it to myself.

Coach (incredulous) Make the decision but then not tell anyone?

Joe (shaking his head) That doesn't sound right.

Coach Sounds really frustrating for you. [demonstrating empathy] What if you were to consider the decision a hypothesis about what should be done and put it out there for people to react to? [This is a straw man option, offered as a way to further the exploration.]

Joe So just say, "Here's what we could do," instead of, "Here's what we're going to do."

Coach Something like that. How would that feel to you?

Joe I could do that. But I don't want to get into consensus decision making. In our business, that would kill you.

Coach Joe, I want to make an observation. I hear you making connections and then drawing conclusions very quickly. You just did that when you went from "Here's what we could do" to the assumption that that would mean consensus decision making. Are those two things necessarily connected? [This is a key moment in the dialogue. The client has just demonstrated the behavior others criticize him for, so the moment is ripe for the coach to point that out. The observation is much more powerful when it is linked to immediate behavior.]

Joe (reflecting) No, you're right. They're not.

Coach (silent; listening) [Another moment of insight for the client, so the coach remains silent.]

Joe I think I probably do that a lot.

Coach What?

Joe Make these intuitive leaps. You know, assuming that one thing follows something else, and maybe it doesn't.

Coach Can you think of other times when you've done that?

Joe Yes. I'd have to think about it, but it seems pretty characteristic of how I operate. [An important self-revelation for the client. Now the coach will try to help the client understand why he operates that way. This helps put his behavior in context.]

Coach You've had to make decisions quickly in your previous roles. Isn't that right?

Joe (nodding) I've always been a good turnaround artist. You know, come into a failing situation, diagnose the problems, make some quick decisions about what to change, cut costs, make the operations more efficient, and get on with it.

Coach And you've been pretty successful at that?

Joe Damn right.

Coach So is that the situation you're in now? In this division? [The coach knows it isn't, but he uses a question to prompt the client to do the reflecting.]

Joe It was when I became president last year. I've pretty much turned things around now.

Coach So how would you describe your challenges at this point?

Joe We have a stable situation now. The challenge is to meet the growth targets, which are aggressive but doable.

Coach What will it take to accomplish that?

Joe What will it take? Hmm. I need to build my management team, get the resources and skills in place throughout the division, and spend more time focused on customers. Those are probably the top three challenges for me at this point.

Coach That sounds different from turnaround management. [This is the point. What the client is doing now is different from what he's done in the past. His leadership style may have been appropriate in his previous roles but not in his current role. Clients often cling to successful previous strategies, even when they no longer work in those circumstances.]

Joe In some ways it is, yes. (pause) You know, it's interesting because in my past four or five positions I've done the turnaround and then left. This time I'm not leaving.

Coach What are the implications of that? [A good question to ask when clients tell you that something is different.]

Joe I guess the main one is that I need to have a team that can manage the division longer term. (pause) I can't make all the decisions, or I'll be the bottleneck. And, you know, I may not have the right management team. Some of the people who've been with me from one place to another may not be right in a growth-oriented environment.

Coach What about you? [This question is meant to be challenging. It plays off the client's observation about his management team, but it also applies to him. Delivering this kind of question requires the right tone. It should prompt the client to think but should not sound aggressive or cynical.]

Joe Am I right for this environment? I'd like to think so, but honestly I don't know. It means going from a shoot-from-the-hip style to something else, more inspirational, I guess, more charismatic, less authoritarian.

Coach (silent; listening) [Wow. A powerful realization on the client's part. Don't say a word.]

Joe I think I can do it, but it's clear that I have to change how I'm making decisions. (pause) For one thing, I need the team to make most of the decisions. Otherwise, they'll keep expecting me to do it, or waiting for me to do it, or thinking I'll override them. Right?

Coach (nodding)

Joe So the key to this whole thing is for me to be less impulsive about making decisions. How the hell do I do that? [Notice that the dialogue has come full circle—back to the question of what he should be doing differently. Now, however, he's clearer about the problem and the need for change. Now the options will be less speculative and more operational.]

Coach We had one idea on the table: offering potential decisions as hypotheses. What else could you do?

As this example illustrates, the art of the dialogue is in managing clients' journeys so they develop insights about themselves along the way. You do that by providing just the right amount of information to prompt exploration; by using questions to provoke thought, examine causes and effects, challenge assumptions, and surface options; by confronting the client's perspective at the right moments; and by reframing what's been said so the client sees things in a new light. Effective dialogue is a combination of questioning, stating, observing, giving feedback, and remaining silent. In this example, the coach asked forty questions, made twenty statements, offered five observations, and remained silent four times. There is no secret formula for how these elements of dialogue should be combined, but in nondirective coaching in particular there should be more questions than statements.

WHY SOME COACHES ARE NOT ARTFUL AT DIALOGUE

A number of coaches we have observed are simply not very skilled at dialogue, and it severely hinders their effectiveness. We suspect that many are talkers and advice givers by nature. They have a strong need to assert their knowledge or be in control of the situation. Highly opinionated people and those with narcissistic personalities often do not make good coaches because they cannot set aside their ego for the duration of the dialogue. Other coaches who are otherwise well intentioned are not good listeners. Some lack finesse in asking questions and asserting appropriately. Finally, a number of coaches we've observed seem unable to hold that meta-level of process awareness in their head. They become so immersed in the conversation that they forget to keep one eye on what's going on while it is happening. You won't be able to coach effectively unless you can, in a sense, step away from the flow of the dialogue and be thinking about pacing, disclosure, and the give-and-take of information as clients progress toward insights. Ultimately, this is what dialogue is about: helping clients gain insights about themselves that they would not have had without the dialogue. Without these moments of insight, clients are unlikely to change and grow. If what happens in coaching conversations is business as usual, then clients will have no reason to behave differently.

THE ETHICAL LIMITS OF DIALOGUE

We have argued throughout this book that coaching is not therapy; however, it is a thoughtful exploration of the client's behavior, choices, assumptions, and skills. Occasionally, the dialogue will lead coach and client into terrain the coach is not equipped to handle (and should not attempt to handle because it violates the ethical limits on coaching). Coaches who are behaving ethically know their limits and do not go beyond them. Even when coaches are licensed psychologists, we would argue that the coaching relationship is fundamentally different than the therapeutic relationship, and those coaches should not engage in therapy while coaching. The proper course of action is to refer clients to therapists if issues arise that should be handled by therapy. In chapter 4, we discussed the "ten red flags"—client behaviors indicating that the problems are outside the domain of coaching. When these or other problematic behaviors occur, the right answer for coaches is to stop the dialogue and find the right resources to help the client. You risk doing harm (and potentially being liable) if you trespass into areas you are not equipped to handle. Here are our suggestions for ensuring that you remain within the ethical bounds of coaching:

- Don't venture into areas where you're not qualified. If psychological issues arise, refer the client to someone qualified to address those issues.

- Don't offer advice unless you have sufficient expertise (don't fake it or make it up). Don't let your ego guide your decisions.

- Don't suggest or support courses of action that would be harmful to the client or to others.

- Don't divulge confidences or betray the client's trust in any other way.

- Remain objective but helpful. Avoid involvement with the client beyond the professional level. Coaching comes from a position of trust, and you must not betray that.

- Be transparent about what you know and what you don't. Be forthright about your ability to be helpful. Always be candid and honest.

We will close this chapter with a sample dialogue showing how one coach handled a situation that was outside the domain of coaching.

Coach	Tom, you've been telling me about your difficulties with the transition. I think if I were you, I would have been angry about being passed over.
Tom	Whatever.
Coach	It didn't matter to you?
Tom	Not any more than anything else. What the hell. Bad things happen to good people, right? It's the way my whole life has been going, so it wasn't a bigger deal than anything else has been.
Coach	I don't understand.
Tom	(shrugging)
Coach	(silent; listening)
Tom	You probably heard that my wife left me. That happened a month ago. Now my son isn't talking to me. Won't return my calls. Hell, it just seems like everything is crashing at once. You know, you just reach a point where it doesn't matter anymore.
Coach	(pause) Have you talked to anyone about this?
Tom	No.
Coach	I think you should.
Tom	Isn't that what you're here for?
Coach	No, it isn't, Tom. I'm here to coach you, but this situation sounds more serious than coaching. I have to be candid with you. I can't help you with the personal problems you're having. That's not what coaching is about, but I'm convinced you need help. Look, if I were having the problems you're having, I would want help from someone who could really help me deal with the situation.
Tom	So what do you suggest?
Coach	Let me make a few calls and get the names of some people you might want to talk to. Would you be willing to do that?
Tom	I don't know.
Coach	Well, think about it.
Tom	Why don't you just tell me what you think I should do?
Coach	Because you'd be hearing from a well-intentioned amateur, and that's not what you need. You need to talk to a professional, somebody trained to help with these kinds of problems.
Tom	All right.

Coach I'll make some calls and get to you tomorrow morning. Will you be all right tonight?

Tom Yeah.

Such situations are always tricky. The key is not to give in to the impulse to offer advice or to accept responsibility for the client's problems beyond the commitment you should make—which is to seek competent professional help. Incidentally, if in this example Tom had said he wasn't sure if he'd be all right tonight, then the coach would need to seek competent help immediately. It's the responsible and decent thing to do.

8

Listening and Questioning

Ask more open-ended questions to obtain more input.
Probe more and spend less time relating your personal experiences.
Give people your undivided attention.
SUGGESTIONS TO COACHES FROM THE "COACHING EFFECTIVENESS
SURVEY," KORN/FERRY INTERNATIONAL

Thirty-four percent of the coaching clients we studied said that their coach is not very skilled at asking insightful questions that encourage them to explore their issues and needs further. Thirty-eight percent said that their coach is not adept at probing both for their ideas and feelings, and 26 percent said that their coach does not listen well and does not build upon their ideas throughout their discussions. Although most coaches seem to be skilled in these areas, these findings are nonetheless disturbing because they show that a significant number of people coaching in the business world lack the most basic skills of coaching: listening and questioning. Much of the art of coaching derives from these critical skills. In this chapter, we explore how coaches can use these two fundamental communication skills to manage the dialogue.

LISTENING

Much has been written about the art of listening. We are most fond of Stella Terill Mann's comment that "listening is a form of accepting." In conversation, the greatest show of acceptance is patient listening. This skill is so fundamental that without it a coaching dialogue is not possible. Even coaches who are listening can sometimes convey the impression that they're not. These are the kinds of signals an impatient coach sends:

- Fidgeting, writing notes, or failing to maintain eye contact while the client is speaking

- Speaking as soon as the client stops talking; "clipping" the ends of a client's sentences

- Interrupting

- Failing to respond to what the client last said (indicating that the coach was thinking about something else while the client was talking)

- Missing important verbal or nonverbal cues in the client's speech or behavior

Professional coaches and counselors are trained to be patient listeners, but most managers are not, and when they act as coaches they often fail to listen as carefully and thoughtfully as they should. Even trained coaches can sometimes lose themselves in the moment and forget to listen patiently. If the client trusts the coach, then a momentary lapse in listening is usually forgiven, but chronic lapses diminish trust and can cause clients to lose faith not only in the coach but in the coaching process itself. Listening is a skill requiring constant practice—and vigilance during the dialogue.

Beyond listening *patiently*, good coaches listen *attentively*—with their eyes as well as their ears. When coaches listen with their eyes, they are observing their clients' nonverbal signals: shrugs, gestures, eye movements, body posture, and so on. When they listen with their ears, coaches pick up on the tone of the voice, pauses, or unusual word emphasis. The full story being told comes as much or more from a client's nonverbal cues as it does from the verbal dimension. For this reason, coaching by telephone is considerably less effective than coaching face to face. Nonverbal communications are an important part of the dialogue—for both parties. Coaches' nonverbal signals are also observed and interpreted by their clients. So it's critical for coaches to understand—and manage—the nonverbal signals they send.

The core of the dialogue is the client's story, and this is fundamentally what coaches listen for. All people interpret their experiences in ways that reflect their worldview and reinforce their self-image. When people talk about themselves, they are revealing elements of their story as they have constructed it. Understanding how clients have built their own stories helps coaches understand why clients behave as they do—and, hence, what their problems and blind spots might be, as well as how they might best be helped. Virtually everything clients say about themselves is part of their story, whether or not they begin with "once upon a time." Even when clients are talking—not about themselves but about their companies, divisions, or projects—they are presenting their construct of reality, their interpretation of events and situations as they see them. That's an important part of their story. As you listen to a client's stories, you should be asking yourself these questions:

- How is this person interpreting his experience?
- How does he assign importance to situations, events, or outcomes?
- How does he define himself?
- How does he view himself as a participant in events?
- How does he view the importance of these events? And his own importance?
- How does he think about his skills? His ability to influence people, events, and outcomes?
- How does he draw conclusions about what has happened and why?
- What did he learn from these events?
- What did he conclude about how to behave in the future?
- What does this tale say about the teller?

The art in listening well is for coaches to hear what their clients are saying without projecting their own experiences onto the story. The danger is in coaches hearing what they want to hear, interpreting the clients' words from their own experience, and then constructing the clients' stories based on how they would construct them. These are the coaches who give advice that's right for them, regardless of whether it's right for their clients, and then fail to see the difference. Coaching is an art, and listening patiently, attentively, and objectively is the core skill. Coaches who do it well can develop enormous insight into the people they are coaching and can use this insight to create a meaningful dialogue with their clients.

So, how do you listen well? The skills include being there, going through the open doors, following the client's agenda, following the bread crumb trail, trusting silence, using minimal encouragers, pointing out the elephants in the room, synthesizing now and then, listening with your eyes as well as your ears, and listening with your heart as well as your head. We will explore each of these areas in more detail throughout the pages that follow.

Being There

Being there means simply to be present and accounted for while coaching is taking place. Coaching is not a multitasking activity. It can't be done on a shop floor in the middle of a production run. It can't occur while the coach is taking phone calls or responding to e-mails or reading the ticker on the big board. When you coach, it's important to concentrate fully on the client, so you need to eliminate external and internal distractions. In a busy world, this is sometimes difficult, so it's best to think of coaching as "sanctuary time," a stepping away from the chaos and noise of the world outside so you can focus on the client.

Some pundits have observed that in contemporary life—with a degree of connectedness that would have astounded, and perhaps terrified, our parents—everyone is beginning to suffer from attention deficit disorder. When you're being pinged every ten seconds by one gadget or another, it's difficult to concentrate, and we are becoming more accustomed to juggling fifteen things at once. But in coaching this simply will not do. It's not possible, with a distracted mind, to engage in a thoughtful dialogue. It's also disrespectful to the person you're coaching. A number of the clients we surveyed in our coaching research reported that their coaches did not fully attend to them during coaching sessions. When asked what their coaches could do to improve their coaching, three of them made the following comments:

- Listen to what is said all the way through before going on to something else. It's okay to be busy, but I would like to feel that I have your undivided attention for a few minutes.

- Better handling of interruptions when a coaching session is taking place. When meetings are held in your office, constant interruptions and taking phone calls reduced the effectiveness of the meetings. Off-site meetings seem to work better.

- Just a bit more relaxing and listening. I don't want to feel there are sixteen people outside the door waiting for us to finish, even if there are. I don't need a quantity of coaching time. I am more concerned with quality of coaching time since this is my biggest area of opportunity. Not much is completed between the two of us when we have one eye on each other and one eye on the door.

Going Through the Open Doors

When clients avoid a subject or seem unwilling to talk about it, you have two options. You can continue to pursue the subject or you can move on to something the client is more willing to talk about. If you do the former, you are knocking on a closed door; if you do the latter, you are going through an open door. In coaching, it is generally better to go through the open doors. When the doors are open, clients are more engaged, more likely to feel comfortable, and more likely to tell you how they feel. Yet we have seen many coaches, like the one in the following dialogue, who are determined to knock down those closed doors, no matter what.

Client   So, anyway, I completed my report and followed all the guidelines they gave me, and Jim still sent it back to be redone. I couldn't believe it. And he sent it to Legal to get their opinion after I told him that I'd already had Legal review it. His basic problem is that he doesn't trust what you tell him.

Coach   You had problems with your previous supervisor, too, as I recall. Is there a pattern here?

Client   You're missing the point. Jim doesn't just nitpick me to death. He does it to everybody in the department.

Coach   Maybe so, but you seem to have a pattern of problems with your supervisors. It's not just Jim.

Client   Whatever. Jim is the guy I have to deal with right now, and I'd like to figure out what I need to do to get him off my back. I'm really frustrated that I can't seem to make any headway with him.

Coach   We'll get back to Jim in a moment, okay? Tell me more about your last supervisor.

This client is no doubt becoming frustrated with the coach, too. In this example, the coach has probably made an insightful observation, but the client is not ready to hear it. That door is closed. Rather than bang on that closed door, the coach should go through the open door (what to do about Jim) and come back to the broader issue later. At this point, the client is emotionally entangled in his immediate problem with Jim, and this is what the coach should follow. Go through the open doors. Return to the closed doors later.

Following the Client's Agenda

Related to going through the open doors is following the client's agenda, which means setting aside your own thoughts about subject matter and sequence and going where the client wants to go. Clearly, this "letting go" is fundamentally what nondirective coaching is about. In fact, it's virtually the definition of nondirective coaching. However, even directive coaches should periodically release their agenda and go where the client leads them. Coaching that is totally directive can make a client feel like a puppet in someone else's puppet show. Even in directive coaching, the dialogue is about the client's story, not the coach's, so the client's agenda must prevail.

To follow the client's agenda, you have to release your own, and this is especially difficult for coaches who need to feel in control or for those who are highly logical and structured. Releasing your agenda can mean feeling lost sometimes, which is an uncomfortable feeling for many of us. It can mean feeling that the dialogue is going nowhere or that you're not adding value. Coaches whose MBTI® preferences include T (Thinking) and J (Judging) can find it maddening to go where clients lead them, especially if the flow does not seem logical. But if you insist on being in control and guiding the conversation constantly, then you are likely to be a poor listener (because part of your mind will be planning the next few steps instead of following what the client is saying) and you are likely to miss some important, but perhaps subtle, clues in the dark folds of the client's story.

Following the Bread Crumb Trail

When clients talk, they leave clues, like bread crumbs left to mark a trail. Good listeners follow the bread crumb trail by picking up on clients' key words, thoughts, transitions, and other dialogue markers that signify an important piece of information.

Client I'm becoming increasingly impatient with Marcia and her team.

Coach Say more.

Client Two days ago, we held an "all hands" meeting to discuss consolidating the Franklin and Wabash operations, and they spent the entire meeting complaining about one thing or another.

Coach What did they complain about?

Client You name it: we're moving too soon, we're not moving fast enough, they want to be more involved in the transition, they don't want the space we've allocated for them. It frustrated the hell out of me.

Coach You sound frustrated.

Client You know, I think I've done everything humanly possible to accommodate them. I've even invited Marcia or another member of her team to come to our planning meetings, although they aren't part of the transition team.

Coach They're not on the transition team?

Client No, no, they're not. But . . .

Coach But what?

Client I was trying to keep the transition team small. I thought if we had too many people on it we'd never get anything done. But I can see how Marcia felt about that.

Coach How do you think she felt?

As this dialogue illustrates, the client is really solving the problem. By "connecting the dots," the coach reflects important thoughts from one moment to the next and furthers the client's thinking: *complaining—complained, frustrated—frustrated, not part of the team—not part of the team, but—but, and Marcia felt—she felt.* When you follow the bread crumb trail, you reinforce the flow of the client's thoughts and use the dialogue as a device for discovery. Note that at the end of this short dialogue, the client has begun to put himself in Marcia's shoes and is discovering the source of her team's frustrations. By listening carefully, the coach is able to guide the client's self-discovery, which is a more powerful way for the client to learn than being told why Marcia's team may be complaining so much.

Trusting Silence

Mark Twain is said to have observed, "The right word may be effective, but no word was ever as effective as a rightly timed pause." Silence is one of the great, underused tools in coaching. We observed hundreds of coaches who seem uncomfortable with silence. They ask their clients great questions and then, while the client is thinking, destroy the moment by talking again. It often looks like this:

Coach	As you've said, your style is really not aligned with the style of this organization. If you aren't able to align yourself with the executive team here, what is likely to happen?
Client	Hmm.
Coach	It's unreasonable to expect all of them to change for you, don't you think?
Client	(pause; thinking)
Coach	I mean, look, their team has been together for a long time, right? They are comfortable working the way they work. As the relative newcomer, isn't it up to you to adapt?

We have to remember that coaching is about change, and people don't change through a harangue. They change because they work through the mental processes themselves and decide to behave differently. We have much more to say about this in the epilogue. Suffice it to say here that the point of coaching is to help clients think. When they are thinking, they are working, and if you interrupt their work, you risk frustrating them and stalling the process. When clients are thinking, let them think! So when you ask a provocative question, remain silent while the client thinks about it. Silence may be uncomfortable for you, but it's also uncomfortable for clients, and they will eventually break the silence with their next thought or question. The guideline we recommend is to ask insight-provoking questions and then wait for at least a ten-count before saying anything else. Trust silence.

Using Minimal Encouragers

Minimal encouragers are those brief statements, questions, and sounds that encourage the client to continue talking. Sometimes, clients come to a full stop in their dialogue. They've made a statement and are waiting for you to respond. However, you think there is more to what they have said, and you want to encourage them to continue talking. An excellent way to do that is to use one of these minimal encouragers:

- Can you tell me more?
- What else?
- How does that work?
- Say more.
- Um-hmm.
- Go on.
- Interesting.
- That's great.
- And then?
- What happened next?

Minimal encouragers can also be nonverbal. You might just nod, shake your head, or wave your hand in a "please continue" manner to encourage the client to keep going.

Client Where I grew up, in Japan, I learned to be respectful toward others and not to be direct. When I came to this country at seventeen, I was told that I had to be more direct, so I learned to do that. Now, that's how I prefer to interact with people.

Coach (nodding)

Client You know, if you have a problem, you just say so. Maybe you fight, and then you kiss and make up later. But in this company, people aren't direct with each other, and they think I'm different for just saying what I think.

Coach Hmm.

Client I'm convinced that's why they don't get anything done around here. Decisions don't get made because no one will just say what he means.

Coach Never?

Client (pausing) You know, I think decisions sort of get made by default in this place. The culture is one where people avoid confrontation, so if you have a problem with someone, it's considered bad form to be direct with them about it. Instead, you're supposed to beat around the bush or something.

Coach Tell me more.

You would not want to use minimal encouragers exclusively, of course. They are excellent tools at the right moment, especially with clients who are economic with their speech or who don't fully develop their thoughts. They are also useful when it's important to keep clients talking—perhaps because they are following an insightful line of thought or because you have observed or concluded something but would rather your clients discover it for themselves.

Pointing Out the Elephants in the Room

The elephant in the room is the big, ugly, hairy, smelly beast that everyone knows is in the room but no one wants to talk about. It's the "gross truth" that will cause discomfort or embarrassment if it's discussed, so people tend to talk around it or pretend it isn't there. Effective coaches know the elephant is in the room and point it out. The only way issues can be resolved is to discuss them, even if they are big, ugly, hairy, and smelly.

Client It's unbelievable that this team hasn't come together and done what it's supposed to do. I've put the best people there. I've given them all the resources they need. I've made it clear what they're expected to do. I won't do the job for them, but short of doing that, I don't know how the hell to get this bunch to perform like they should.

Coach I think you are the problem.

In this case, Terry was coaching a hard-charging senior executive who tended to throw his weight around like the proverbial bull in the china shop. He was not used to people being so direct with him and was not ready to hear this feedback, so it was a pivotal moment in the coaching. In our view, coaches must be truth tellers, as they see it. Their value is in being as candid and forthright with clients as the clients can handle.

Coaches who soften the blow simply to protect their clients' egos are not being helpful. There are times in the coaching dialogue when candor is all that will move the client's discovery process forward, and if you fail to point out the elephant in the room, then you fail the client.

Synthesizing Now and Then

One way to show that you've been listening is to synthesize the dialogue from time to time. A synthesis is different from a summary. In a summary, you merely repeat, in condensed form, what's been said. A synthesis is a wholly new formulation of what's been said. Literally, it means to combine separate elements into a coherent whole. When you synthesize the dialogue, you create a new picture from the elements of the dialogue, a picture the client may not have thought of previously. So synthesizing is one powerful way to develop and share insights, as the following example shows.

Client	I don't think Eduardo has had much experience speaking before large groups of employees, and we will have nearly five hundred people at the event.
Coach	You seem anxious about that.
Client	I don't want to put someone up in front of the group who isn't going to do a spectacular job. Marina has more public speaking experience, but very few people at the event will know who she is.
Coach	So what are your options?
Client	I suppose we could videotape the chairman and show the video on several large screens.
Coach	What else?
Client	We could look for an outside speaker, someone who has a marquee name and knows how to wow a large crowd.

Coach   Would your people find anyone like that relevant?

Client   Probably not.

Coach   So if I put this all together, I'm hearing that you're not comfortable with any of the options you've considered, including the one you haven't talked about, which is you giving the presentation yourself. Is this about your own fears of public speaking?

Listening with Your Eyes as Well as Your Ears

How clients say things and what they do in between saying things is at least as important as what they say. Listening with your eyes means carefully observing your client's body language, gestures, pauses, and tone of voice, and then using what you observe to further the dialogue.

Coach   You look like you haven't slept. Are you all right?

Client   I don't think it's important. It hasn't . . . well, let's just say it won't be a problem in the future.

Coach   It hasn't what, John? You hesitated there.

Client   I was going to say that it hasn't, uh, caused the kind of problem I thought it would.

Coach   I'm glad to hear that, but I'm a little confused. You don't sound relieved.

Client   Well, you know I was hoping to be named manager of the design engineering group.

Coach   And you were.

Client   Yes, but they've just announced a reorganization that means I'll still be at the same level. My new position was reclassified downward.

Coach   Hmm. So what won't be a problem in the future?

Client   I won't have to worry about being promoted. Clearly, they've decided against it, and I'm stuck at this level.

Coach   Hmm. I'd like to know a bit more. What else did they say when you were told about the promotion?

It's difficult in words to illustrate a visual phenomenon, but we hope this brief sample of dialogue illustrates the importance of observing clients carefully and using those observations to deepen your and the client's understanding of the situation. Listening with your eyes means noticing when clients rub their hands, tap their fingers, fidget, look at their watch, scratch their chin, look off in the distance, smile, or do myriad other things that communicate pleasure, fear, discomfort, frustration, happiness, uncertainty, and so on. Clients are often unaware that they are doing these things. When you point them out, you often help clients gain insight into how they feel about what's happening to them.

Listening with Your Heart as Well as Your Head

Finally, you should also listen with your heart as well as your head, and this means listening for how clients feel—being attuned to their emotional frequencies, so to speak. When you listen with your heart, you empathize with clients and thus demonstrate that you understand how they feel and can put yourself in their shoes. In normal conversation among business people, *empathy* is a word that's often misunderstood and seldom practiced, in part because many business people confuse empathy with being "touchy-feely" and feel that connecting with someone else's emotions is inappropriate at best, and scary at worst. Given the widespread confusion over empathy, it would be useful to define the term. According to *Merriam-Webster's Collegiate Dictionary*, empathy is "the action of understanding, being aware of, being sensitive to, and vicariously experiencing the feelings, thoughts, and experience of another of either the past or present without having the feelings, thoughts, and experience fully communicated in an objectively explicit manner."

The complexity of this definition may explain why the term is so often misunderstood. Gerard Egan (1998), a professor emeritus of Loyola University of Chicago, offers a simpler definition in his book *The Skilled Helper:* "Basic empathy involves listening to clients, understanding them and their concerns to the degree that this is possible, and communicating this understanding to them so that they might understand themselves more fully and act on their understanding" (p. 81). The operative word here is *communicating*. Empathy occurs when coaches are able to communicate their understanding of their clients to their clients. Empathy is one of the key ways coaches reflect what they've heard or observed—verbally or nonverbally—and it often does reflect the emotional aspects of clients' stories.

Client   (pausing) You know, I think decisions sort of get made by default in this place. The culture is one where people avoid confrontation, so if you have a problem with someone, it's considered bad form to be direct with them about it. Instead, you're supposed to beat around the bush or something.

Coach   And that frustrates you. [recognizing the emotion]

Client   Absolutely! Why can't people just say what they mean? I keep leaving meetings with the senior executives wondering if I understood what they were saying. It's like you have to read between the lines because nobody will just tell you what they think. Is he okay with my decision or not? I don't know! Does he think I'm doing a good job or not? I don't know!

Coach   It must be very unnerving not to know where you stand. [Another way to empathize is to hypothesize how the client might feel.]

Client   (nodding) I feel like saying, "If you don't think I'm doing a good job, then just say so. We can talk about it. If I disagree, I'll say so. If you disagree, you say so."

Coach   You would be happier if people were candid with you about how you're doing. [projecting how the client would feel if the situation were different]

Client   Absolutely. It saves time. No beating around the bush.

Coach   Have you asked people for very direct feedback?

Client   Yes. I mean I've said, "Tell me how I'm doing, and if you think I need to do something differently, just tell me." What I get in response are vague assurances that I'm doing okay, with maybe a suggestion or two, but then I hear through the grapevine that somebody's unhappy about my decision to let Simpson go, and somebody else thinks I'm too hard on my staff, and whatever.

Coach   You're frustrated because people won't be candid with you if they think you're doing something wrong. [The classic way to show empathy is to say, "You're feeling _____ because _____."]

Client   That's right.

Coach   I wonder why that is. Are people not candid with everyone? Or primarily with you?

Client   I don't know.
Coach   Perhaps we should find out.

We should note that being empathetic does not mean being nice, or trying to make the client feel better, or anything of the sort. It means understanding the client's emotions and communicating your understanding in a way that helps the client gain more insight. In this example, the client does move quite a distance—from "decisions get made by default" to "somebody thinks I'm too hard on my staff." In the end, however, the coach is not buying the client's conclusion that the entire culture is non-confrontational. What will eventually emerge in this dialogue is that the client discourages others from giving honest feedback because she resists hearing feedback and becomes antagonistic when people try to give her feedback. The coach's empathy enables her to accept this difficult truth about herself and thus begin to change.

In *Emotional Intelligence*, Daniel Goleman (1995) notes that "all rapport, the root of caring, stems from emotional attunement, from the capacity for empathy" (p. 96). When you empathize with clients, you show that you have heard them with your heart, not merely your head; that you have connected with them on an emotional level; and that you understand how they feel. These are the prerequisites of caring, which is itself a prerequisite of trust. For clients to trust you, they must know that you care about them as people and are committed to helping them succeed. Coaches who don't care remain at an emotionally detached distance. They may understand cognitively what the client's issues and opportunities are, but they will never truly grasp the essential person unless they can also understand the client's emotional landscape.

We will close this discussion of empathy with a brief note about *empathic accuracy*. Empathizing is important, but it must be accurate. After all, if you mislabel the client's emotions, you don't create an emotional connection; instead, you demonstrate that you are not attuned, that you don't get it. So if you have trouble reading other people's emotions or aren't sure what emotion the client is experiencing, then it's best to test your empathic accuracy with these kinds of questions:

♦ You seem _____. Is that how you feel about it?

♦ You seem to be _____ about this. Is that how you would describe it?

♦ You feel _____ about this. Does that seem right to you?

♦ You are feeling _____. Am I seeing this correctly?

Listening is largely a matter of patience and focus. You have to be patient enough to release your agenda and be with the client while you are coaching and focused enough to minimize distractions and truly hear what the other person is saying. It requires a degree of single-mindedness that many coaches lack, as evidenced by the kinds of suggestions that many of the clients we surveyed made to their coaches.

- Strive to listen more empathetically (i.e., restate statements and the underlying meaning in a question format).

- Don't be afraid of being a bit more empathic when appropriate.

- Listen more attentively and demonstrate more that you truly are listening.

- Listen more to let the person know that she is being heard. Repeat back what is understood.

- Listen more instead of forming opinions first.

- Listen to what is being said before speaking.

- Listen well before giving feedback.

- Develop better listening skills. Do not be judgmental too early in the process.

- Listen completely before reacting to a situation.

- Listen carefully to what I am saying.

- I like her ambition to solve the problem, but Gloria does not always listen to all the facts before jumping in with suggestions.

- Releasing agenda: listen effectively. Know that you don't have to control every situation.

- Maintain genuine empathy for the people you coach and the situations you are asked to address. Listen with all of your senses.

- Listen, listen, listen.

QUESTIONING

Albert Einstein said, "I have no special talents. I am only passionately curious." Although not intended as such, this quotation describes the finest coaches. They are passionately curious about the people they are helping, and they exercise their curiosity by asking probing questions. A good question can open a closed door. It can stir people's memories; stimulate them to think about things in ways they've never thought about them before; and provoke insight and change by causing them to examine their aspirations, motivations, choices, assumptions, priorities, and behavior. Questions are the most important tools in a coach's toolbox, and the skill with which coaches use questions reveals the difference between the novice coach and the master. As Egyptian author Naguib Mahfouz said, "You can tell whether a man is clever by his answers. You can tell whether a man is wise by his questions." Wise coaches have a repertoire of questions and know which kind of question to ask at any point in the dialogue to stimulate the client and move the dialogue toward insight.

Much has been written about the difference between open and closed questions. Open questions are those that encourage the respondent to provide expansive answers; closed questions are those that can be answered in one word or two. "Did you attend college?" is a closed question; it can be answered "yes" or "no." "What did you enjoy about college?" is an open question; to answer it, the respondent has to provide more information. We are not going to dwell on open and closed questions because the distinction itself is straightforward. Yes, you should use open questions to encourage clients to open up and closed questions when you seek a simple, more definitive response. Beyond that, the open and closed distinction is not terribly useful.

More useful is understanding the types of questions that can help clients explore themselves and their motivations more deeply, or challenge and provoke them to question their own perspectives, or encourage them to dream. These include motivation questions, ideal outcome questions, implication questions, sensory questions, and Columbo questions. However, to set up these kinds of questions, you often need to gather more facts, so you may need to start by asking some situation questions.

Situation Questions

Situation questions are the common, fact-gathering questions that Rudyard Kipling cited in his poem:

> *I keep six honest serving-men*
> *(They taught me all I knew);*
> *Their names are What and Why and When*
> *And How and Where and Who.*

Invariably, coaches need to ask some of these basic questions to learn more about the facts of clients' lives and their work, organizations, roles, plans, problems, and so on. However, situation questions do not provoke insight. They merely engage clients' memories. They are like oral fact sheets, and clients derive very little benefit from answering situation questions. Moreover, if you use too many situation questions in a row, you can start to sound more like an interrogator than a coach. For both of these reasons, we suggest keeping situation questions to a minimum. Use them when you need information, but then move on to the more provocative questions we discuss next.

Motivation Questions

Motivation questions include the following:

- What led you to do that?

- What were the factors in your decision?

- What would you prefer? Why?

- What is most important to you?

- Why is that important to you?

- If you had it to do over again, what would you do differently?

These types of questions are useful for exploring clients' motivations, decision processes, and priorities. They can yield considerable insight into how clients think and what is important to them. Consider the difference between these pairs of questions:

Situation   Where did you go to college?
Motivation   Why did you choose to go there?

The situation question yields a simple piece of information. The motivation question can disclose the client's youthful dreams, educational interests, career goals, life ambitions, state or other affiliations, and so on. The situation question offers slim pickings; the motivation question yields tremendous bounty. It tells you a great deal about the person.

Situation   What is your primary goal for your business unit?
Motivation   Why is that goal your most important one?

Again, the situation question yields nothing more than a simple fact. The motivation question can yield a response that tells you what challenges the business unit is facing, what the unit must achieve to meet those challenges, what resources or constraints the unit may have, how the client has prioritized among the various options, and so on.

You will notice that motivation questions often follow a situation question. First comes a fact, then an understanding of the thinking that led to the fact. For coaches, the value of motivation questions is that they reveal how clients think. For clients themselves, the value is that they stimulate an examination of motives, priorities, interests, and decision criteria. Moreover, you can use follow-up questions to deepen your understanding of the client's motivations and any changes that have occurred:

Motivation   I'm curious. Why did you choose to accept that offer?
Follow-up   Knowing what you know now, would you still have
                accepted the offer?
Follow-up   What if the conditions had been different? What would
                have made it more attractive to you?

Follow-up   How do you think that experience changed you? What became more or less important to you afterward?

Ideal Outcome Questions

Ideal outcome questions, like the ones that follow, help coaches explore clients' goals, dreams, and visions of the future.

- What are your goals and aspirations?
- What is the best possible outcome?
- What would you ideally like to see?
- What would the best circumstances be?
- Where would you like to be in a year? Two years?
- If there were no constraints, what would be possible?

The real value of these questions is not just that they encourage clients to think about the future but that they ask clients to raise the bar and posit an ideal future. The difference between "What do you think you can achieve?" and "If there were no constraints, what would be possible?" is the difference between the mundane and the sublime, especially for people who see more barriers than opportunities, who lack self-confidence, or whose dreams have always been muffled by circumstances they have more control over than they imagine. These people may be sailing through life, so to speak, with a virtual sea anchor dragging behind them. Part of the value of coaching can be to help them dream again—and then explore ways to achieve more than they thought possible. To aid in this transformation, you need to follow up on ideal outcome questions with questions that help clients see options:

Outcome	What would you ideally like to accomplish?
Follow-up	What would it take for you to do that?
Client	It's not possible.
Follow-up	Imagine for a moment that it were possible. What would you need to do?
Client	But they won't let me.

Follow-up   Imagine that they weren't a constraint. If it were entirely up to you, what would you need to do?

In this sample dialogue, we've shown how you can respond to clients who are skeptical about reaching an ideal goal. Obviously, some goals are unattainable for some people because of real constraints that cannot be overcome, but in our experience clients imagine more constraints than they actually have, and accomplishing something less than the ideal goal is nonetheless a great outcome and is usually more than they thought possible. If your challenge in coaching someone is to raise her aspirations, then ideal outcome questions are a good tool.

A variation of the ideal outcome question is the straw man question. In these types of questions, you ask clients to imagine a situation that does not currently exist (much as we did in the previous example) and then figure out how to close the gap between that imaginary state and current reality.

Client   It's pointless to even present this proposal. The board will never buy it.

Straw Man   What if they were open to it? Imagine for a moment that the board was open to this kind of proposal, what would they need to see from you in order to say yes? What would make this a compelling proposition?

Straw man questions are useful when clients perceive insurmountable barriers and are not allowing themselves to think beyond the barriers. We have found that straw man questions have an amazing ability to get people to release real or imaginary constraints long enough to problem solve what they would do if there were no constraints. After they problem-solve, you ask clients how they could remove or overcome the constraints.

Follow-up   What could you [or others] do to make the board more open to your proposal?

Implication Questions

Implication questions ask clients to explore the potential consequences of actions or events.

- What would happen if [the event] occurred?

- If you do (or don't do) [this action], what could happen? What are the consequences?

- What are the implications of [doing one thing or another]?

- What would be the impact of [doing one thing or another]?

- How serious would it be if [this event] occurred?

- How bad could it be? How good could it be?

Implication questions are among the most effective types of questions for challenging clients. Implication questions can cause them to question their assumptions, enable them to envision a brighter or darker future, and contemplate the effects of taking or failing to take a particular course of action.

Client	It's pointless to even present this proposal. The board will never buy it.
Implication	If you don't pursue this proposal, what's going to happen? Or, if you don't pursue this proposal, what will the company stand to lose?

Implication questions can be positive or negative. They can explore the upside of a potentiality or the downside.

Upside	How big could this be? If you pursue this course of action, what's the best that could happen?
Upside	What if you could achieve two or three times more than you imagine?
Downside	How serious could this be? If you pursue this course of action, what's the worst that could happen?
Downside	What if you achieve only half of what you expect? Then where would you be?

You can use implication questions to help the client calibrate the importance or significance of a course of action.

Client	I'm not sure we can replace the team leader at this point.
Implication	Well, if you don't, what impact will that have on the team's performance?
Client	Oh, not much, really. This team is functioning pretty well on its own.

The principal use of implication questions is to encourage clients to think through the consequences of their actions, both for themselves and for their team or organization.

Implication	If you could exceed your targets in Germany, wouldn't you be able to attract some heavy hitters to your initiative? What would be the implications for the division as a whole?

Implication questions encourage clients to think. They are probably the most thought provoking of all questions.

Sensory Questions

Questions like the ones listed next invoke the senses and help clients explore their feelings.

♦ How do you see [this situation]? What do you envision? How do you look at this?

♦ How does that sound to you?

♦ What does that feel like?

♦ What are your feelings about [this person, thing, or situation]?

Sensory questions provoke a more visceral response from clients, one that is grounded in what they have sensed or experienced or could imagine sensing or experiencing. Appealing to a client's sense of sight, sound, or touch engages parts of the brain not normally engaged in discussion. Sometimes, to help clients re-create the sensation, you might even ask them to isolate the sense.

Sensory	I'd like you to sit back and relax for a moment. Close your eyes and try to remember what happened when you heard the news. Where were you? Imagine that you're back there now. What do you see?
Sensory	Close your eyes for a moment and imagine that you've already achieved the goal. What does that look like?
Sensory	Close your eyes for a minute. Just rest your head in your hands and try to remember what you heard during the meeting. What were people saying?

These kinds of questions may seem touchy-feely, and we suppose they are. But they are an often powerful way to help clients re-create an important moment and remember facts or feelings they had forgotten. Long-term memories often form because the situation produced strong emotions when it occurred. When you ask clients sensory questions, you often help them reconnect with those emotional events and thus remember things more clearly than if they don't make the sensory connection.

Columbo Questions and Statements

Finally, we refer to the following group of questions and statements as *Columbo questions*. We remember Peter Falk's Lt. Columbo as the disheveled detective who people tended to underestimate because he was so unassuming. But if Columbo seemed dumb to some perpetrators, he was dumb like a fox. Columbo questions work because they are a way of asking for clarification of something a client has said. They are also a way to be skeptical without appearing to be skeptical. Here are some examples.

- ◆ How does that work?

- ◆ Do you think they'll go along with that? I'm really curious about why they would. What's in it for them?

- ◆ Why would you approach it this way rather than that way?

- ◆ Help me understand that. [This and the next statement are better than asking "Why?" because they don't sound challenging or evaluative.]

◆ I don't understand. *Or*, What I don't understand is why [this situation] is true [or not true]. Help me out with that.

◆ Please explain. *Or*, Tell me more about [the situation or problem].

Of course, you have to use the proper tone when making Columbo statements and questions. You have to be genuinely intrigued by or interested in something the client has said.

What Else?

One final question deserves its own heading: What else? We sometimes see coaches who are satisfied with the first response they get to a question and don't probe further. Many times, the best second question to ask is "What else?" You can keep asking this question a number of times to encourage clients to keep thinking and dig deeper.

Coach As you think about your future, Jane, what would you like to do next?

Client I'd like to lead a product development team. I think I'm ready for that, and I have some ideas I'd like to explore that could take us in some new directions.

Coach What else?

Client At some point, I'd really like an overseas assignment. I think international experience is an important step on the road to advancement in a global company. I don't want to be seen as one-dimensional or knowledgeable only about domestic markets.

Coach What else?

Client Hmm. I don't know. (pause) I hadn't thought about it, but I guess I'd like to work directly for a CEO, someone who could teach me about running a large corporation.

Coach You'd like to be a general manager someday?

Client You know, I would. And I think I have what it takes, but I need more experience.

Asking this simple question repeatedly indicates that you think there's more gold in that mine and that you're not willing to stop digging until you've found all the ore there is to be found. It forces clients to go beyond the easy answers and develop ideas that had been undeveloped and articulate thoughts they had not articulated before. This is a simple but powerful way to continue the dialogue and force clients to work a little harder.

COLLABORATING WITH CLIENTS

Collaboration means to *co-labor*, to work together toward the accomplishment of a shared goal. Coaching is (or should be) a collaboration between the coach and the client, a journey undertaken by mutual consent in which the desired result is the client's development, growth, or enlightenment. For it to be a collaborative process, coach and client must jointly discover the relevant facts and perspectives and their implications for the client's life and work.

We have been arguing that dialogue is the principal vehicle for this mutual journey, and in this chapter we have discussed how two primary skills—listening and probing—help coaches guide the process of discovery without overcontrolling it. In the next two chapters, we will discuss the coach's complementary skills: sharing observations with clients (chapter 9) and pushing and pulling (chapter 10). It takes this entire suite of skills to create a dialogue that informs, enriches, and engages clients enough to help them change.

9

Sharing Your Observations with Clients

Continue to encourage others to expand beyond their current comfort levels.

Give more positive feedback. Focus on what was done right and not always on what was done wrong.

Help the coachees see where they could have done something different. When you see for yourself what other options there were, it forms a more lasting impression.

SUGGESTIONS TO COACHES FROM THE "COACHING EFFECTIVENESS SURVEY," KORN/FERRY INTERNATIONAL

In chapter 8, we argued that much of the art of coaching lies in listening and asking insight-provoking questions. Indeed, in nondirective coaching, you may spend more than 90 percent of your time doing just those two things. However, clients will also want to know what you think and what you have observed about them, and in this chapter and the next we discuss how to share your perspective with your clients. *Asking* and *listening* may be the primary tools you use to manage the dialogue, but you also need to do the right kind of *telling* at the right time. In directive coaching, ways of telling (giving feedback, advising, teaching, etc.) play a more prominent role in how coaches help clients learn and grow, but even with the nondirective approach, it's important for coaches to observe their clients and use various telling tools to advance clients' understanding of themselves, build their skills, and modify their behaviors.

As you observe clients, either in their work settings or in your sessions with them, you will develop a perspective on what they are doing well and what they need to change. You share your direct observations of them through feedback. You also observe clients by noting how they talk about themselves, their environment, and their experiences, and you sometimes share those observations by *reframing* something a client says or believes. Reframing typically means using language that is different from your clients' to create a different picture for them. They see something one way, and you reframe it in a way that gives them a new perspective on it. In this case, your observations are not on the behavioral level, as with feedback, but on the cognitive or conceptual level. Finally, one effective way to observe clients is to synthesize your observations of them in a way that may create a totally new picture for them. We call this *reflecting*, which means, in effect, "to hold up the mirror." In this chapter we discuss effective ways to give feedback, reframe, and reflect.

GIVING FEEDBACK

On the field of play, coaches typically give very direct feedback based on their observations of players: "You're not following through with your racket, Donna! Swing all the way through the stroke." "Jensen! Keep your eye on the ball. Whatsa matter with you?" This kick-in-the-butt style of feedback is, fortunately, less common in business but still occurs. Terry recalls staying at a hotel some years ago and walking behind two businessmen down a hallway. They had just left a conference room, and one man said to the other, "George, you need to keep your mouth shut. You're making everybody mad." Feedback is sometimes very direct and very frank.

Some business coaches adopt this macho, in-your-face style, and it seems to work for them, but in our view this approach is more about imposing upon and intimidating people than it is about coaching. Some clients may want to be abused by their coaches, but in our experience most prefer a mutually respectful relationship in which feedback is given with a certain amount of grace, tolerance, and understanding. That said, figure 6 shows a framework for giving feedback that we have found to be simple, practical, and effective.

Observation

Good feedback is based on observation, not opinion. It is factual rather than evaluative. It is given as close to the event as possible so clients can

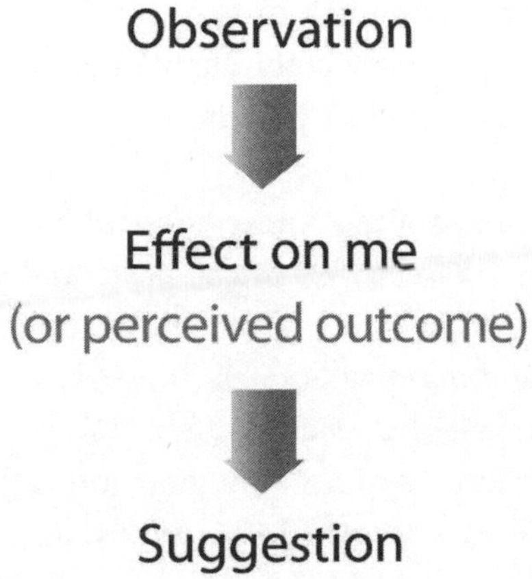

Observation

Effect on me
(or perceived outcome)

Suggestion

Figure 6: Giving Feedback

recall it. Finally, it is behavioral, concrete, and specific so clients can understand exactly what you are referring to. Here are some examples of good observations:

Coach John, I just saw you talking to Carolyn. When she asked how the tests were going, you responded in a composed, thoughtful manner. I didn't see any of the frustration or anger we talked about last week.

Coach Fran, I have an observation about the meeting we just left. I noticed on three occasions that you interrupted the client when she was speaking. First, you cut her off when she was explaining their strategy for marketing in the Midwest. Then you interrupted her when she was responding to John's question about their IT systems. You cut her off again toward the end of the meeting when she was summarizing the next steps.

Bear in mind that these statements are not feedback—they are merely the observations that form the first part of feedback. An entire feedback sequence has three parts: observation, effect, suggestion. When you make the observation, you are simply stating what you saw, but this is an important first step.

Effect on You or Perceived Outcome

Next, you should say what effect the client's behavior had on you or the outcome you think it may have had on others.

Coach   You came across as much more cooperative and less moody and volatile than I've seen you in the past. And Carolyn seemed to appreciate it. When you interact with people that way, you build more trust and more willingness to work with you. That's how I felt, and I think it's how Carolyn felt.

Coach   I found your interruptions annoying and, although I can't speak for the client, she seemed to be annoyed, too. When someone interrupts you repeatedly, it feels disrespectful.

Citing the effect on you or the perceived outcome on others of the client's behavior does several important things. First, it indicates why you think the observation is important. After all, if there were no significant positive or negative outcomes, there would be no point to the observation. You chose to observe this behavior because it had real or apparent consequences on you or others. That makes it important to the client. Second, citing the consequences of the behavior helps clients better understand what effect their behavior is having. They may not have known that they were doing whatever it is you observed, or they may not fully appreciate the impact their behavior has. In any case, the observation and the effect raise their awareness, an important first step in learning.

Suggestion

Finally, feedback is not complete until you close the loop by suggesting what they should continue doing (if it's positive) or what they should do differently (if it's negative).

Coach   I don't know if you felt frustrated or angry about the tests, but you managed your emotions well. You should keep doing that.

Coach   I suggest you try to be more aware of "turn taking" in conversations and allow the other person to finish completely before you start talking. And if you catch yourself interrupting, apologize to the person and ask her to continue.

Sometimes, as in the first example, you are observing something the client did right, and your suggestion may be nothing more than "keep doing it." Otherwise, your suggestions should be as specific and actionable as possible, as in the second example. The point is to help the client see behavioral alternatives. If you don't know what the client could have done differently, then say so. In our experience with coaches, the part of feedback most often neglected, oddly enough, is the suggestion. We often have to coach the coaches by saying, "So what do you suggest?"

Putting It All Together

Actual feedback is not quite as rigid or one-sided as our examples here imply. Generally, feedback occurs as part of the dialogue and is an exploration that includes the client's thoughts, as shown here:

Coach	John, I just saw you talking to Carolyn. When she asked how the tests were going, you responded in a composed, thoughtful manner. I didn't see any of the frustration or anger we talked about last week.
John	Thanks. I was really trying to control myself. It's damned hard, I can tell you. It's not how I felt.
Coach	Well, you came across as much more cooperative and less moody and volatile than I've seen you in the past. And Carolyn seemed to appreciate it. When you interact with people that way, you build more trust and more willingness to work with you. That's how I felt, and I think it's how Carolyn felt.
John	Yes. At least she didn't run the other way when she saw me coming.
Coach	I know you're still frustrated or angry about the tests, but you managed your emotions well. You should keep doing that.

Similarly, dialogue with Fran might run something like this:

Coach	Fran, I have an observation about the meeting we just left. I noticed on three occasions that you interrupted the client when she was speaking. First, you cut her off when she was explaining their

strategy for marketing in the Midwest. Then you interrupted her when she was responding to John's question about their IT systems. You cut her off again toward the end of the meeting when she was summarizing the next steps.

Fran   I didn't realize I was doing that.

Coach   As you think back on the meeting, do you recall the moments I'm referring to?

Fran   Yes, I guess so. But it's just the way I am. I get into the conversations and just blurt out what's on my mind.

Coach   Be that as it may, I found your interruptions annoying and, although I can't speak for the client, she seemed to be annoyed, too. When someone interrupts you repeatedly, it feels disrespectful.

Fran   Yes, I can see that.

Coach   I suggest you try to be more aware of "turn taking" in conversations and allow the other person to finish completely before you start talking. And if you catch yourself interrupting, apologize to the person and ask her to continue.

Fran   Well, like I said, I just get immersed in the topic. It's not like I'm trying to interrupt people.

Coach   So the challenge for you is to become more aware when it happens.

Fran   Yes.

Coach   Okay, let's work on that.

We suggest that you don't give people too much feedback at once, even if you have numerous observations. A lot of feedback can be overwhelming and, if too much of it is negative, it can be discouraging. It's best to prioritize your feedback and give people only the most important two or three observations at one time. Be sure to engage in enough discussion around each point so clients are able to explore the behaviors thoroughly and understand what they can do differently. If you have given someone feedback on a particular behavior before, especially in an area where the client should do something differently, and the same ineffective behavior occurs, then you need to emphasize that this is more feedback on the same issue. If clients have had the same feedback repeatedly and have not changed their behavior, then you need to explore why.

People sometimes ask us if they should always give positive feedback before giving negative feedback. The answer is that you should always give positive feedback if you have any to give, but it's dangerous to fall into a pattern of positive then negative. Clients are smart and will detect the pattern. Some of our former students called this pattern "the poison sandwich." Soon, they'll start discounting the positives because they are waiting for the negatives. If you have only negative or corrective feedback to give, then give it. You can still be encouraging without having to fish for a compliment the client knows is false. Similarly, if you have only positive feedback, then give it. In any case, try to give feedback as close as possible to the event so it's fresh in clients' minds as they hear your observations and suggestions.

Ineffective Feedback

Feedback that is not immediate or rooted in observation can be maddeningly ineffective and unhelpful to clients. Following are some examples:

Coach   You did a poor job on that report, Clark. [This is evaluative and insulting. It doesn't help Clark understand what he did; it merely disparages his efforts. Evaluation is not observation, and people can't change unless they know what to change.]

Coach   Clark! Great job on that report! Way to go. [Although this is positive and encouraging for Clark, it is also evaluative and fails to enlighten him about what he did well. Positive feedback is great, but without specific observations it is not helpful to clients. Again, evaluation is not observation.]

Coach   Fran, you interrupted the client all through that meeting. Everybody was really annoyed with you. [They might have been annoyed with Fran, but you can't speak for everyone. Generalizing how everyone felt is dangerous. Stick with what you have observed and felt, although it is fair to observe what you saw others do: "After you interrupted her the third time, the client glared at you and then glanced at her watch. She didn't say anything else after that."]

Coach   You need to do a better job of managing your time. [Evaluative and too vague.]

Coach   David, several months ago, I noticed you . . . [Forget about it. That's too long ago.]

Coach   Fran, how do you think you did in that meeting? [A good question but not as a setup for negative feedback. We've heard a number of coaches use this gimmick. The idea is to get clients to surface the pros and cons themselves. However, this ploy feels manipulative—and is! Clients don't like being led around by the nose. If you have feedback, be candid and give it.]

Getting Feedback from Others

It's often useful to ask clients to solicit feedback from the people they work with and then summarize for you what they've heard. Clearly, this is especially useful if your clients are doing something important and you can't observe them yourself. So you suggest they ask for feedback from people who did observe them. Later, when you meet with your clients, you can ask these kinds of questions:

♦   What feedback did you receive? What did people say?

♦   What do you make of the feedback? How useful was it? What did you learn?

♦   What could you have done differently?

♦   How would you do it next time?

The important role you play in debriefing clients' feedback is to help them extract the lessons learned and identify what they can and should do differently next time (or what they should continue doing that worked well). You can also help them identify themes emerging from feedback they receive from diverse sources or resolve inconsistencies if the feedback seems contradictory. Coaching is an important learning experience for clients; however, they may not fully appreciate what they've learned until they discuss it with a coach.

When Clients Resist or Reject Feedback

Some clients do not want to hear what they perceive as bad news, or their defense mechanisms kick in when they feel they are being attacked.

In truth, it's difficult for most people to hear negative feedback. It can be a threat to our identity and our self-esteem. Bear this in mind as you give feedback to others. The cliché is that "feedback is a gift," but in truth it isn't always a gift, and even when it's offered in the right spirit, some people find feedback very difficult to hear. The fact that you have a coaching relation-ship with your clients implies that you have permission to give feedback, that feedback is at least in part what clients want from you. So clients are more likely to accept feedback from you. Nonetheless, some will argue about it, explain the "special circumstances" in which the event happened, or attack the feedback giver ("He's always had it in for me"). When this happens, it's generally best to use the occasion to focus on how they are ac-cepting feedback rather than the specific feedback itself.

Coach David, I don't know whether this person's perception is accurate or not, but you're rejecting the feedback out of hand. You may be missing an important opportunity for learning. What if there is some truth in this perception? Would you be concerned if other people saw it the same way?

Coach Well, let's assume for a moment that the feedback does have some merit. What would that imply? [This is the straw man approach. You try to get the client to accept the possibility that the feedback could be accurate and then move beyond the accuracy question to the implication question.]

Coach Accurate or not, this is how one person saw it. Remember that feedback is not reality; it's just one person's perception. But let's focus on that for a moment. Why do you think Susan saw it this way? [In this approach, you clarify that feedback is not reality; it's just a perception. Then you move on to the reason for the percep-tion.]

Coach Lisa, I need to observe something. In our last three meetings when we've talked about feedback you've heard from people, I've noticed that you tend to explain it away. You always have reasons why the feedback is wrong, why the person didn't understand what you were trying to do, and so on. You don't resist hearing feedback from me, but I observe you resisting it when it comes

from other people. I think this is a serious issue. People are trying to help you, and you're not hearing them. What's going on?
[Sometimes, the best approach is to confront the resistance head
on. In this example, the coach is also being confrontational, which
we will discuss in the next chapter.]

In giving feedback, you must be *gentle* enough to be perceived as caring
and yet be *candid* enough to be perceived as caring. The apparent contradiction in this statement contains the art of giving feedback. Feedback is often as
difficult for the coach to give as it is for the client to hear. It's hard to sit across
from someone you are trying to help and give them feedback that you know
may be hurtful and cause them distress. Yet if you soften the feedback and
avoid giving people the tough messages they sometimes need to hear, then
you protect them at great expense. The only way to be helpful is to be candid
in a caring way. You do that by empathizing, by showing that you know the
feedback is hard to hear, by staying with them after giving the feedback so you
can help them process it, and by being encouraging and supportive.

Reframing

Reframing is like looking at the moon through a telescope and then using different color filters to see the image in a different perspective. Different filters show a completely different picture of the same thing, and that's
what you do when you reframe something a client has said or a perspective
the client holds. In effect, you put a filter on the image so clients can see it
in a new light. When you give clients feedback, you are responding to what
you have observed of the clients' behaviors. When you reframe, you are
responding to how you have observed the client constructing or "framing"
a picture of reality.

When clients tell their story, they are selecting some parts to tell (and
are leaving other parts out) and are putting the parts they've chosen together in a meaningful way that supports their interpretation of reality.
Consider, for example, how one client, Camilla, frames this event:

Camilla The copier outside my office jammed, so I ran up the stairs to
the next floor and finished copying and assembling my report.

Twelve copies. So I got to the meeting about five minutes late. Mark was annoyed with me about that. He wouldn't even make eye contact. Jim had to introduce me to the client, Sue Bernard. The rest of the meeting went downhill. They listened politely to my presentation, and then it turned out that a few pages in my report were upside down. I don't know how that happened. Anyway, at the end of the meeting Mark went to lunch with Sue and never did talk to me.

Camilla's sequence of events here includes some of what happened but not all of it. She left out the following:

- Two other people in her company were also late to the meeting and in fact arrived after she did.

- Mark, her boss, was meeting with a new client for the first time and was focusing on the client as the meeting began. He later indicated that he had not noticed that Camilla was late and was not annoyed at her or anyone else.

- Mark complimented Camilla on her work as he introduced her part of the presentation.

- The client asked Camilla several questions about the area she reported on. Mark smiled at Camilla several times as she responded to the client's questions, but Camilla didn't notice because she was speaking to the client.

- The meeting ran over its scheduled time, and at the end of the meeting Mark and the client had to leave quickly to get to the restaurant, where they were scheduled to have lunch with three other client representatives.

Camilla's situation is probably familiar to all of us. In the Myers-Briggs® typology, she prefers Judging and hates being late to meetings. She felt guilty because she was running late, even though the reasons were beyond her control. Nothing seemed to be going right that morning, so she painted the gloomiest picture of people's reactions when she came in. Her guilt was the filter that caused her to view the situation the way she did. Moreover, she worries obsessively about Mark's view of her. She wants to do a good job and is probably more concerned than she ought to be about what her boss thinks of her. The coach had been working with Camilla for a while and knew how she tended to frame reality, so this is how he reframed it:

Coach	Sounds like you had a really bad morning.
Camilla	To put it mildly.
Coach	But I'm not sure about your reading of Mark. Maybe he was just focused on the client the whole time. [reframing her interpretation of Mark]
Camilla	I don't think so. He looked annoyed.
Coach	Did you ask him if he was annoyed with you? [checking her perception]
Camilla	(pause) No.
Coach	Then you are assuming he was annoyed but really don't know for sure.
Camilla	I guess.
Coach	Could it be that you just had a bad morning and everything seemed doom and gloom? You know, things didn't go right. You hate being late to meetings. So you feel bad going in. Then you've inadvertently turned some pages upside down in your report. You were probably embarrassed about that. Am I right?
Camilla	Yes! I couldn't believe I'd done that.
Coach	Because you want everything to be perfect.
Camilla	(nodding)

Differing with the Client's View

As in Camilla's case, what coaches often do is reframe a client's bleak view of reality. "I see you painting a very bleak picture," the coach might say, "maybe it's not so bleak." On occasion, you may witness the same event your client does and have a very different view of it. When that happens, you should not contradict the client's perspective by saying something like, "Oh, that's not what happened at all." Instead, you want to acknowledge the client's perspective and then differ with it: "Hmm. That's interesting. You felt that Mark was annoyed with you when you came in. I guess I didn't see it that way at all."

Sometimes, you differ with the client's perspective by putting yourself in someone else's place. For example, if a client said the following, you might differ as we've indicated here.

Ramesh	Everyone on the team wants a quality solution. No doubt about it. They might not like working late every night, but it's the price we have to pay to get the highest-quality solution. Everyone knows that. And if we have to redo some piece of analysis, then so be it. They'll keep redoing it until they get it right. That's not too much to ask, believe me.
Coach	I don't know, Ramesh. You're working your team fourteen hours a day and sometimes more, five days a week, and you've required them to work some weekends. If I were on your team, I would see that as excessive, and I'd be questioning whether we need a 100 percent perfect solution. Maybe 80 percent would do.
Ramesh	They can take it. It's only for four months.
Coach	Maybe they can't. If I were working for you, I would not be happy about the lack of balance in my life. You are seeing yourself as a leader who is uncompromising on quality, but others might see you as uncompromising with people. Day after day after day. If I were on your team, it would be too much, and I wouldn't sign up to be on another team with you.

As this example illustrates, a more confrontational reframing is sometimes necessary, and we will have more to say about this in chapter 10. The coach can't speak for the people on Ramesh's team, but she can imagine herself as a member of the team and imagine how she would feel. To do this, you have to use your understanding of human nature to imagine how the client's behavior would feel to others. Of course, it's best if you can also talk to those other people and ask how they feel, but this is not always possible. When you put yourself in someone else's shoes, however, you have to feel certain that your view of the situation represents the view that the people actually in the situation are most likely to have.

Using Implication Questions to Reframe

One way to reframe is to state your differing perception. Another way is to ask questions that pose a reframed reality and ask the client to consider it. Probably the best form of this question is the implication question. As we noted in chapter 8, implication questions are ones that take the form "If [something] happens, what would the consequences be?" Another way to pose an implication question is to say, "What would be the implications if [something] occurred?" When you use an implication question to reframe the client's view of reality, you ask the client to imagine the consequences, favorable or otherwise, of moving forward with a course of action.

Client   I've decided to move the entire staff from Charlotte to Kansas City. We have eighty-three people in Charlotte, and I'm sure not all of those people will choose to move, so I'll have to hire replacements in Kansas City, but in this labor market that should be no problem.

Coach   How many of those eighty-three do you expect will move to Kansas City?

Client   I'm confident that at least half of them will. Maybe three-quarters.

Coach   What if only a handful agreed to move?

Client   I'm sure that won't happen.

Coach   What if it did? What would the implications be? For you and for the company?

This kind of reframing works best with clients who form conclusions or make decisions too quickly and on too little evidence. You become a helpful thought partner by reframing the situations so clients are forced to think through them more deeply. Over time, you will help these clients become more thoughtful by helping them learn how to explore different perspectives. We have found that clients often view their situations from such a narrow perspective that they fail to see how other people will react or how others are affected by what the clients do. They sometimes don't consider all the possible outcomes of their actions, so reframing is a very useful coaching tool.

The sharper the contrast in perceptions, the more powerful reframing tends to be, but remember that it's best to offer alternative viewpoints as a means of exploration, not as a way to refute the client. Whenever you state or imply that someone's beliefs or perspectives are wrong, you invite an argument and may make them defensive. So the best approach is to pose questions or alternative viewpoints as a different perspective rather than the right perspective.

Generalizing and Specifying

Finally, you can sometimes help clients see a different perspective by generalizing from their particulars or specifying from their generalizations. Generalizing is a good way to help clients see the bigger picture and to test their perceptions.

Client I told Connie last week I didn't see any reason why we couldn't change the logo. We need something fresher and more hip than the look we have.

Coach How did she feel about it?

Client She's worried about losing brand identity, but I don't think that's an issue. I think customers are ready for a change.

Coach I think one of your strengths is challenging tradition. You seem to be good at taking a creative look at areas other people wouldn't question. [generalizing from the client's behavior to a trait or ability; this may give the client a new view of himself and may reframe how he views his capabilities and potential contributions]

Generalizing is particularly helpful for clients who clearly prefer Sensing on the Myers-Briggs typology. People who prefer Sensing tend to be practical and concrete in their orientation. They are more detail minded than their opposites types: Intuitive types tend to focus on the big picture and sometimes don't attend to the details. Conversely, specifying is often a more insightful form of reframing for people who prefer Intuition, precisely because they sometimes do not make the leap themselves from the general to the particular. They sometimes overgeneralize and don't test their assumptions by examining the particulars.

Client I'm not going to work with that group anymore.

Coach Why not?

Client   You can't trust them.

Coach   Well, I know you had a legitimate problem with Ted, but I wasn't aware of any other instances.

Client   No, there haven't been, but that one was enough.

Coach   You're assuming the whole group can't be trusted just because of what Ted did. Maybe they're not all like him. Have you had any problems with Tom? Or Rudy or Marianna?

Client   No.

Coach   So the problem may be Ted, not the group as a whole.

Client   I guess you're right.

Reframing is a tool for challenging the client's assumptions, beliefs, conclusions, and views of situations and people that do not seem accurate or well thought out. Sometimes, unless clients examine their assumptions, rethink their beliefs, and question the conclusions they've come to, they will not change, and this raises an important point. Coaching is about helping clients change. Generally, clients need to change their behavior, but they frequently will not or cannot do that unless they also change how they view themselves and the world around them. Reframing is one of the most powerful tools coaches have to help clients think about and revise their perspective.

REFLECTING

Reflecting means to "hold up the mirror" to clients and give them a view of themselves they might never have seen otherwise. When you reflect, you synthesize your observations of a client in an image that ideally illuminates the client's needs and leaves an indelible impression in the client's mind. The best reflections are powerful and memorable. When you can create the right image for clients, you coalesce all your observations around a single perspective that helps clients work on what they need to change. To illustrate reflecting, we will offer some cases from our coaching experiences, beginning with the woman who made herself small.

The Woman Who Made Herself Small

Gina was an accomplished young woman with a Ph.D. and excellent job skills, but the coach noticed in working with her that she had the peculiar habit of scrunching down in her chair when she met with people. She would fold her arms in front of her, as though in self-protection, and seemed to pull back into the corner of the chair to keep distance between herself and others. After observing this behavior for a while, the coach told Gina what he had observed and then gave her a reflection.

Coach You are a woman who makes herself small.

Gina You think I do this all the time?

Coach I can't say that, but every time I've seen you, you've been scrunched over like that. Also, you tend to discount yourself when you talk to others.

Gina How do I do that?

Coach You say, "I'm not sure about this," or "I may be wrong," or "That's only my opinion." You diminish yourself by qualifying what you say. You make yourself small.

To help her see this, the coach arranged for her to be videotaped interacting with other people, and when they watched the tape together, Gina saw how she "withdrew" physically from people and how self-effacing she was in her speech. This insight enabled her to deal with some serious self-confidence issues, and she eventually stopped making herself small. During the period of her coaching, however, the idea of "making yourself small" became a theme that she and the coach discussed frequently. In fact, it became the main focus of her coaching.

The Tin Man

Like the Tin Man in *The Wizard of Oz*, Paul H. had no heart. He was a senior administrative manager in a large corporation and had frequent complaints from his staff about being insensitive. Turnover in his group was high, and many of those who remained said they went through the motions but hated the job. It paid well, so they stayed, but they did what they had to do and left as early as they could. Paul knew that he needed to do something differently but didn't know what.

Paul I'm not sure what these people want.

Coach Have you asked them?

Paul I'm not as insensitive as people think I am. I know what's going on, but work is work. You keep your personal life at home. (pause) Jeanine was crying at her desk last week. I guess I was supposed to stop and ask her what was wrong, but I don't know what to say in a situation like that. I'm not everybody's parent. I'm the boss. When you have work problems, bring them to me. If it's not about work, deal with it on your own.

Coach   Paul, let me tell you how you're coming across. You're like the Tin Man in *The Wizard of Oz*. You have no heart.

Paul   That's not true. I have a personal life like everybody else.

Coach   That may be, but you're coming across like the Tin Man. Did you stop and ask Jeanine what was wrong?

Paul   No.

Coach   Was she aware that you noticed her and didn't say anything?

Paul   I suppose so.

Coach   Was anybody else aware? Did they see you looking at her and then moving on without stopping to ask what was wrong?

Paul   Probably so. We have an open office environment out there.

Coach   Well, you gave a classic demonstration of being insensitive. You're the Tin Man.

As you can see, the coach was not particularly subtle in delivering this reflection, but Paul was the type of person who needed to hear it bluntly and plainly. The coach knew Paul would not be offended by the observation, so he repeated it a number of times. The image stuck, and in their further work together, Paul talked about getting a heart. One of the values of a good reflection is that it crystallizes the client's development needs and gives both coach and client an image to refer to as they continue their work together.

Joan of Arc

This client was the classic martyr. She sacrificed everything for others. She would volunteer to work late if others couldn't because they wanted to go watch their children play soccer. She agreed to work weekends to revise reports. And she turned down a promotion because it would have meant more travel, and she didn't want to inconvenience her husband. She did not view what she kept doing as extraordinary, but after listening to her story for a while the coach made this observation:

Coach You're Joan of Arc.

Joan What do you mean?

Coach You keep sacrificing everything so you can please others.

Joan Anybody else would do the same.

Coach I doubt that. Besides, you're the one working weekends all the time, and then going home to take care of your family.

Joan I don't think I'm doing anything special.

Coach I disagree. The people you're doing this for should erect a monument to you in the town square. You're sacrificing a lot for them. What are you doing for yourself?

Images like this one can sometimes be so startling that they jolt clients into a sudden insight. Joan fought this image for a while but agreed to start making a list of the things she did for others and the things she did for herself. Initially, she saw the things she did for herself as "being selfish," but as she compiled the two lists she came to realize that her standard mode of being was to please others regardless of the cost to herself. Once she saw the pattern, she was able to break free of it.

The Funambulist

Jessica H. was a very bright young professional who carefully weighed her words and actions. She came across as very thoughtful, but people felt that she had much more potential than she was realizing. When you talked to her, you had the sense that she had enormous untapped potential, that whatever she showed you was merely a fraction of the talent she had available but did not use. After working with her for a while, the coach made this observation:

Coach Jessica, a word that comes to mind when I think of you is funambulist.

Jessica What does that mean?

Coach Literally, a funambulist is a tightrope walker. But it also means someone who is mentally agile. That's you. You're bright and mentally nimble. But you also walk the tightrope. You're cautious, as though you're afraid to lose your balance. I don't see you taking risks, for instance. You haven't in your career or your work, and you don't with me. Everything is measured and careful. I think your caution will prevent you from having the impact you could.

Jessica   I guess I'm afraid of falling.

Coach   Yes, you could fall. You could also soar.

As it so happened, Jessica feared success. The funambulist image opened a door for her, however, and she was then able to explore her caution through the rest of the dialogue.

The Jackhammer

Jack was an executive who drove his own perspective relentlessly. People complained that Jack was not a good listener, but the coach felt that poor listening was only part of the problem. After observing Jack interact with other people in meetings, the coach reached a conclusion:

Coach   Jack, you're like a jackhammer in the meetings I've seen you in. I can understand why people have told you you're a poor listener. You drive your point of view relentlessly.

Jack   Yeah, I guess I do that.

Coach   You're amazing to watch because you're tireless.

Jack   (nodding) When I have something to say, I say it.

Coach   No kidding.

Jack   So it's too much, I guess.

Coach   Well, if I were on the receiving end of it, I would feel like I couldn't get a word in edgewise. That's for sure.

Some people might have been offended at the jackhammer analogy, but Jack had a tough veneer and got the message. The solution, which was "seek to understand before seeking to be understood," was right for him but hard for him to implement. Eventually, he learned to turn off the jackhammer and listen, but it took constant reminders because his natural style is to drive, drive, drive.

The Black-or-White Woman

Another interesting case involved a woman who viewed herself as being at odds with the culture of the company she worked in. She saw herself as a very direct person ("If I have a problem with you, I'll tell you; if you have a problem with me, you tell me") in a culture where people were not that direct. She was frustrated by the fact that things got done in a circuitous manner with a lot of private conversations and negotiations. In her view, the culture was highly political, while she preferred direct confrontations. Other people in the company, however, saw her as combative in her interactions with people, and they felt that she was not collaborative. In sorting through this, the coach had an insight.

Coach   Cory, I think you tend to see things as being either black or white. There are no shades of gray for you.

Cory   What do you mean?

Coach   You want people to be direct as opposed to indirect, but others don't see the same distinction. To them, disagreement is not about conflict or avoidance, black or white; it's about approaching people the right way, raising issues so they don't offend anyone and yet get resolved, and working harmoniously so that goodwill and cooperation are preserved. You're a black-or-white woman working in a world filled with shades of gray.

This image helped Cory see the either/or distinctions in the way she thought. It was a pretty subtle learning point for her, and the coach needed to show her other instances in which her thinking tended to be black or white. She was uncomfortable with ambiguity and tended to disparage anything she couldn't readily understand. However, this became the overriding theme of their work together, and she later developed more of an understanding of ambiguity if not outright comfort with it.

The Screensaver

Our final case involves Peter. His presenting problem was that he was not an inspirational leader. A few interactions with him helped the coach understand one of the fundamental problems: Peter showed very little affect when he spoke to people. No matter what the conversation was about, Peter's face was like a blank slate. There were no facial expressions or reactions. If you joked, he did not smile. If you were angry, he did not react. If you were sad, he showed no concern. No matter what happened in a conversation with Peter, his face did not change. His coach told him this, but it had little impact. Finally, his coach said the following:

Coach   Peter, you're like a screensaver. When you talk to people, your expression never changes. If you had a screensaver of your face, you could be talking to someone, leave the room for coffee, come back later, and no one would know you were gone.

This example illustrates an important point about reflecting. You should never use an image that will be insulting or damaging to the client. However, your images should be accurate and provocative. The more provocative they are, the more likely the client is to find them memorable and to work on the problem. In this case, Peter was shocked by the image but not offended by it, and the coach knew Peter would not be offended because he had worked with him long enough to accurately judge Peter's ego strength and resilience. The image was shocking enough, however, for Peter to work seriously on the problem. He practiced conversations in front of a mirror, worked with a voice coach, and learned to be more visually expressive in his conversations with people. Peter hadn't grasped the magnitude of the problem until the coach observed that his expressionless face was like a screensaver.

Whether you are giving clients feedback, reframing their view of the world, or reflecting an image of them that may provoke insight, you are using your observations of them to enhance their understanding of themselves and rethink how they behave, how they present themselves, and how they interact with others. When you combine observation with listening and asking insightful questions, you have a powerful repertoire of skills for coaching. In the next chapter, we will discuss how you can use additional telling skills to push and pull clients through the dialogue. We will also discuss the important use of process checks to ensure that your coaching remains adaptive and relevant to your clients' needs.

10

Pushing and Pulling

Give more detailed hints for improvements.

Provide suggestions to the people who are being coached to help them identify what they need to do to improve.

Be more straightforward in communicating the "not quite so nice" feedback instead of sugarcoating it so much.

SUGGESTIONS TO COACHES FROM THE "COACHING EFFECTIVENESS SURVEY," KORN/FERRY INTERNATIONAL

In the previous chapter, we focused on one of the most powerful ways in which coaches share their perspective with clients: observing their behavior and giving them feedback, observing their thought processes and reframing how they view themselves and their world, and giving them reflections of themselves that synthesize the coach's impressions and give clients a potent image that can help drive change. In this chapter, we examine additional forms of telling: advising and teaching, confronting, and encouraging clients. We also discuss a critical tool in adaptive coaching: the process check.

Advising, teaching, and confronting are ways in which coaches can push clients. When you advise or teach clients, for instance, you are giving them a perspective that you hope will move them from one place to another—from one attitude to another, from one skill level to another, and so on. The driving force behind this movement is your knowledge, expertise, experience, or authority. When you confront clients, you are trying to move them by directly contradicting or challenging them, and the driving force is your will.

You can also move clients by *pulling* them, so to speak, and you do this primarily through encouragement. When you encourage people, you reward their successes (and sometimes their noble failures) and give them positive reinforcement for the things they've done right. The word *encourage* comes from the Old French *cuer*, which means "heart." When you encourage clients, you are filling them with courage; giving them heart; imbuing them with the mental or moral strength to venture, persevere, and withstand danger, fear, or difficulty. Encouragement has a powerful effect on clients and is probably not used enough.

ADVISING CLIENTS

Everyone loves to give advice. People enjoy feeling like experts and being valued for what they know (or appear to know). Ann Landers and her sister, Abigail Van Buren, made careers of it. Solving other people's problems is one of life's great vicarious pleasures. Of course, this begs the question: Who gets the most from advice—the giver or the receiver? Nineteenth-century American writer Josh Billings said, "Most of the advice we receive from others is not so much evidence of their affection for us as it is evidence of their affection for themselves." The principal danger of advice giving is that it can be a self-administered aphrodisiac, doing more to satisfy your own ego than to help clients. So we will borrow our advice on advice giving from the Roman poet Horace, who said, "Whatever advice you give, be brief." Here are more tips on giving advice.

Don't Offer Advice Too Early in the Relationship

Clearly, there is a role in coaching for advice giving. Sometimes clients ask for it, and in some types of coaching relationships, advice giving is expected. When professors coach students, for instance, the professors are expected to offer advice because of the explicit master-novice relationship. The same is true in parent-child relationships and in many supervisor-subordinate relationships. Whenever one person in a relationship is presumed to know more than the other and when one purpose of the relationship is to convey knowledge or build skill, then advice giving is not only acceptable, it's expected. In other types of relationships, such as colleague-colleague or friend-friend, advice giving may be part of the relationship, but some level of trust must be built before this is true.

In a master-novice relationship, there is a presumed or implied right to advise; however, in a relationship between peers there is no such right. It must be earned. If you and I are colleagues, I may not believe that you are a credible advisor. If I don't and you offer me advice, I will reject it and think less of you for not being savvy enough to know that I wouldn't accept advice from you. This is also true in coaching relationships. There may be an implied right to advise, depending on the extent to which the client views the coach as a "master," but there may not be. The coach may have to earn the right to advise by first being a good listener and a capable and insightful thought partner. For this reason, it's best not to offer advice too early in a coaching relationship unless a client specifically asks for it.

Coach Maria, you said that the two groups are really not aligned.

Maria That's right. Everyone would claim to be customer focused, but the engineers are really more concerned about the elegance of their designs. They always see more potential functionality than the finance team thinks customers are willing to pay for.

Coach So you have another meeting on Thursday. Right?

Maria Thursday from three to five, right.

Coach How are you going to handle that issue?

Maria I'm not sure. I've tried discussing it rationally, but each group thinks the other group doesn't understand the problem. What would you suggest?

Feed the Hunger

Clearly, when clients ask for advice or a suggestion, you should give it. However, we've seen coaches who instead ask another question:

Coach Well, what are your options? *Or*, I have some thoughts but I'd like you to come up with some alternatives first.

Neither of these responses is adequate. The coach may legitimately want the client to do most of the brainstorming, but it still seems unreasonably coy to avoid answering a direct question. When clients are hungry, you need to feed the hunger. In other words, when they ask you a question, answer it!

Resist Telling War Stories

Next, be cautious about offering advice that is entirely grounded in your experience.

Coach   How are you going to handle that issue?

Maria   I'm not sure. I've tried discussing it rationally, but each group thinks the other group doesn't understand the problem. What would you suggest?

Coach   You know, I faced a similar situation several years ago when I worked for Atlantic General. I was a division manager at the time and was responsible for the Southeast region, including Florida, which I loved, by the way. Have you ever been to St. Petersburg Beach? Anyway, I had a marketing group then that was totally at odds with our product specialists. What I did . . .

Maria can only hope the coach's story doesn't go on too long. Coaching is not a license to tell interminable war stories or provide oral histories of your life. Too much of that can feel to clients like going to a friend's house for dinner and having to sit through their three-hour, six-hundred-slide presentation of their last vacation, complete with humorous narration. When you give in to too much personal storytelling, you risk boring your clients and diminishing your value. It's best to confine advice to best practices or lessons you've learned from your experience.

Don't Put Yourself in the Client's Place

Some coaches have the annoying habit of assuming that they are the client. They presume to put themselves in the client's place and offer advice on what they would do.

Coach   How are you going to handle that issue?

Maria   I'm not sure. I've tried discussing it rationally, but each group thinks the other group doesn't understand the problem. What would you suggest?

Coach   Maria, if I were you, I would get both groups together and ask them to present their point of view. You might even ask each group to defend the other group's perspective, so they step into each other's shoes for a while.

The advice being given is a reasonable option, but it is framed in a way that undercuts its value. The "If I were you" construct is annoying to a number of people and limits the client's options to the single path the coach would choose. You aren't the client and can't presume to be. Moreover, there is a danger in presuming to be the client, which is that you risk assuming the problem is yours to solve, and you may convince yourself that your way is the only way to do it. Ex-CEOs who become coaches, for example, run a great risk when they coach other CEOs. They may miss "the thrill of the hunt" so much that they not only put themselves in their client's place but start wishing they were actually in their client's place and start acting like the CEO. Some coaches have trouble separating the "If I were you" construct from actually wishing they were the client. It's best to keep some distance.

If You Know You Don't Know, Say So

Next, resist the temptation to offer advice when you don't know what you're talking about. Some coaches seem to be confident that they can "wing it" if they're asked a question they really don't know the answer to, but it's best to be totally transparent.

Coach   How are you going to handle that issue?

Maria   I'm not sure. I've tried discussing it rationally, but each group thinks the other group doesn't understand the problem. What would you suggest?

Coach   I don't know. I've never faced that problem. Why don't we think it through?

Obviously, "faking smart" when you really don't know the answer is risky because you may steer clients in the wrong direction. If you give advice and it's wrong, you may lose all of your credibility with the client, and "faking smart" is a good way to be wrong. Acknowledging that you don't have all the answers often builds trust because you've been honest and you're showing that you're human. If you're candid about what you don't know, then clients will have more trust in what you do know.

Be Culturally Sensitive in Your Advice Giving

Finally, it's important to consider the cultural differences between you and your clients when you offer advice. Differences between you and your clients in culture, gender, age, nationality, and so on can affect how clients view what you tell them, how appropriate your advice is, and whether the advice is accurate for that person. We have much more to say about diversity and coaching in chapters 12 through 15. Suffice it to say here that if you advise someone from a culture that values harmony to be a lot more assertive, you may be giving them inappropriate and culturally insensitive advice. When you are not sure whether your advice is culturally appropriate, it's better to ask rather than tell. When you ask clients how they might handle a situation, they automatically invoke their own cultural filters. When you advise them, you have to invoke the cultural filters and may be wrong.

Advice giving is fraught with danger. In Shakespeare's *Hamlet*, Polonius was a character who seemed compelled to give people advice. Look what happened to him.

TEACHING CLIENTS

When clients need to learn something the coach knows or need to build their skills, then the challenge for coaches is to teach them (or find someone else who can). The latter is often the right answer. If you lack the knowledge and skills yourself, then your responsibility as a coach is to help your clients find the right teacher, master, program, seminar, or other learning aid. However, if you do have the knowledge or skills to be helpful, then you need to know how to teach clients effectively. Teaching is obviously a complex topic, but coaches who are not professional teachers can nonetheless do an adequate job by keeping in mind a few basic principles.

Different Learning Styles

First, people learn in different ways. For the sake of simplicity, we will call these learning styles *know, show,* and *throw*. Some people prefer to learn by *knowing*: they read about the topic; absorb the subject matter cognitively; and then deepen their knowledge by discussing the subject with others, researching the subject, and sometimes writing about the subject. These kinds of people might say that they don't know what they think about something until they write it down. The act of writing (or speaking to others about the subject) is their way of processing their learning and synthesizing it in ways that are meaningful to them. Knowers typically respond well to content-based lectures, books, and thoughtful discussions. If you are teaching this type of person, then you should provide books or other written materials as well as a bibliography or list of other resources.

Other people learn best by being *shown* how to do something. They thrive on models and often describe themselves as visual learners. They need to see how things work and prefer coaches who can model the skill or behavior for them. People who prefer to learn by being shown how to do something typically enjoy demonstrations and other forms of instruction that walk them through the steps or illustrate what must be done.

Finally, some people like to learn by *doing* whatever it is they need to learn. They are generally very tactile people and prefer to touch, handle, and manipulate the thing in order to learn how to use it. They may want to see it done first, but they are generally impatient during any demonstrations and just want to "jump in and get their feet wet." The mantra of people who prefer to learn by being thrown into the situation is, "You can't learn to swim by watching from the side of the pool while the coach swims."

Knowers are the people who buy a new DVD player and study the manual before doing anything else. Showers are the people who buy a new DVD player and then ask someone else to show them how to use it. Throwers are the people who toss the manual aside and try to figure out how to use their new DVD player by experimenting with the buttons on the remote. To some extent, of course, each of us has the characteristics of the knowing, showing, and throwing types of learners. However, we do generally prefer one form over another. When you are coaching and need to teach a client a skill, you first have to consider what kind of learner the client is. Then adapt your approach accordingly.

Reducible and Nonreducible Skills

Another important consideration in teaching clients is the subject matter itself. Some subjects can be reduced to logical parts or sequential operational steps. For instance, if you are teaching someone how to operate a drill press, you can reduce the operation of the drill press to a series of steps, a sequence in which things must be done, or a series of steps required to operate the equipment safely. If the thing to be learned can be reduced to a sequence of steps, then you teach by teaching the steps, following the logic required to operate the thing so learners can grasp the bigger picture of its operation and learn what should happen in what order. One caution is important, however: often what looks to an experienced practitioner like a series of steps is really a more complex activity to a novice, and countless educational mistakes have been made by people trying to teach complex skills in a step-by-step fashion.

The process is not so simple with nonreducible subjects such as learning how to build strong client relationships, how to resolve conflict between groups, or how to develop an effective business strategy. With nonreducible subjects, there generally is no single right way to do things and no order in which things must be done. People take individual approaches, and although there may be principles and best practices regarding how best to do a particular task, doing it well still requires some art and judgment. There is no formula for building client relationships (although a few authors might suggest otherwise).

The Two Basic Approaches to Teaching Clients

When you are teaching clients a subject that can be reduced to steps, then you should show them the subject, explain how it works, and then have them practice it. Show, explain, practice. Showing gives people the big picture and aids the visual learners. Explaining helps people understand the principles behind the operation of the thing. Practicing gives them the visceral feel of the thing and reinforces what they saw you do. Because practice makes perfect, as the old saying goes, it's important for clients to practice doing the thing as many times as is feasible, and they should practice it with you observing and giving feedback and encouragement. When they falter, tell them specifically how and where they did so and how to do it right. When they succeed, pat them on the back and reinforce what they did correctly.

When you are teaching a subject that is not reducible to steps, it's often best to begin by observing what the client has already done. Look at his previous work or observe him doing whatever it is you want to teach. Then share your observations, talk about what's working and what's not working, and discuss and explore alternatives. It's often good to model the skill and talk about what you're doing and why you're doing it as you are performing. You may also have some best practices or general principles to share, but clients by and large are going to learn by doing, getting feedback, and doing again. Your observations about their past performance in the areas they want to improve is critically important to this learning process.

CONFRONTING CLIENTS

Advising and teaching are relatively benign ways to push clients (unless you bore them with unwanted advice). However, confronting can be direct, dramatic, and, well, confrontational. It is the maximum strength form of pushing clients. As we are using the term, confronting means to deliberately and directly challenge or contradict clients in ways intended to compel them to rethink an attitude, perspective, or conclusion. Confrontation is likely to be a little-used tool in your coaching toolkit, but it's an important one on the rare occasions when you might need to use it.

When to Use Confrontation

Three circumstances may occur during a coaching dialogue in which the correct coaching response could be to confront the client: when a client is deceiving herself, when a client is doing or saying something contradictory, or when the client is too facile at explaining away an issue. The first of these, self-deception, is not unusual. To one degree or another all people engage in some self-deception. We overlook our own blemishes and selectively ignore indications that we are not as smart, attractive, professional, generous, and right as we like to think we are. Some self-deception is not only normal; it's probably healthy. It becomes debilitating, however, if it shields us from uncomfortable truths and prevents us from accepting a real need for change. When you are coaching someone and observe an inordinate amount of self-deception on the client's part, then it may be appropriate to confront the client by pointing out the self-deception.

Client I don't have any problem sharing power.

Coach I have to say, Dennis, that's not what I've observed. On the contrary, you seem to worry most when you don't have total control over a situation.

• • •

Client That was primarily my idea! How did Bob Franklin become team leader?

Coach Correct me if I'm wrong, but didn't Bob develop the prototype?

Client Yes, but he used my ideas to solve the design problems that kept us from creating a working prototype in the first place.

Coach Maybe they don't care where the ideas came from. Maybe they only care about who was able to make the concept workable.

Client It still doesn't feel right to me.

Coach Maybe not, but Bob Franklin may deserve more credit than you're giving him.

You may also choose to confront clients when they contradict themselves—when what they say is inconsistent with what they do or when they contradict something they said previously. You need to be careful not to point out a contradiction as a way of saying, "Gotcha!" The purpose is to help clients see when their thinking is muddled or when contradictory behavior is a source of the client's problems.

Patricia I am a firm believer that you have to treat everyone fairly. You can't show any favoritism or bias toward anyone on the team.

Coach I know you feel strongly about that, but how does it look when you always award the highest bonuses to the same three people?

Patricia They're consistently the highest performers.

Coach I have no doubt that's true. But let's be candid. Don't you always give them the best assignments? And didn't you tell me that you spend more time coaching them than anyone else on your team?

I think you mean well, Patricia, but I also think you set up those three people to succeed.

Without this confrontation, Patricia may not have realized her unconscious bias in managing her team. It's not uncommon for people to espouse certain theories but have other "theories in use." In other words, they say one thing but do something else. Pointing out these inconsistencies can be illuminating to clients.

Finally, confronting clients is a useful tool when their explanations of their behavior are too facile and they aren't accepting responsibility for something they clearly are responsible for.

Dan   I'm glad she left.
Coach   I thought she was one of your top performers.
Dan   She was, and that's the worst part of it. But in the end she just wasn't a team player.
Coach   I don't buy it, Dan. I spoke to Kathy several times. I've seen her in action. She was very much a team player in my book.
Dan   You didn't know her like I did.
Coach   That's true, but I still don't think that's why she left. I think she had trouble with your management style. And, let's be totally candid here: I think you were threatened by her. She was a strong succession candidate.
Dan   You're way off the mark here.
Coach   Maybe so, but you keep losing good people, and we need to understand why. If you can't retain your top people and build some solid successors to your position, where does that leave you?

As the previous examples illustrate, confronting clients can be gentle and less forceful ("Correct me if I'm wrong, but didn't Bob develop the prototype?") or bolder and more forceful ("I think you were threatened by her"). There are a number of ways to confront clients. Generally, coaches should err on the side of gentle, less forceful methods, but occasionally clients will not respond to anything other than a direct confrontation. To explore this idea further, we will describe a continuum of ways to confront clients.

Ways to Confront Clients

Figure 7 illustrates the ways in which coaches can confront clients. On the left side of this continuum, at the number 1 position, are question and reflect. These are the milder, more indirect ways to confront. In this mode, you express curiosity about inconsistencies between the client's words and actions or may interpret the client's behavior in a way that is mildly challenging to his point of view. The purpose is not to put the client on the spot but to call something into question that you believe needs to be reexamined. Here are some examples of what you might say to mildly question or challenge clients:

Figure 7: Continuum for Confronting Clients

Coach   Jim, you told me last week that you were determined to see this through. What's changed?

Coach   Liz, you have very high standards and are one of the most success-oriented people I've ever met. But I have this image of a turbine engine that just never stops. How much risk is there that you'll burn yourself out or burn out the people on your team?

Coach   Fernando, do you think the other district managers are deliberately excluding you, or are you pushing them away? How much of your own behavior is causing the isolation you feel?

Mild confrontations like these are easier for clients to hear than more challenging ones, so there is less likelihood of defensiveness or other reactions in which clients resist your perspective and push back in ways that make it even more difficult for them to listen to and consider the challenge. As we suggested earlier, the mild, indirect mode of confronting is preferable in most circumstances because it is less likely to engender a defensive reaction. You give clients more latitude to disagree with you, more room to maneuver, so to speak, so they don't feel cornered. Most people are more willing to entertain a contrary notion if they don't feel compelled to accept it but instead are invited to think about it.

In the middle of the continuum is disagreement and outright challenge. Clearly, these are stronger forms of confrontation. You use them when clients are not responding to milder forms of confronting and when you believe they need a stronger antagonist to question their position or viewpoint. Here's how disagreements and challenges might look:

Coach Jim, last week you told me you were determined to see this through. Now you're saying it doesn't look feasible. Some things have come up that will prevent you from moving forward. That just doesn't seem right to me. I don't see any reason why you shouldn't continue.

Coach Liz, you have very high standards and are one of the most success-oriented people I've ever met. But I'm concerned about you burning yourself out and burning out your team. In my experience, people have trouble sustaining the kind of pace you've set. Are your recent health problems related to this?

Coach Fernando, you and I have been talking about this problem for several months now, and I know the other district managers. I just don't think it's true that these people are deliberately excluding you. I just don't see it. What else could be happening?

In the middle part of this continuum, you are essentially saying things like, "That doesn't sound right to me," "I don't think that's true," or "That hasn't been my experience." In disagreeing with clients, you are challenging them directly and encouraging a more vigorous debate about the ways in which you disagree with them. In fact, the purpose of this kind of confrontation may be either to cause a debate or get clients to rethink something they believe. Your tone should be respectful, not combative, and you should focus more on the ideas than the person.

The far right part of the continuum, the number 3 position, is the most forceful and direct way to confront. Here, you are consciously opposing the client's perspective and perhaps even evaluating the client. This level of confrontation is "in your face" and bold.

Coach Jim, last week you told me that you were determined to see this through. I'm not seeing you do that. What I'm seeing is the same old pattern we've been talking about. You back down when you run into roadblocks. What's it going to take for you to break that pattern?

Coach   Liz, you have very high standards and are one of the most successful-oriented people I've ever met. But you are burning yourself out and you're burning out your team. People just can't sustain the pace that you've set, and your own recent health problems are evidence enough that you can't continue at this pace, either. You need to let up before something really serious happens.

Coach   Fernando, you and I have been talking about this problem for several months now, and I disagree that the other district managers are deliberately excluding you. On the contrary, I think you do a lot to push them away. You're blaming others for a problem that is largely of your own making.

Confrontations like these are among the most dramatic things coaches can do, and you can't be this confrontational unless you have already established a very high level of trust with clients. Being this bold too soon in a coaching relationship would destroy trust (because the client would rightly question your judgment). You have to earn the right to be this bold with clients. What gives you the right is that 1) you have already demonstrated that you care about the client and are acting in her best interests, 2) you have shown that you maintain confidences so she knows that whatever you say to her will not go elsewhere, and 3) your purpose in being so bold is to be helpful, not harmful.

Even when you have a high degree of trust, you should not be this bold unless you know the client is resilient. Resilient people have the power to endure difficult messages and bounce back when things are tough. If you choose to be strongly confrontational with a client, you must know beforehand that she will not disintegrate under the onslaught to her ego. The key factor is the client's ego strength. Resilient people have a strong enough self-concept to endure negative messages. Someone with less ego strength may crumble under a strongly negative message, begin to question her worth, and enter a negative spiral of self-doubt and vulnerability to other negative messages. The key questions to ask yourself are, "Can this person take a direct message?" and "Will she rebound from it and, in fact, come out stronger?" If you have any doubts yourself, do not use the bolder forms of confrontation.

In our experience, the strongest forms of confrontation are used very infrequently. In Terry's nearly three decades of coaching, he has had to do it only about a dozen times. The milder forms of confrontation work well enough in most cases. In coaching, as in medicine, it is wise to adhere to the main tenet of the Hippocratic oath: "Above all, do no harm." Always err on the side of milder forms of confrontation first. Then, if necessary, escalate to the stronger forms. What follows are two case examples of confronting clients. Note in both examples that confronting clients does not entail being rude or mean. In every form of confrontation, you should always be respectful and considerate.

An Inauthentic Life

In this case, the coach worked with a partner in a professional firm who appeared to have withdrawn from his fellow partners. He was mentally disengaged from the partnership and was not contributing at the level he had previously. Moreover, he was isolating himself socially from the firm—he had stopped attending partner meetings and even informal social gatherings. His behavior was puzzling, so the firm engaged a coach. As they began working together, the client revealed to the coach that he was having trouble in his marriage. He had been having an affair, he said, and was about to file for divorce. As the coach listened, he realized that this client was very conflicted about his behavior and the choices he'd made. He'd withdrawn from the partnership partly to hide the affair and partly because he was ashamed of what he'd done. In the course of their discussion, a picture coalesced in the coach's mind.

Coach   I think the fundamental issue, Charles, is that you've been leading an inauthentic life.

Charles How do you mean?

Coach   I think much of your life has been about taking the moral high ground. You've been a highly principled person, both in school and in your profession. But recently you've made some decisions that you are clearly conflicted about. You've been living a lie in your personal and professional life, and I think the shame you feel has caused you to withdraw from your partners and friends, in a sense to isolate yourself from people you care about and respect because you're ashamed of what you're doing.

Note that the coach balanced "you've been living a lie" with statements like "much of your life has been about taking the moral high ground" and "you've been a highly principled person." The purpose in this confrontation was to show how the client's recent behavior was at odds with his fundamental character. The notion that he had been leading an inauthentic life was a profoundly disturbing one to this client and caused an abrupt about-face in his behavior. Shortly after this confrontation, the client put an end to the affair and tried to reconcile himself to his wife. He had been feeling, but could not articulate, a deep ethical dilemma. Once the coach surfaced it for him, he radically changed the direction he'd been taking and eventually reconciled himself to the partnership as well.

A Matter of Time Management

In this case, Bernard, an office manager for a large company, was receiving coaching on his leadership in the office. However, during one meeting with the coach, Bernard opened the discussion by saying, "I'd like to talk about my wife." He revealed that they were having trouble in their marriage. His wife felt that he was not spending enough time at home, and Bernard worried that she might leave and take their three-year-old son with her.

Coach   You're clearly feeling anxious about that.

Bernard   Yes, I'm worried about it.

Coach   Tell me more about her complaint that you don't spend enough time at home.

Bernard   Well, she's right, of course. This is a new office, and I have a lot of responsibility. I've been spending probably twelve hours a day here. I come in at six, typically, and leave at seven or seven-thirty. Sometimes later.

Coach   Which, if I do the math, is more than twelve hours a day.

Bernard   Yes, well, I guess that's right. I do what I have to do. It's a new office, as I said. We have only eight people now, but the company expects us to generate as much revenue as offices with two or three times that number. Last year, we grew by more than 300 percent! Can you believe it? This year won't be as much, certainly, but we are still the fastest-growing small office in the company.

Coach   You seem really proud of that.

Bernard   We all are. It's a huge accomplishment, especially because we're in a relatively undeveloped market.

Coach   So you're very busy at work.

Bernard   Constantly. There's never enough time to do what I need to do, much less what I'd like to do. We need to hire more people, but I can't do that until we increase our customer base.

Coach   So you're doing your own job plus—

Bernard   Plus building the business, plus servicing some new accounts, right. It's overwhelming sometimes. I spend a lot of weekends just catching up on e-mails.

Coach   And your wife thinks you're spending too much time working.

Bernard   She complains about it all the time, and I can see her point, really, but I'm doing all this for her and Josh. At this point in my life, I have to do what I'm doing, you know, but I'm making good money and building a lot of security for our family.

Coach   Uh-huh.

Bernard   It's a time management issue, and that's what I guess I need help with. I really do want to spend more time with my family.

Coach   (pause) Hmm. I don't think that's true.

Bernard   (pause; shocked)

Coach   I think you're fooling yourself, Bernard. If you wanted to spend more time with your family you would be.

Bernard   But I do want to spend more time with them!

Coach   No, in a strange way, you don't. If you wanted to do that, you would be. You're making choices. No one's twisting your arm. You are choosing between your wife and work, and you're choosing work.

Bernard   That's not true.

Coach   It might make you feel better to think it's not true, but it is. All the evidence says that you find work much more satisfying than spending more time with your wife and son.

This was one of those moments in coaching when absolute candor was required. Bernard needed to be shocked out of his complacent notion that he was doing the right thing for his wife and son and that somehow he had a "time management" issue. The fact is that clients do make choices, and those choices are revealed in the decisions they make. Bernard needed to see how he was deceiving himself, and the coach felt that a strong confrontation was necessary. It worked. In the dialogue that followed, Bernard accepted the fact that he was making a choice and that if he wanted to save his marriage he had to rethink his priorities.

ENCOURAGING CLIENTS

As we said at the beginning of this chapter, encouraging clients is a way to pull them, to motivate them to go forward and to reward the progress they've made, which encourages them to make even more progress. That clients want more positive reinforcement than they are getting is evident from these client responses on our Coaching Effectiveness Survey. Remember that these are suggestions from clients to coaches about how the latter could be more effective.

- Increase the amount and frequency of positive feedback to individuals.

- Recognize excellent performance and superior effort, even if they fail.

- Recognize good performance on a more regular basis.

- Be more supportive and give out "atta boys."

- Always highlight the positives of situations and then explore how to improve.

- Continue to encourage others to expand beyond their current comfort levels.

- Have more positive feedback. Focus on what was done right and not always on what was done wrong.

- Use more encouragement and "pats on the back."

- Recognize achievements.

- Be more open to offering praise as well as helping with problems.

- Compliment successes both large and small.

- Attempt to express approval and encouragement more frequently when specific jobs have been well done.

People hunger for encouragement, although they don't want mindless cheerleading or false praise. Pats on the back and encouraging words from coaches must be perceived as genuine and deserved. They can't be so frequent as to defy credibility, nor so lavish as to provoke doubt. What people want is an authentic acknowledgment when they have done something well and an appreciation for their efforts, even when those efforts result in a noble failure.

Encouragement fills the heart with courage. It gives people the inner resources to keep trying and the strength to endure hardships and barriers. It's important to recognize wins, even if they are small ones. Small wins accumulate, but without ongoing encouragement, clients may become disheartened if the wins seem too small or too infrequent. Some coaches excel at giving encouragement; others are much more parsimonious with their praise. The right answer is to read each client's need for encouragement and adapt accordingly. The error most coaches make is to encourage too little. So err by encouraging too much.

DOING PROCESS CHECKS

In this chapter we have discussed ways of moving clients by pushing and pulling. In truth, we've spent more time on pushing than we have on pulling because the former is considerably more difficult to carry off with finesse. Pulling by encouraging clients is almost second nature to most coaches (although they still may not do it enough). Another way to pull clients is to engage them in reflecting on the coaching process itself, to make them willing accomplices in the shaping of the ongoing dialogue, and you do this through process checks.

The simple principle operating in the process check is to make the coaching process transparent and adaptable to the client's needs and wishes. You do this in part by telling clients what you're doing or what you think the process should be:

♦ Before discussing the results of your feedback surveys, I'd like you to tell me how you view yourself as a leader. That may help both of us understand the feedback better.

♦ I'm not sure we've fully defined the problem yet, Sean. What do you think?

♦ In your development plan, I think we ought to identify not only what you want to achieve but how we will measure progress. That way, we'll both know when you've accomplished your goals.

You also make the process transparent by asking clients how they feel about it:

♦ What do you think we should discuss next?

♦ Where would you like to go from here?

♦ How useful was it for me to review your business plans?

To keep the dialogue on the right path, the most helpful path, you have to know which path you are on, and your assumptions about how helpful you are being may be wrong. In our work with coaches, we have seen numerous instances in which the coach was heading off in a direction that did not seem productive. Often, the coach started offering advice on a problem that seemed peripheral to the client's actual needs. In our roles as coach supervisors, we would sometimes stop the process and ask the coach to do a process check using these kinds of questions:

♦ Is this helpful to you? *Or*, Am I being helpful?

♦ Should we be doing anything differently?

♦ Are we on the right path?

♦ Are we focusing on the right topic?

♦ What would be most helpful to you right now?

The answers to these questions would frequently be, "No, this isn't helpful," or "No, we're really not talking about the right thing." You have to remember as a coach that, along with the dialogue you and your client are having, the client is having an interior monologue or stream of consciousness that may parallel what the two of you are discussing but often sidetracks into related memories, assumptions about where this discussion is going, thoughts or emotions that stream from something that's been said, and even thoughts about the drive home or dinner that night. The client's interior monologue often holds the key to the real issues and problems, as well as real but unspoken barriers, fears, hopes, and dreams. The way to tap into this stream of consciousness is to step away from the content flow of your discussion and ask a process question: "Is this helpful?" By asking if the process is helpful, you invite clients to make mid-course corrections that are usually more helpful to them than what you were doing. Making those midcourse corrections is fundamentally what adaptive coaching is all about.

What if you ask clients if what you are doing is helpful to them and they say that it's not? Are there risks inherent in process checking? We don't think so. No matter how clients answer process questions, there is no bad news. If you are on target and are being helpful to your clients, that's great. If not, then at least now you know and can change your approach. The worst thing you can do is assume you're on target and assume you're being helpful and then learn later that the client felt the coaching was a waste of time.

Being transparent about the process and being willing to adapt to your client's needs and wishes have other benefits: they build trust and help ensure that your coaching will have real impact. There is also tremendous value in admitting when you are lost, when you don't have the answer or an opinion, or when you lack experience. You may be the coach, but you don't have to have all the answers. You just have to be a thoughtful dialogue part ner and a good listener. Don't assume that you always know the right way to go or that your assumptions are always correct or that the path you're taking is the right one. Instead, do a process check and then adapt accordingly. That will keep you on the right track.

11

Closing Coaching

Keep your promises. You are a highly skilled listener during coaching sessions. These listening skills are in large contrast with the follow-up, which gives people the impression you don't care about their development.

Actively follow up the actions agreed upon.

Allow the people being coached to make the final decision for what they need to do and take responsibility for their decisions.
SUGGESTIONS TO COACHES FROM THE "COACHING EFFECTIVENESS SURVEY," KORN/FERRY INTERNATIONAL

S ome coaching relationships end without closing. The coach and client become busy, and the coach doesn't follow up. The best of intentions evaporate in the midst of problems, competing commitments, telephone calls, e-mail messages, meetings, and dozens of other daily distractions that result in whole populations of workers having more starts than finishes. As we said at the end of chapter 6, it doesn't have to be that way. The most effective coaching occurs when the process reaches a satisfying sense of closure, and this is as true for individual coaching meetings or events as it is for the coaching relationship as a whole. Managing closure is a key coaching skill.

In chapter 7, we said that dialogue is an act of exploration that helps clients determine what they must do to navigate the rest of their journey safely and successfully. In coaching relationships that extend for months or even years, the dialogue forms a continuous—and sometimes discontinuous—chain of interactions that, together, constitute the journey. Each of these dialogues should conclude in a satisfying way and yet form a bridge between the previous dialogue and the one yet to come. This is to say that each dialogue should have a distinct opening, middle, and ending. In chapter 6, we talked about how each dialogue should begin. In this chapter, we discuss how each one should end. We also discuss the follow-up that should occur between meetings and, finally, how effective coaches bring closure to the coaching relationship itself.

CLOSING INDIVIDUAL COACHING SESSIONS

Fitness experts recommend that every workout begin with a warm-up and end with a cooling-down period. Coaching sessions are like this as well. In the warm-up, you reengage, remind each other where you ended last time, review commitments and action steps, and warm up to the main body of the session, which is the helping dialogue. Toward the end of the session, the coach needs to sense the "winding down" in the energy or flow of the discussion that signals the need to start closing. Sometimes you sense closure when the client seems to have exhausted her capacity to explore further; sometimes, the agreed-upon time for the meeting has elapsed; and sometimes, a natural break occurs when you have fully explored a topic and neither of you has the time, energy, or willingness to begin exploring another. When you sense that the time has come to close the dialogue for now, you need to start "cooling down" the discussion and bring it to a satisfying conclusion. Our key point here is that closure is a process you should manage. It should not just happen.

In our experience, a satisfying closure has these four elements: 1) identification of the key points or learnings in the preceding dialogue and a synthesis of them into a shared perspective on what emerged from the dialogue; 2) an articulation of any new commitments the client has made; 3) identification of next steps each person agrees to take, including when you will meet again and how you will follow up; and 4) a process check on this session, and sometimes on the coaching process as a whole.

Synthesizing Learnings

As you sense the dialogue winding down, it's important, first of all, to recapture and synthesize the key points of the discussion. You need to review the ground you have covered together and reach a mutual understanding of the lessons you learned, the key discoveries you made, or the insights you reached. One reason for summarizing the key points is to ensure that you don't lose track of something important, something you need to re-member or may need to follow up on. Another reason is to ensure that you have a shared view of what took place. It's not unusual for two people who have had the same conversation to remember it differently. So when you summarize the key points of the dialogue you are, in a sense, negotiating a shared understanding of what was important and what should be remem-bered. Finally, if you ask your clients to summarize the key points, then you also gain some insight into what they considered important— and it may differ from what you considered important, as this example shows:

Coach   Richard, we said we would stop at eleven o'clock, and it's nearly ten 'til. As we wrap up, would you summarize what we talked about today? From your standpoint, what were the key things we talked about this morning?

Richard I think the key thing is that I just need to step out as the new leader of this company and not worry so much about being sec-ond-guessed.

Coach   Uh-huh.

Richard I'm not entirely comfortable with the role yet, and I'm not sure everyone else is comfortable having me in the role. Until a few months ago, I was one of their peers.

Coach   Yes, but now the decision's been made. You're the new president.

Richard (nodding) I just need to get my own self-doubts behind me and not worry about what people are thinking.

Coach   People are waiting for you to really take charge.

Richard (nodding) So I just need to get on with it. The other thing we spoke about was my comfort, or lack of it, in being visionary. I'm not going to be the charismatic leader Stuart was, but I under-stand the need to set a clear direction and get everyone behind it.

Coach   We talked about how you might do that.

Richard Right. I need to go out into the offices and talk about where I see the business going. And I need to do that with more energy and optimism than I usually convey. Not that I'm not optimistic, but my natural style is not to wave the flag and lead people in the company cheer.

Coach   No, and you don't need to go to those extremes to motivate people. They mainly want to feel that their leader is positive about
the future and is confident that the company will attain its goals.

Richard   Exactly. Well, I'm comfortable with that. (pause) So those are
the two key things I want to take away from this morning.

Coach   Those were two key points. I recall one more. We also talked
about the fact that you tend to avoid conflict if you can, and people have interpreted this as being indecisive.

Richard   (laughing) I was trying to avoid that one.

Coach   Sorry about that.

Richard   Well, it's true, I don't like conflict. I do everything I can to put it
off and then hope it will go away on its own. (pause) No, it's clear
that I can't keep doing that. In some ways, this will be the hardest
thing for me to overcome. It's just not something I enjoy doing.

Coach   Most people don't enjoy conflict. In your new role, however . . .

Richard   I know. I'm going to have to fight those fights when they happen.

This synthesizing process should not be just a mundane summary
of the key things you talked about but instead a real search for a shared
understanding of what emerged from the dialogue. In effect, you are
jointly answering the questions What did we just talk about? and What
insights did we gain? Notice that in response to each of the client's comments in this example the coach helped shape their joint understanding.
Sometimes, the coach's comments were supportive: "People are waiting
for you to really take charge." Sometimes, the coach reminded the client
what they did: "We talked about how you might do that." And sometimes
the coach reinforced a key learning point: "You don't need to go to those
extremes to motivate people. They mainly want to feel that their leader is
positive about the future and is confident that the company will attain its
goals." As clients synthesize what they gained from the dialogue, coaches
have a prime opportunity to shape their mutual understanding of the outcomes and to reinforce key lessons learned or behavioral changes the client should make.

We have found that it's generally best to keep your own notes during a
coaching session so you have a record of the key points, insights, or conclu-

sions as you saw them. You should have your own perspective on what's important and what isn't. However, it's best to ask clients to summarize and use your notes to determine whether they've left anything out.

Articulating Commitments

Next, if clients have reached any conclusions during the dialogue about what they will do differently or how they will change their priorities, then it is useful in closing a session to ask them to articulate those new commitments. As we noted earlier, the moment when clients decide to change is both pivotal and fragile. Decisions have a way of disintegrating unless they are reinforced and acted upon reasonably quickly. Life events, work distractions, and the sheer difficulty of change may weaken clients' resolve. To counter this tendency, it helps if clients express their commitments out loud. It often helps further to put those commitments in writing. It helps even more to share those commitments with others. The more public the commitment, the more likely the client is to stick with it because of peer pressure and the desire to be seen as someone who has the discipline and perseverance to see things through. Here's how it might look:

Coach	Richard, what are you going to do differently as a result of our talk this morning? What commitments are you willing to make?
Richard	(reflecting) I suppose the most important one is that the next time I'm faced with a conflict situation I'm not going to put it off. As much as I don't like it, I'll jump in to resolve it as soon as possible.
Coach	Do you have any conflicts right now? Anything that needs to be fixed immediately?
Richard	Yes, I've got a district manager I've got to deal with.
Coach	What's the issue?
Richard	He's retiring in place. (pause) He's just not showing the energy or commitment to the job anymore, and I either need to turn him around or ask him to leave. It's causing morale problems in his district. I know it's been going on, but I just haven't wanted to confront him about it.
Coach	So that's one situation you could deal with tomorrow.
Richard	(reflecting) I'll get it on my calendar.

Moving clients to concrete action steps is an important step in making commitments real. You need to strike while the iron is hot and convert intentions to actions. As you get clients to articulate their commitments, you can also return them to their personal development plan and reinforce what they are trying to accomplish. As we have discussed, clients' personal development plans should consist of their goals based on their developmental needs, the steps they have agreed to take to reach those goals, and how they will measure success. After clients have established their personal development plan in the first place, you should revisit that plan in subsequent sessions and 1) gauge their progress toward their goals, 2) reinforce those goals, 3) problem-solve if they are encountering barriers, and 4) renew their commitments to the plan.

Agreeing on Next Steps

In closing your coaching sessions, you should also agree with clients on the next steps both of you will take. Clearly, these next steps may include the kinds of commitments we just discussed. They can also include actions or exercises you ask clients to complete before your next meeting. In our coaching engagements, we frequently give clients "homework" to do before the next meeting. This homework might include the following:

- Asking the client to meet with each of her key stakeholders (superiors, peers, or subordinates) to ask what they expect from her and what she could do to work more effectively with each of them.

- Having the client record each instance in which he lost his temper and the circumstances that led to that event.

- Asking the client to find ways to recognize and reward any of his direct reports who do something noteworthy between sessions, to justify why he did not recognize and reward some employees, and to identify what he could do to support the performances of those he did not recognize.

- Asking the client to read a book and respond to a self-test in the book in order to better understand some issues she is facing. Some books we often assign as homework include *Emotional Intelligence* by Daniel Goleman (Bantam Books, 1995), *Reinventing Your Life* by

Jeffrey E. Young and Janet S. Klosko (Penguin, 1994), and *Learned Optimism* by Martin E. P. Seligman (Pocket Books, 1990).

- Asking the client to complete a "life timeline" that helps him identify the parts of his life when he was most and least satisfied and the types of life and career choices that are most rewarding to him.

- Having the client analyze his executive team and determine the appropriate leadership response to each team member according to each person's level of skill and will.

- Having the client complete a psychometric instrument, such as the California Psychological Inventory™ or the Myers-Briggs Type Indicator®, and reflect on the implications of her results. (You must be qualified to administer these instruments. If you aren't, you may find someone in your organization who is qualified. Both instruments are available from CPP, Inc.)

We have used these and many other assignments between sessions to help clients learn more about themselves, explore alternative behaviors, and gain insight into where they are effective or ineffective in what they've been doing. We don't have a standard set of homework assignments that we take off the shelf, so to speak. Instead, we invent the right assignments for each client during the coaching session, and after some sessions there may be no homework for clients to do. It depends on the client, the client's needs, and the circumstances. As with everything else in coaching, you have to be adaptable.

In addition to doing homework, clients may have a number of additional next steps to take between coaching sessions, including practicing a new behavior (or trying to modify or eliminate a current behavior), meeting with other people in their "ecosystem" to get feedback, writing a report on their progress, and so on. In our view, every coaching session should end with some commitments on the client's part to do something next. Coaching sessions are way stations on the path to development, but they are not development itself. Clients may learn a lot during the coaching dialogues, but their development largely takes place in how they act and what they try to do differently in between those dialogues. So it's important that clients not view the time in between sessions as "time off."

Doing a Process Check

The final element in effective closure to every session is doing a process check. Essentially, you want to ask the following:

♦ Was this session useful to you?

♦ What would have been more helpful?

♦ What would you like to do next time?

These kinds of questions help you understand if you are being effective as a coach and if the client feels you're on the right track. As we said earlier, there is no bad answer to these questions, because if you're not being helpful or you are on the wrong track, it's better to know that sooner rather than later. Of course, these questions also help you adapt to your clients' preferences, so they are fundamental to adaptive coaching. Next, you might also ask some broader questions about the coaching relationship.

♦ Am I being helpful overall?

♦ Should I be doing anything differently as your coach?

♦ Could I do anything that would be more helpful to you?

These questions serve as a sort of midterm coach evaluation and, again, there is no bad answer. You should ask these questions periodically just to gauge whether you are providing the kind of value as a coach that you hope to provide. We've also used another form of this question:

♦ Am I being helpful overall? Please be candid with me because I really want to be helpful to you. On a scale of one to ten, with ten being the highest, how would you rate my effectiveness as a coach?

We've found that some clients are uncomfortable with this question, but most aren't and will tell you truthfully what they think. If their response is anything less than a ten, then your next question is:

♦ What could I do to reach a ten?

The purpose of this question is not really to receive a quantitative evaluation. You're really trying to discover what more you could be doing that would be helpful to the client. However, we have worked with some coaches who are uneasy about this question, particularly when they are not employed as coaches but are instead going out of their way on the job to coach a colleague or a direct report. Their attitude is, "I'm the one doing the helping. Why should I be evaluated for something that is essentially voluntary on my part? I don't have to do this." We believe that whether coaching is or is not part of your job, and whether or not you are a volunteer, if you're going to provide the greatest value to the people you're coaching, you should ask these kinds of questions. First, having the feedback helps you become a better coach. Second, it helps you understand how each particular client wants to be coached, and if you can learn to adapt to their needs and preferences you have a better chance of having real impact with each person.

FOLLOWING UP COACHING SESSIONS

In between coaching sessions, the client's development journey continues, and coaches should follow up on their clients' progress in various ways. In programmatic coaching, it is especially important to be structured and systematic in your follow-up, but we believe that even circumstantial coaching should include a reasonable degree of follow-up after every coaching session or event. A number of the coaching clients we surveyed in our research indicated a greater need for consistent follow-up.

- Establish documented goals and completion dates for your coachees and follow up regularly with those individuals.

- Jeanine is very good at helping with problems or finding out what is happening, but she needs to follow up on what the resolution was for the problem.

- Follow up completely on agreed action items.

- Improve on following up with coachees after coaching sessions.

- Follow through with all aspects of your coachees' goals.

We suspect that a number of coaches are not good at following up because they are unpaid volunteers, so to speak. They have their own job priorities and many other responsibilities and demands on their time. No matter how well intentioned a coach may be, after the coaching session ends, real life then intrudes upon the coach, and it may be difficult to follow up consistently when there are so many other demands on the coach's time. Be that as it may, if you are going to be effective as a coach, then follow-up is necessary.

Of course, following up with clients can be as informal as dropping by the client's office to see how things are going. Telephone calls, voice messages, and e-mail messages are also good tools for following up. Face-to-face meetings and telephone calls allow for interaction, but we have found that many clients appreciate voice or e-mail messages as well. An e-mail reminder before a client goes to an important meeting can be the kind of reinforcement of behavioral change that he finds helpful. Some clients may not want to clutter their e-mail with messages from their coach, but in our experience these clients are rare. An e-mail message from one's coach is different from the unwanted "spam" messages that truly do clutter people's mailboxes. It's best, of course, to talk about how clients would prefer for you to communicate with them, but you should not neglect these informal kinds of periodic follow-up.

One important reason for following up is to check on clients' progress, especially when they are trying to make behavioral changes. Generally speaking, the greater or more critical the behavioral change, the more frequent and persistent your follow-up should be. Is the client sticking with the program? Is she doing the things she said she would do? Is she running into any barriers or roadblocks? Is she maintaining her commitments? Besides asking the client these questions, you may also talk to the people who work with her. With her permission, you may want to interview selected colleagues or direct reports or other members of the "ecosystem" surrounding your client and ask these kinds of questions:

◆ Has the client told you what she is working on?

◆ Have you seen any change? If so, what?

◆ What is this person doing differently? Is it more or less effective?

◆ What else could this person do to be more effective?

Naturally, follow-up discussions with people who work with your client must be treated sensitively and confidentially (unless by prior agreement with your client they will not be). Furthermore, the client should know that you may be following up with people who work with her. In talking to the people who work around your client, you are essentially returning to the poles of the needs compass that we discussed in chapter 3 and calibrating the client's progress by returning to your original sources of information on the client's needs.

In our research on effective coaching, we learned that a great many clients prefer a more systematic and disciplined approach to coaching. As we shared earlier, one client's lengthy suggestion to his coach describes almost perfectly the programmatic approach to coaching:

> *Create a long-term plan of action that goes through the following process:*
> *a) Highlight areas of improvement.*
> *b) Highlight long-term goals—both personal and professional.*
> *c) Create a specific plan of action to address the weaknesses and move toward the goals.*
> *d) Create a structured mechanism to review the above.*

The last item in this wish list is about following up. It's insufficient, really, to help clients determine where they need to improve, help them establish goals, help them create an action plan for their development—and then not follow up on their progress and provide ongoing support, encouragement, and modeling. You may be an excellent coach in most respects, but if you don't meet with clients more frequently than once a month, and you are absent in between meetings, you will be much less effective in helping clients change. Following up after coaching sessions is a crucial part of the process.

BRINGING CLOSURE TO THE COACHING RELATIONSHIP

Inevitably, the curtain must fall. You will have reached your agreed-upon objectives, or your clients will have gone as far as they can with your help, and it's time to end the coaching relationship. We would hope these relationships close with feelings of gratitude, satisfaction, and accomplishment rather than relief, regret, and disappointment (if the latter occurs, you could not have been doing good process checking along the way). If indeed the coaching relationship has been a good one, then it is beneficial for both coach and client to end the coaching relationship in a way that gives each person a satisfying sense of accomplishment and closure.

In successful coaching relationships, the coach and the client will both have invested a lot in the success of the effort, so it makes sense to review what you hoped to accomplish and what you did accomplish. Reviewing goals and outcomes is important, because it helps bring closure to the goals you achieved and reminds you of the client's continuing developmental journey if there is more to be done. Professional coaches often ask clients for an evaluation of them at this point, and we think this is a good idea, too. If coaching is an important professional activity for you, then you should seek as much feedback as you can. Coaches have ongoing developmental needs, too.

The last words in the coaching relationship should be positive and encouraging. There should be a sense of the distance clients have come, the changes they've made, and the goals they've achieved. There should also be a sense of the continuing journey. Learning and development are lifelong pursuits, although some people may choose to sit out the journey. The clients who benefit most from coaching are those who recognize that no matter where they are in life and their career they will never reach a place where they have nothing left to learn and no place left to grow. Indeed, the people who decide they have nothing left to learn are virtually uncoachable anyway and are unlikely to have successful coaching relationships in the first place.

For the fortunate clients whose outlook allows them to seek help from a coach and continue to develop themselves, the conclusion of a successful coaching relationship should be a cause for celebration. It is one more positive step on a journey that may take them far and may help them be more successful and happier than they would otherwise. So the best way to bring closure to the coaching relationship is to celebrate. Obviously, people do this in different ways, depending on what is meaningful to them. A simple handshake and a smile may be celebratory enough, but some coaches and clients do a celebratory dinner or something similar. If the coaching has resulted in real change for clients and an improvement in their work and lives, then acknowledging and celebrating those results is a fitting way to bring the coaching relationship to a satisfying and rewarding close.

PART

3

Driving Deep and Lasting Change

Most coaches, HR professionals, and talent experts would agree that behavioral change is difficult for adults, and especially difficult for executives who have been largely successful in their careers. We would further assert that a transformative leadership development approach, the kind that leads to lasting change, requires not only a coachable executive and an adaptive coach but a process for understanding human change and a framework for reconciling the individual and the organization. In this part of the book we discuss the challenging process of helping clients effect lasting changes in themselves and in their behaviors—with the ultimate goal of improving their performance at work.

We begin this section with a human change model. Most coaches follow one coaching process or another, and their process should be aligned with adult learning theories as well as the literature on steps required to truly change behavior. The model that we advocate consists of four steps:

Building Awareness: The Path of Vision

Building Commitment: The Path of Courage

Building Practice: The Path of Discipline

Building Accountability: The Path of Continuous Learning

In chapter 12, we elaborate on this human change model. The path we describe—from awareness to commitment to practice to accountability—is the foundation for helping clients move from where they are to where they want to be. There are many different approaches to coaching, and we discuss some of them in chapters 13 and 14, but regardless of the approach a coach takes, lasting change is rarely possible unless clients follow this path.

Beginning with chapter 13, we borrow a metaphor from our colleague, Kevin Cashman, who argues that effective leadership development occurs when you combine coaching from the inside out (growing the whole person) and from the outside in (the external act of leadership). "As much as we try to separate the leader from the person," Cashman says, "the two are totally inseparable. Unfortunately, many people tend to split off the act of leadership from the person, team, or organization. We tend to view leadership as an external event. We only see it as something people do." But leadership is more than this, he argues. Leadership "comes from a deeper reality within us; it comes from our values, principles, life experiences, and essence." (Cashman 2008, p. 22) So to coach leaders effectively, you must integrate building the whole person (inside out) with building the person's leadership skills and performance in the organization (outside in).

Cashman's approach to growing people from the inside out often means helping them achieve a personal transformation, and we describe his approach in chapter 13. We also briefly discuss the core concepts of two other approaches to transformational coaching—the psychoanalytic approach and the family therapy or systems thinking approach. These approaches have their roots in psychology and cybernetics, but coaches do not need to be experts in these approaches to benefit from the insights they offer. Indeed, coaches who are informed practitioners are aware of these core concepts and use them from time to time in their coaching as the situation warrants.

Chapter 14 describes Cashman's approach to coaching from the outside in, which, because it focuses on what leaders do, is more aligned with traditional performance coaching. Here, coaches are not trying to transform the client as much as they are trying to help improve the client's performance by focusing on behavioral changes that will make a difference or cognitive processes that are causing the client to misperceive what is happening in his environment. Along with describing some of Cashman's techniques, we briefly discuss some core concepts from behavioral coaching, cognitive coaching, and appreciative inquiry, one of the applications of positive psychology. As in chapter 13, these approaches to coaching offer useful insights for adaptive coaches.

We know that the most effective coaches adapt to the preferences of their clients; furthermore, we believe, as Kevin Cashman asserts, that deep and lasting change requires attention to inside-out and outside-in leadership issues. The most effective coaches are those who help clients integrate inside-out with outside-in leadership development and who do so in an adaptive manner, focusing on inside-out methods when that's most relevant and vice versa.

12

Helping Clients Change

Understand the fact that the receiver may or may not be able to change due to various reasons and work on how to make things happen.

Each individual needs a different plan. And change is something that may happen slowly. You need to have patience. Even though it may look very simple for you, for others, even though they know the change is for their good, it can take more time to change.

Be aware that a coaching process may have to change in the moment if the person being coached is reacting negatively to the process. Adapting a coaching process to the individual being coached is preferable to the "right" way.

SUGGESTIONS TO COACHES FROM THE "COACHING EFFECTIVENESS SURVEY," KORN/FERRY INTERNATIONAL

Change is difficult, mysterious, and uncertain, which creates an enormous challenge for us when we try to coach others. The fact that people fear even the smallest change was poignantly illustrated by the late Eric Hoffer—migrant worker, longshoreman, street philosopher, and author. In his 1963 book, *The Ordeal of Change*, he tells the story of how a slight change in his life precipitated a feeling of foreboding:

Back in 1936 I spent a good part of the year picking peas. I started out early in January in the Imperial Valley and drifted northward, picking peas as they ripened, until I picked the last peas of the season, in June, around Tracy. Then I shifted all the way to Lake County, where for the first time I was going to pick string beans. And I still remember how hesitant I was that first morning as I was about to address myself to the string bean vines. Would I be able to pick string beans? Even the change from peas to string beans had in it elements of fear. (p. 3)

We fear change because it undermines our security. It threatens to upset our routine and eliminate (however temporarily) the comfort zone we create around the behaviors and habits we have become accustomed to. We aren't certain the change will be better for us. We don't know whether we will adapt well to it. It may require new skills we don't have and can't master. It will be uncomfortable for us because it's not part of our routine. We may have to think harder about what we're doing; we won't be able to go through the motions, because we aren't sure which motions to go through. Change is difficult. If it were easier, no one who knows how bad smoking is for them would smoke cigarettes, average life expectancies would rise because fewer people would be overweight, there would be no need for Alcoholics Anonymous, and more New Year's resolutions would be kept. Moreover, toxic bosses who recognize the deleterious effects of their operating style would transform themselves into outstanding managers, and ineffective but motivated leaders would become inspiring, galvanizing, and charismatic.

Radical life changes are even more difficult. Eric Hoffer (1963) speaks of this in his book: "In the case of drastic change the uneasiness is of course deeper and more lasting. We can never be really prepared for that which is wholly new. We have to adjust ourselves, and every radical adjustment is a crisis in self-esteem: we undergo a test, we have to prove ourselves. It needs inordinate self-confidence to face drastic change without inner trembling" (p. 3). Drastic changes could include the following:

- Changing your work life so you spend more time with your family

- Changing your management style so you are less of a command-and-control manager and more of an empowering manager

- Changing your approach to your projects so you are more creative, more open to new ideas, and more innovative in your solutions

- Changing your personality so you are less emotionally volatile and have more composure when things go wrong

- Changing the way you relate to others so you build trust sooner and are better able to create sustained, trust-based relationships

These kinds of changes are drastic because they require very different routines and ways of behaving, and the capacity to accomplish such change may not be within us. To successfully accomplish these changes—not only immediately but forever—we would have to radically alter the way we behave, make decisions, set priorities, and perhaps relate to other people. This is not easy. Now imagine trying to coach other people to make these changes:

- Coach an ambitious, career-oriented direct report of yours who is working too many hours and starting to have problems at home to change his work habits so he spends more time with his family. (What if he doesn't want to change?)

- Coach a manager whose department is suffering because of her rigid, hierarchical, command-and-control management style so she becomes more of an empowering manager. (Is she truly capable of releasing control?)

- Coach a professional whose work is no longer acceptable because she seems to have fallen into a rut to change her approach to her projects so she is more creative, more open to new ideas, and more innovative in her solutions. (How easy is it to help someone else become more creative?)

- Coach a supervisor whose abrasive personality is grating on people and causing high turnover to be less emotionally volatile and have more composure when things go wrong. (Maybe his personality is part of who he is. Is it even possible for him to be more composed? How emotionally intelligent is he?)

- Coach a struggling salesperson who can't sustain customer relationships to change the way he relates to people so he is better able to create sustained, trust-based relationships with customers. (Do you understand enough about human relationships to know how to help him become better at sustaining relationships with his customers?)

Without a doubt, most of us could coach others in these situations and have at least *some* positive impact, but would it be lasting? Can you honestly say that you'd be certain to help the person you're coaching permanently change her behavior? Changing yourself is hard; coaching others to change is even harder because you can't be present all the time. You can't know the external and internal pressures on them. You can't help them manage their moment-by-moment priorities, decisions, trade-offs, and temptations. More important, you can't manage their commitment to change or their persistence in doing things differently.

Some coaches fail to have impact with people because they either don't understand human change or lack the patience to see it through. For example, a command-and-control manager might think that coaching is giving feedback and orders. If you point out what people are doing wrong and tell them how to do it right, isn't that enough? An empowering manager, on the other hand, might think that just helping people think about their performance, encouraging them to do things differently, and providing resources for them is enough to make a difference. If you take off the handcuffs and empower people to do it themselves, and if you discuss it with them and give them the resources they need, isn't that enough? Sadly, it usually isn't. Human change is complicated, as anyone who's successfully completed an AA twelve-step program can confirm. Permanent change in people over twenty-one years of age is usually a monumental struggle.

It reminds us of the story of the physicist and psychologist who are arguing. The physicist contends that psychology is too soft and touchy-feely. It's not even a science, the physicist asserts. On the other hand, physics is a difficult field that deals with the most fundamental questions in nature—the elemental particles that form the physical world, the laws that govern how the world works, the formation and death of stars, and the creation of the universe. The psychologist says, "You're right. By your definition, psychology is not a science. It deals with human beings and how they work, and that's so much more complicated than physics."

A HUMAN CHANGE PROCESS

Given that human change is difficult and coaching people to change is even more difficult, what can coaches do to help others change? The most important thing to understand is that change rarely happens either spontaneously or instantaneously. Change—lasting, transformative change—takes time, in part because it means rewiring the brain, and the older people get, the more difficult the rewiring is and the longer it takes. Human change is a process, not an event. Consequently, it's helpful for coaches to think in terms of process as they try to help the people they're coaching.

Coaches generally follow a process that, ideally, is well grounded in the principles of human change. The reasons we need a process are many: to create a roadmap for our clients to follow; to introduce transparency and predictability into an otherwise soft development activity; and, most important, to help clients effect lasting change, which is the purpose of coaching. Of course, a particular coach may be giving performance feedback, debriefing a developmenting 360-degree feedback report, brainstorming with a group on how to improve quality, advising a colleague about improving customer relationships, or counseling a young person about her career options and helping her think through them. Whatever the specific coaching task in each of these cases, fundamentally, the coach is trying to help the other person change—improve performance, make better choices, do something differently, avoid ineffective behaviors, or change an attitude or perspective.

The problem, as we have noted, is that change is difficult for most people, and data from Korn/Ferry's Coaching Effectiveness Survey show that most coaching is only moderately effective. Forty-two percent of clients report that their sessions with their current coach have not had much positive impact on their work performance, and 51 percent of those surveyed said they would like better coaching than they are currently receiving. The irony, of course, is that coaches can't make people change; they can only offer guidance and help. Change is the client's responsibility, and no change will occur, no matter how helpful or brilliant the coach, if the client isn't able to make it happen. But as coaches we can guide clients through the difficult process of change and facilitate what is inevitably, for clients, a process of self-discovery and commitment. Figure 8 shows the human change process we recommend based on thirty years of coaching inside large organizations.

One important caveat about this process is that it is a rational one. In our experience, it applies in most business settings with people who are rational, well-functioning adults. It does not necessarily apply in circumstances in which people are not rational or have psychological issues that should be treated by a therapist, not a coach. Furthermore, although the process appears as a linear series of steps, in fact change is usually messy, and the process is actually iterative, which means that steps may be repeated and can potentially proceed out of order. Finally, even this rational change process will

BUILDING AWARENESS
Establish Baseline & Gather Information

BUILDING COMMITMENT
Create Urgency & Generate Commitments

BUILDING PRACTICE
Practice New Behaviors & Gauge Impact

BUILDING ACCOUNTABILITY
Seek Feedback & Achieve Alignment

Figure 8 : The Four-Step Human Change Process

not work unless the client is able and willing to change. The coach is a helper, not a driver. People begin the change process when they become aware of the need for change. Once they become aware of the need, they must develop a strong sense of urgency about changing. They must be motivated enough to act on their desire to change and see it through, in spite of the obstacles and roadblocks that inevitably appear. The change process usually involves exploring what change would mean to them, reflecting on what they must do differently, and problem solving about overcoming barriers—all of which help build their commitment to change.

If they can successfully commit (because they have done some problem solving and know what to do), then they can begin to practice those different thoughts, attitudes, and behaviors—to start following the new path. Once they have started this path, they will need to build accountability by sharing with others, requesting continual feedback, and reinforcing new behaviors. Otherwise, they risk lapsing back into their old, familiar habits. If you wish to have impact as a coach, you must make sure that the people you are coaching go through each step. It would be nice if there were simple shortcuts, but there aren't.

BUILDING AWARENESS: THE PATH OF COURAGE

Awareness is the necessary foundation for change and development to occur. The ability to seek truth and the willingness to embrace it require courage. This can be more difficult than it sounds because people tend to disregard or sublimate disconfirming information—something that contradicts what they already believe—especially if it disconfirms their self-image. John may believe he's a good manager, for instance, so if he gets feedback that he's not, he may resist hearing that message. He may ignore it, blame the problems on someone else, or attack the messenger. It may take repeated messages or feedback from someone John respects for him to hear what others are saying. This is the value of a coach. If you have built a good coaching relationship and are skilled at giving feedback so that even tough messages are delivered with obvious caring, then you can help John and people like him hear and accept disconfirming messages.

A useful tool for thinking about how you can help others become more aware of the need for change is the familiar Johari Window in figure 9. This framework was developed by professors Joseph Luft and Harry Ingham. The four boxes of the window indicate what both you and John know or don't

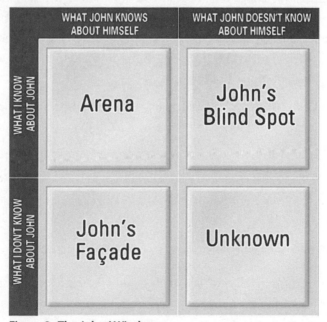

Figure 9 : The Johari Window

know about him. The **arena** is the area of shared knowledge. You know that John is a manager; he knows that, too. You know that John's latest performance assessment shows that his management skills are among the lowest rated in the company. He now knows that, too, because he's seen the report. Though he may be in denial about the results, they are indisputably what they are, and you both know it. This information is in the arena.

Where you can help John most is with his **blind spot**—the area of things you know about John that he doesn't know. Maybe you have talked to some of John's direct reports and you have more insight into what's been happening. Perhaps you've observed John yourself, so you can tell him what you've observed and enlarge his arena by sharing your perceptions. Or maybe you have other information—from customers, performance measures for his department, or observations of his peers—you can provide that may help John develop a better understanding of how his management skills and style are viewed. Reducing the blind spot is one of a coach's important roles.

Where you need John's help is regarding his **façade**. This includes the things John knows about himself that you don't know. Maybe he's actually had more direct feedback on his management style and he hasn't shared it with you yet. Or maybe he's been having some misgivings himself. Maybe he's more aware of the issues than you realized. You help him reduce his façade by asking questions. For example:

♦ John, how is it going? What's working well in your department and what isn't?

♦ Where do you think you're strong as a manager? Where do you have developmental needs?

♦ If you could be doing two or three things better as a manager, what would those be?

♦ What do your people think about your management style?

How much John tells you is usually a good indicator of how self-aware he is and how willing he is to acknowledge his developmental needs. As coaches, we find these kinds of questions extremely useful.

Often, a very useful area to explore with people like John is the **unknown**—the area in which neither of you has any insights. You do this, again, by asking questions. You might also ask John to do a 360-degree management skills assessment and then look at the results together. You could do a roundtable discussion with John and his direct reports—so both of you can hear their observations and ask questions. This kind of roundtable may be high risk for John, but it usually has high returns if it's handled well and his direct reports have no fear of retribution.

Your purpose in building awareness is to help the person you're coaching understand what needs to be changed. Clearly, no change is possible unless the person first accepts that something should be changed. These are the kinds of questions you ask yourself as a coach as you reflect on the other person's level of awareness:

♦ How do you need to change?

♦ What could you be doing better?

♦ What is the source of the need to change—is it within you or is it coming from external pressure?

♦ What problems are you having? What opportunities are being missed?

♦ What is wrong that needs to be fixed?

♦ What are you doing that is dangerous, ineffective, or inadequate?

♦ Do you recognize this?

♦ To what degree are you aware of any developmental needs? To what degree do you accept responsibility for them?

♦ Where are your blind spots? What are you missing?

♦ What kinds of things have you already tried to do?

BUILDING COMMITMENT: THE PATH OF VISION

No change or development is sustainable without envisioning what's possible if we commit to change and what's at stake if we maintain the status quo. The ability to imagine what's possible and what's at stake requires vision. It also requires a sense of urgency, thoughtful problem solving, and—ultimately—a decision to begin taking action.

Urgency

Of course, nothing whatsoever will happen just because people are aware of the need to change. How many times in your life have you been aware of something you needed to do differently but were not able to do it—or at least weren't able to sustain it? The fact is that people won't change unless they feel a compelling need to do so. Their *felt need* must be urgent enough to prompt them to act. Furthermore, it must be urgent enough to help them overcome their fear of change. Millions of smokers are no doubt aware of the dangers of cigarette smoking. The medical establishment, the courts, the government, the media, and educators have made it abundantly clear to anyone who's listening that smoking is harmful. Awareness is not the issue. Urgency is. People won't feel compelled to stop smoking until they feel an urgent need to do so. They may *decide* to stop smoking. They may even buy the patch or the nicotine chewing gum or find some other aid to help them stop. But they won't follow through on their decision and make a permanent change unless their sense of urgency is strong enough to overcome the physical and psychological dependencies smoking creates.

Similarly, a manager with an abrasive style may become aware of the need to change but will not act on it unless she feels an urgent need to do so. What could create a sense of urgency for her? Fear is one of the primary motivators. She may fear that if she doesn't change she will lose her job or won't be promoted. But even if her manager tells her she needs to change, she is still likely to weigh the other pressures on her and think "Is it *that* serious? They promoted me to this position. I've done well so far. I keep making my numbers. Besides, they don't know my people. My people have to be pushed. If you don't set tough standards and weed out the nonperformers, then you won't meet the goal. Is that what they want? No way. At the end of the day, they'll accept who I am because I hit the targets." In her case, the threat may still not be strong enough for her to fear the consequences sufficiently.

Fear is one of the primary motivators because it reflects the deep-seated human need for safety and security. As Abraham Maslow noted in his famous hierarchy of needs, beyond physiological needs, humans need to be safe and secure (Maslow 1998). We need to feel that we are safe from harm. When fears arise that threaten our safety, we are compelled to act and have a far stronger sense of urgency. So, what are we afraid of? Certainly death and lesser forms of physical harm. We also fear punishment. We fear losing ground, losing face, or being left behind (social exclusion). We are afraid of failure.

Suddenly faced with the prospect of failure or social exclusion, we will feel a stronger sense of urgency to change what we're doing. A smoker, for instance, may have a physical checkup in which the doctor notes a spot on his lung or sees the early signs of emphysema. Or the smoker's father may die of lung cancer after a long, wasting illness. Sometimes such events are sufficient to create a strong sense of urgency based on fear. If the abrasive manager is sent to an interpersonal skills program and told that she has ninety days to become less abrasive and improve the morale and productivity in her group, she may have a strong enough sense of urgency to change. In these examples, the person's felt need is based on fear—a negative emotion—and the tools for increasing the felt need are based on real or implied threats. However, while fear can be a powerful motivator, a person's sense of urgency can also derive from fulfillment, fellowship, followership, or faith.

Fulfillment reflects the common human need for achievement. Virtually all human beings need to feel that they have accomplished something, that they are valuable, that their efforts result in something they and others can be proud of. People with a high need for achievement push themselves to excel in some way—to get an advanced degree, to win the competition, to achieve higher status, to be recognized as an expert, to become certified in some important field, or to use their hard-earned expertise in some way that benefits others. Maslow felt that the desire for achievement and recognition underlies the two highest needs on his hierarchy—self-esteem and self-actualization. One way to increase a person's sense of urgency, therefore, is to appeal to her need for achievement, to help her attain a higher level of self-esteem or self-actualization through change. Most Olympic athletes are driven largely by an inner desire for fulfillment through the accomplishment of something difficult and demanding. The need for fulfillment may also arise from discontent with the way things are along with the desire for something new, better, or different. Inventors, innovators, entrepreneurs, visionaries, and revolutionaries of all kinds are driven by a passion to create something new (or destroy something intolerable), to discover new ways of thinking, experiencing, or being. Their dissatisfaction with the status quo or their vision of something that does not yet exist fills them with a sense of urgency that drives change. Another of the needs in Maslow's hierarchy is social inclusion, the need for fellowship. We are social creatures and are driven in part by our need to affiliate with other people. This manifests itself in our desire for acceptance and belonging, by our responses to peer and group pressures, and by our conformance to the cultural norms of the societies, families, organizations, clubs, and other groups we belong to. People may feel the urgent need to change because they want the approval of their peers, because they want to be admired and loved, or simply because it's the fashion (it's what their friends are doing). You have only to look at how teenagers respond to fashion changes to see how powerful a force this can be.

Sometimes the urgent need to change comes from followership—from being inspired or motivated by a leader. For some people, an inspirational leader represents a cause, a movement, a philosophy, a passion, or a direction they lack. Following the leader enables them to find meaning and passion in what the leader represents and how she can motivate them to act. Martin Luther King Jr., Gandhi, Susan B. Anthony, John F. Kennedy, Eleanor Roosevelt—these are leaders whose ability to inspire moved millions of people, generally as a force for good. Clearly, it is also possible for leaders to move scores of people as a force for evil—Adolf Hitler, Josef Stalin, David Koresh, Jim Jones. Followership can become so consuming a force for change in some people that they lose themselves completely in the leader's destructive aura.

Finally, some people may feel an urgent need to change because of their need to believe in something greater than themselves. The search for meaning in their lives, the desire for universal truth and understanding, or the sense of connectedness with God, nature, or revered persons—these can be powerful incentives for change. People can come to embrace certain principles—justice, truth, righting wrongs, improving lives—and be driven by a vision that changes how they see the world and thus how they behave. Occasionally we see profound midlife changes in someone who has come to embrace a particular religious faith late in life. In this regard, the missionary is a coach who builds the sense of urgency through faith.

It is virtually certain that change will not occur unless a person feels a strong enough sense of urgency. However, urgency can be preempted by necessity when a radical event necessitates change whether the person likes it or not. If a person is fired or laid off after a long term of employment with the same company, for instance, necessity may force him to change regardless of how urgently he felt the need for change prior to losing his job. Similarly, a right-handed person who loses the use of her right hand has no choice but to change and learn how to be left-handed. Traumatic, life-changing events are usually the vehicles of necessity. They can include experiencing the death of someone dear, battling a catastrophic illness, becoming a victim of crime or war, being displaced from one's home, and so on. It should be apparent that these kinds of circumstances compel change through a kind of shock treatment.

In the absence of such traumatic events, people feel a less-compelling need for change. Fortunately, most coaches work with people who aren't faced with catastrophic situations, but this means that developing a sense of urgency may be challenging. To succeed, you have to know what would be most compelling to the person you are coaching. What would cause him or her to feel a greater sense of urgency? Fear? Fulfillment? Fellowship? Followership? Or faith? As coaches, we devote most of our time to this area—helping the people we're coaching explore their sense of urgency. The questions you might ask are these:

♦ How important is this?

♦ What will happen if you don't change? What would be the negative consequences?

♦ What could you lose? What will happen if you continue doing what you are doing now? How much worse could it get?

♦ What will happen if you do change? What are the positive consequences? What could you gain? How much better could it be for you?

♦ What would have to be different for you to be able to change?

These are implication questions. They are some of a coach's most powerful tools.

Problem Solving

In problem solving, we ask people to explore how they will change, what they will have to do differently, what barriers they might encounter and how they will get around those barriers, what skills they need to have and how they will develop those skills, what the next steps are, and so on. In short, we ask them to think through what change will actually mean for them.

Problem solving is the roll-up-your-sleeves grunt work in the human change process. It's where you become pragmatic, specific, and action oriented—and it's where many people falter as they confront what change will actually mean to them and how they will have to be or act differently. In some ways, it is the toughest part of making personal change, because it's where the rubber meets the road, as they say. It's where the dream becomes real, where the goal is transformed into the often harsh reality of what the person must now do differently. There are three parts to this problem solving. First, the person needs to envision and think through the alternate future (what he needs to do differently to achieve the change goal). Then he needs to explore potential barriers. Finally, he needs to develop an action plan, with specific next steps. Your role as the coach is to guide people through this problem solving. You might use these questions:

Alternate Future

♦ What do you need to do differently?

♦ Specifically, what would that look like? How could you do it?

♦ What options do you have?

♦ What must you do to get the job done?

♦ When will you have to do it?

Potential Barriers

♦ How and why could this change be difficult for you?

♦ What could get in your way?

♦ What barriers could you face? Externally? Internally?

♦ How will you overcome these barriers?

♦ Do you have the skills to do this?

♦ Do you have the resources?

Action Plans

♦ What is your plan?

♦ What, specifically, should you do?

♦ Do you need anyone else's buy-in? Support? Encouragement? Cooperation?

♦ If so, how will you bring them on board?

♦ What are your next steps?

♦ How will you make those next steps happen?

In our experience, when people fail to improve or change in some other way, it is often because they haven't thought through what they must do differently or really considered the implications of the change. In other words, they haven't done enough problem solving. People sometimes ask for coaching because they haven't been able to do something they've wanted to do and they don't understand what's keeping them from doing it. In 90 percent of the cases, they have failed either because they didn't have a strong enough sense of urgency or because they didn't spend time problem solving.

Problem solving is not a particularly strong area for many coaches. In Korn/Ferry's Coaching Effectiveness Survey, 37 percent of the client respondents said that their coach was not effective at identifying the barriers or situational constraints that interfered with their performance or ability to change; nor was their coach effective at helping them set action plans so they would know specifically what they had to do to accomplish their goals. Problem solving is an area where many coaches need to improve their own skills.

Decision

The decision to change is both pivotal and fragile—pivotal because it represents the point at which the person decides to change, fragile because that decision can evaporate in an instant. A common, mistaken belief is that the decision to change is the most important part of this process, that once people have decided to be different, they will be. In fact, the decision is the weakest link in the chain. The journey after the decision is fraught with pitfalls and barriers in the form of habits, temptations, diversions, problems, and daily life—the rituals and noise of which can dissolve even the staunchest resolve.

The decision is fragile because nothing yet has happened—nothing concrete to test the person's resolve, nothing specific in the form of new behaviors, nothing challenging in terms of barriers, skill gaps, resource deficits, and resistance from other people, all of which can weaken the person's resolve and erase the decision. People who decide to do something differently often experience a psychological release when the decision is made. It seems like a climactic moment: "There, I've done it! I'm going to change." Yet until the decision is tested, until it is acted upon, until the challenges have been faced and overcome, the decision is as fragile as a newly born calf in a stampede.

Nonetheless, it is crucial for coaches to help the people they're coaching reach this fragile point. Once they've reached the decision, most people have enough commitment to it to continue—at least for a while. Among the key questions a coach can ask at this stage are:

◆ What have you decided to do differently?

◆ Why are you doing this? What do you expect to gain from it? What will it do for you?

◆ What will be different for you afterward?

◆ What's the ideal outcome?

◆ What are your new goals?

◆ When will you start? When do you expect to be finished?

If people have truly completed the preceding steps, then making the commitment to the change and initiating action is the logical next step. This is not to say that it's always easy, but it can be easier—if they've truly taken themselves through the preceding steps. Commitment falters, however, if they don't feel a strong enough sense of urgency, if their decision was half-hearted, and if they haven't done enough problem solving. So the coach's role at this point is to test those preceding steps. What you're testing is the person's will. Is he committed to this change? Does she have the will to do it? The kinds of questions you might ask include the following:

◆ Now that you've thought through your plan, are you committed to doing it?

◆ Do you have the will to do it?

◆ How strong is your commitment?

♦ What will happen to your commitment over time?

♦ What if this is harder than you imagined?

♦ What if things don't turn out the way you wished?

Note that there are two important parts to this step: expressing the commitment and then taking action. It's important that the commitment be expressed. Saying "I will do this" is a crucial early step in acting on the change the person is committed to making. It's best if that commitment is made publicly, because people have a deep psychological desire to appear consistent to others and to live by their commitments. As Robert B. Cialdini (2006) observes in his book *Influence: The Psychology of Persuasion*, "Once we have made a choice or taken a stand, we will encounter personal and interpersonal pressures to behave consistently with that commitment. Those pressures will cause us to respond in ways that justify our earlier decision" (p. 57).

BUILDING PRACTICE: THE PATH OF DISCIPLINE

All change and development, by definition, require practice to be sustainable. The ability to sustain change over time requires discipline. Building practice means taking action. A plan is still a plan until it is acted upon; then it starts to form the new reality.

One of the most helpful things you can do as a coach is to help your clients take those important first steps. After they start taking action, they are no longer thinking about improving; they are improving. If it's going well for them, their success will reinforce their decision, and they are likely to build momentum to keep going. Conversely, if they have some early failures, they will need your help to work through them and maintain their resolve. In fact, it is often best to plan for some relapses, or at least the possibility of relapse, and then develop a plan that minimizes the damage or loss if and when a relapse occurs. Rather than encourage relapses, this actually minimizes the impact of a slip and allows clients to feel successful, to feel that they've handled it well. If the setbacks are not planned for, it leads to feelings of failure and discouragement, which could snowball into complete failure.

BUILDING ACCOUNTABILITY: THE PATH OF CONTINUOUS LEARNING

The measure of our efforts is determined by the impact on each stakeholder of the process. Executive coaching literature often tells us that coachees rate the rewards and outcomes of coaching much more highly than their organizational sponsors. Internal and external metrics and feedback loops must be established for all stakeholders at the outset of the coaching engagement, and later must be revisited to ensure that all stakeholders are confident that the objectives of the coaching process have been met. The ability to assure and address accountability requires continuous feedback and learning—in part because lasting change can be extremely difficult to achieve.

Until the change becomes the new reality, it remains difficult, because even though the person may have changed, his environment is likely to be the same. Tomorrow, the office will look the same as it did yesterday. The same quality problems will exist on the production line. There will still be an urge to get angry when things go wrong. The temptations will still be there. So will the habits and accoutrements of the old routines. The brain will still be wired the same way and will urge people to think, behave, and respond as they have in the past. In short, it will be "business as usual."

So it's crucial that people undergoing change have the positive aspects of change reinforced in their environment and by the people around them, including their coach. You should reinforce every little step, which helps build momentum. Enough small steps will eventually create a critical mass, and the new reality will be established. Lasting change is generally not possible unless the person receives support and encouragement from others and unless the reasons for and benefits of the change are reinforced repeatedly during the period in which the changed behaviors are still unusual and the old, usual behaviors are still habitual. The diagram shown in figure 10 illustrates the dynamic process of integrating new learning into one's normal behavior.

Everyone begins in the lower left, the area of unconscious incompetence. They don't know that they aren't skilled. They move to box 2 (conscious incompetence) by developing *awareness* of their lack of skill. Coaches help them move from box 1 to box 2 by giving them feedback about their performance or otherwise helping them understand that they need to develop greater skill. Being in box 2 is generally unsettling for people, especially

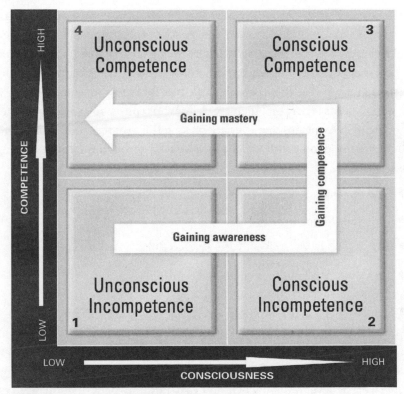

Figure 10: Learning and Behavorial Integration

if having the skill is important to them. If their *sense of urgency* is high enough, they will *decide* that they need to change (to develop their skills). *Commitment* and *practice* take them from box 2 to box 3 (conscious competence). While they are highly skilled at this point, box 3 is also an unsettling area to be in, because they have to continue to consciously use the skills in order to build and maintain their competence. Finally, through the processes of *practice* and *accountability*, they attain the highest level of learning—unconscious competence or, better yet, *mastery*. At this point, they have integrated the new skills into their normal behavior and no longer have to consciously think about what they are doing.

This learning and behavioral integration process applies whether you are learning to play golf, learning to lose weight and keep it off, learning to be a more empowering manager, learning to be more creative, or learning to improve your ability to build strong relationships with your customers. In short, this process applies to anything that you could be coached on or coach someone else on. It should be apparent, then, how critical accountability and reinforcement are. It is the process where the behavioral integration occurs; it helps clients become unconsciously competent. Surveys of people being coached indicate that this is also a weak area for many coaches. Nearly 40 percent of clients report that their coach does not consistently follow up after coaching to help ensure that they are making the progress they wanted. To better help the people you are coaching, follow through on your coaching sessions and ask these kinds of questions:

♦ Are you doing what you said you would do?

♦ Are you sticking with it?

♦ How does the change feel? What's going well?

♦ Is it working? If not, what more could you do?

Incidentally, the coach should not be the only source of continued support for people trying to change. People need as broad a support network as they can reasonably get, including friends, colleagues, spouses or significant others, children, other coaches and mentors, and so on. They need other people who believe in them when they may not fully believe in themselves, and they need the positive aspects of their change reinforced and encouraged by other people in their environment. If the going gets tough, they need others who will empathize with the difficulty they're having and continue to provide positive support and reinforcement through the most difficult days of change. As their coach, you should help clients build this support network and teach them how to use it.

DIAGNOSING CHANGE FAILURES

When coaching fails to result in the improvements or changes you wanted, what has gone wrong? First and foremost, remember that improving is the client's responsibility, not the coach's. The coach's ability to influence the client will always be limited. Nonetheless, here is a quick diagnostic checklist for identifying the problem.

1. Did the person have sufficient awareness of the need for change? If not, can you or anyone else do anything to help increase awareness?

2. Did the person make the commitment to change—and express that decision? If not, was the person's sense of urgency truly high enough? Maybe it wasn't. Revisit the sense of urgency by asking implication questions. If the felt need is strong enough, then ask the person to make a firm decision.

3. Did the person do enough problem solving? Did she identify and remove the barriers? Did she create a specific action plan? If not, reengage in problem solving. Don't stop until the person seems to have a clear sense of what must be done, has thought through and removed the barriers, and has a clear sense of the path forward, including next steps.

4. Did the person commit to the change and then start practicing? If not, then the sense of urgency may not be strong enough or the person still may not have done enough problem solving. Return to these steps of building commitment and building awareness.

5. Finally, did the person have adequate accountability and reinforcement? If not, you may need to help the person you're coaching build greater awareness, commitment, or practice (specific actions). Or you may need to help her reenter the process at some previous step and, in essence, start over. Remember that the weakest link is the decision and that the two points where someone is most likely to falter are urgency and problem solving.

Coaching would be less challenging if it were easier for people to change, but it's not. There are no shortcuts except traumatic ones. Nearly all the time, you need to follow the steps outlined in this human change process—and even this will not guarantee success, because human beings are complicated and the coach's powers are limited. Ultimately, the only people who can change your clients are themselves.

Nonetheless, following the change process described here will help you be a better coach. Remember that each step requires the one before it. There can be no commitment without first having awareness. There can be no practice and action without a sense of urgency, problem solving, and the commitment to change. And there will be no lasting accountability unless practice and commitment have taken place. As noted, this process is often iterative, which means that steps may need to be repeated, but it always begins with awareness and commitment and should always end with accountability and reinforcement.

The coach's work is to guide people through this process. It may be simple or complex, quick or tedious. It may involve simple skill development or complicated personal issues. But whatever your particular challenge or opportunity to help someone, your coaching will be more successful if you follow the principles of this four-step process for helping people change. Coaching people can be difficult because old habits are hardwired into people's brains. They become complacent, comfortable in familiar patterns and routines, and resistant to change that requires integrating new and unfamiliar behaviors. Being creative and following a new, uncharted path are just plain hard for nearly everyone under normal circumstances.

Remember that adapting to clients' coaching preferences makes coaching more likely to succeed—because it helps people the way they want to be helped—and also makes lasting change more likely because you are helping people meet the right needs in the right way at the right time.

13

Transformational Coaching (from the Inside Out)

In chapter 5, we identified different approaches to coaching depending on how you prefer to give help (directive or nondirective), when you prefer to give help (programmatic or circumstantial), and what you prefer to focus on during coaching (specific or holistic). Our research on coaching shows that coaches often prefer to coach using a style of coaching—directive, circumstantial, specific, for instance—that differs from what their clients prefer (nondirective, programmatic, holistic). When such mismatches occur, clients don't benefit from coaching as much as they might because they aren't being helped the way they prefer to be helped. Our central thesis is that coaches should be adaptive. They should strive to understand how their clients want to be helped and then adapt their approach to coaching accordingly.

Sometimes, what clients want amounts to a relatively simple fix. They're uncomfortable giving presentations, and they want a coach to help them become better speakers. Or they've been told that they don't run effective meetings, and they want help on that specific skill. These situations typically call for circumstantial, specific coaching, and their coach is often their manager, one of their peers, a trainer, or a friend who is skilled in these areas. Or they may buy a self-help book and try to improve these skills on their own. Conversely, what clients want or need sometimes amounts to a more involved and complex personal transformation. They manage team tasks well but aren't inspiring and don't engage the people they direct. Or they are overly competitive with their peers, and some of their decisions seem too self-serving, so people question their motivation. What these clients need—and may not recognize at first—is a more substantive transformation of themselves as leaders and managers.

Coaching intended to be transformative is likely to be programmatic and holistic. It focuses on the whole person, and success depends on a series of thoughtful interventions carried out over some period. Typically, those thoughtful interventions are driven by a theory about human change and development, and by a body of knowledge and practice that informs what the coach does to help clients transform themselves, the type of guidance the coach gives, and how the coach measures success. In the past decade, a number of approaches to coaching have been promoted, including many based on psychological theories and practices—psychoanalysis, human development, family therapy and system thinking, social psychology, emotional intelligence, appreciative inquiry, positive psychology, and yoga and meditation. Indeed, for every psychological theory or practice, someone has proposed it as an approach to coaching, and many of those approaches, like psychoanalysis, are intended to produce transformational change.

One of the most useful metaphors we have found for describing the process of deep, transformational change in people appears in Kevin Cashman's book *Leadership from the Inside Out* (2008). Cashman argues that "the missing element in most leadership development programs is . . . *growing the whole person to grow the whole leader*" (p. 26). His emphasis on growing the whole person is the essence of holistic coaching as we defined it in chapter 5. To grow the whole person, Cashman believes that coaches need to help clients connect "with their core talents, core values, and core beliefs." Hence, the helping process begins from the inside out—from the core of the client's being, which he may have suppressed, lost sight of, or never truly understood. By focusing on core talents, values, and beliefs, we help clients explore their authentic self, the wellspring from which true leadership grows.

But this is not enough. Clients also need to examine themselves from the outside in, from their environment, from the circumstances in which they live and lead, from their actions in that environment and the results they seek to achieve. In the outside-in approach, you build clients' awareness of other people's perceptions as well as the opportunities and constraints in their world that influence how they behave. The goal, says Cashman, is to integrate the inside-out and outside-in perspectives. "Leaders who work on achieving congruence—alignment of their real values and their actions—are more energetic, resilient, effective, and interpersonally connected." Coaches can help their clients achieve that integration by moving adaptively between the inside-out and outside-in perspectives, as shown in figure 11.

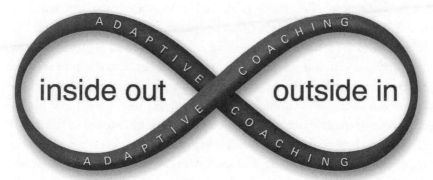

Figure 11: The Infinity Loop

Cashman and his colleague, Janet Feldman, view the coaching process as a continually shifting interplay of the inside-out and outside-in perspectives. Coaches may begin by exploring a client's core talents, values, and beliefs and then explore how congruent those are with her goals, interactions, challenges, and decisions in the world in which she operates. Or they may begin with feedback the client has received from her boss and coworkers and then discuss that feedback in the context of her core talents, values, and beliefs. There is no single departure point; there are many. There are no prescribed pathways; there are many options. It is the continual weaving back and forth that enables clients to discover the congruities that help them achieve mastery and lead authentically as well as the incongruities that block them and deny authentic leadership.

This is an inherently adaptive process, which is the reason we appreciate Cashman's inside-out and outside-in metaphor of leadership development and coaching. Without a fixed departure point, this process avoids dogma about a *right* way to coach, *right* frameworks to use, *right* ways to offer guidance, and *right* solutions to the client's problems. Moreover, because it forms an infinite loop, this process captures the elegance and utility you gain when you continually integrate contrasting perspectives and enable clients to explore themselves holistically.

One potential trap in coaching is to stay at the surface level of goals and actions, to say, for instance, "Here is what your boss expects you to achieve. Let's talk about how you're going to do that." Although that kind of discussion can be helpful sometimes, it fails to develop the whole person because it avoids asking whether those goals and actions are congruent with the client's core values and beliefs. Most people can fake good behaviors, like David, one vice president Terry coached. David received feedback that he made all the decisions himself and didn't solicit ideas from the people in his group or truly listen to them when they offered suggestions. David knew that he was supposed to ask for people's ideas. He understood that his direct reports were more engaged in their jobs when he listened to them and acted on the best of their suggestions. He "got it" but that wasn't him. He could fake the good listening and leadership behaviors because he knew what they were, but inevitably he went off the rails when his true nature asserted itself. In the end it didn't matter what mask David wore because at his core he believed that his ideas were the best ones, and he relished making all the decisions because he loved being in control. The only way to help David was to enable him to see the incongruities between his core values and beliefs and his behavior while trying to play the good leader. Ironically, he was an inauthentic leader and everybody knew it but him. Alternating between the inside-out and outside-in perspectives helped David discover that he was being inauthentic and come to terms with the kind of leader he really was, which was a critical step in his journey toward becoming a better leader.

In the previous chapter, we argued that the human change process has four parts: awareness, commitment, practice, and accountability. Figure 12 overlays that change process on the infinity loop of inside-out and outside-in adaptive coaching, showing how the integrative process can flow not only between the inside-out and outside-in perspectives but also between different parts of the change process. For instance, a client who has been coached for a while may be managing herself and trying out new behaviors (shown under the "Practice" heading on the inside-out part of the loop). In taking those steps she may receive feedback from others on a new issue that has emerged as she's tried on those new behaviors ("Awareness" on the outside-in part of the loop). That feedback may prompt her to reexamine her core

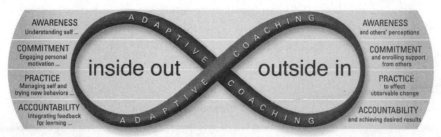

Figure 12: Change Through the Infinity Loop

beliefs and appraise her level of personal commitment to further change, and so on. The process shown in figure 12 is iterative and not necessarily sequential or tidy. It is an evolutionary journey of learning and development that demands skill and adaptability from the coach and curiosity, commitment, and courage from the client.

COACHING FROM THE INSIDE OUT

To explore one application of transformational coaching in greater depth, we will elaborate on Kevin Cashman's inside-out and outside-in approach in greater detail and then compare it with other transformational coaching approaches. Two essential concepts in inside-out coaching are *self-awareness* and *authenticity*. Cashman believes—and the research supports—that authentic leadership arises from the client's self-awareness, so uncovering each client's strengths and developmental needs is fundamental to developing effective, emotionally intelligent leaders. Dysfunctional leadership occurs when a client's behavior is misaligned with his core values, when he is not using his core talents to best purpose, or when he doesn't understand how best to bridge the gap of self-awareness and interpersonal impact. When any of these conditions occur, clients may be ineffective but not understand why. They may grow frustrated with the gap between their aspirations and their accomplishments. The gap between their intentions and the outcomes gives them and others around them the feeling that the outcomes could have been better.

So inside-out coaching is an attempt to help clients discern and explore the inner dynamics supporting outer success. It's about helping the client grow as a person in order to grow as a leader. You want the people you coach to gain greater self-awareness and grasp who they are (and are not) at a very authentic level. This can mean discovering some fundamental truths about themselves (e.g., what they truly value most) as well as revealing some shadows that impact themselves and others. This kind of exploration can be challenging for some clients, and for this reason we advocate taking a mindful approach to inside-out coaching. The client needs to be psychologically prepared for it—open to looking inside, willing to disclose some perhaps uncomfortable aspects of himself, and able to challenge some long-held beliefs about himself in an effort to uncover core truths.

Building Awareness from the Inside Out

As you build a client's awareness from the inside out, you are invoking the north pole of the needs compass—the client's self-perceptions. Recall in chapter 3 that the north pole of the needs compass includes exploration of how clients see themselves. In this step, the coach is facilitating a process to provide more insight about clients' motivations and meaning in order to discern their unique path. During this step the coach helps clients explore and discover their core, essential self. Together, they sketch a picture of the clients' signature strengths, talents, values, and aspirations. This is where clients either discover or clarify what drives meaning in their work and life.

Core Purpose

Building awareness from the inside out often begins with reflection about the client's core purpose, which Cashman (2008) refers to as the connecting thread of one's life.

> Core purpose frames all our life and career experiences into a meaningful whole. When we understand purpose, all the challenging experiences of our lives serve to forge identity, character, and meaning. Although life may be challenging, every experience becomes our teacher, and every challenge an opportunity through which we learn and live more purposefully. When we lack purpose, immediate circumstances dominate our awareness and overshadow our reason for being. (p. 26)

Janet Feldman (2010) tells this coaching story to illustrate the importance of building awareness from the inside out:

We had a client who was a high-level sales leader in a pharma-ceutical firm. During this step of the coaching process, he articulated his core purpose: to create an incredible environment for others to be successful. However, as he examined his talents, values, and contri-butions, he recognized that he is not the most innovative or creative leader. One day he called and shared a story about how he connected his purpose to an otherwise dreaded task he was assigned. He was asked to prepare a presentation on compliance. Initially, he dreaded it. Sales people are often the least compliant given their natural ten-dencies to create solutions on-the-fly and resist rules and policies that infringe on their ability to sell. Compliance was a topic he saw as annoying and tiresome. However, he realized that compliance builds trust and integrity, and he was able to relate to compliance in a new way because his purpose was to do the same with his teams. He wanted to create an incredible environment for teams, and those en-vironments require trust and integrity. When people like this client can understand what they're about and can relate what they're doing to their core purpose, they discover that it serves a greater purpose. When you know what's purposeful for you, you can convert chal-lenges or annoyances into something worthwhile.

Why are you here? What are you trying to accomplish? What drives you and adds meaning to your life? These kinds of questions help clients reflect on their core purpose. Clients who are already highly self-aware may have a clear sense of their core purpose. In our experience, many clients who are highly coachable (C5s and C6s) have already thought about what adds meaning to their lives and what they want to accomplish, but the less-psychologically minded clients (C1s and C2s) often struggle with these questions and don't have insightful answers to them. By helping them discover, question, explore, and refine their core purpose, you can create a very meaningful experience for them. Cashman and Feldman have found that the following exercises are useful in helping clients reflect on their core purpose.

The Lifeline
In the lifeline exercise, you ask clients to use a large piece of paper (e.g., butcher paper or a sheet from a large desk pad). Have them draw a

horizontal line across the page so it bisects the paper. Then have them partition that line by identifying the parts of their life that, for them, are clear segments. For instance, one client's segments might include:

Childhood in Chicago

Junior high in Springfield

High school

Columbus Junior College

The Army—base camp

The Army—Fort Hood

Ohio State University—B.S. in Chemical Engineering

First job: Dow

Second job: BASF

Some segments may be larger than others. There are no rules about what constitutes a life segment; it's whatever is meaningful to each client. When a client has identified her life segments, have her draw vertical lines extending from the top of the page to the bottom. Then ask her to reflect on each of those segments of her life and, for each segment, note every positive memory above the horizontal line and every negative memory below the line. This part of the exercise is best done alone. We often ask clients to do it over a long weekend when they can spend meaningful time by themselves. As you debrief the exercise with them, ask them to expound on each of their memorable experiences using the following questions:

- ◆ What does each segment tell you about yourself? About what you enjoy or don't enjoy? About what was meaningful to you during each period of your life?

- ◆ What talents were you using during each experience?

- ◆ What was important to you? What values were being served?

- ◆ What contributions were you making to others?

♦ What was the impact on you?

♦ What did you learn from these experiences?

♦ What insights did you gain about yourself as you created this lifeline?

This exercise enables a pretty thorough look at the clients' most powerful experiences in life—when they were making a difference by contributing their talents to something important to them. In our experience this exercise always yields interesting insights for clients, and you can use it at any time in the coaching process. Clearly, it's best for clients who are comfortable examining their life and sharing some deep insights with their coach. Its purpose is to help clients explore the whole of their lives and to develop insights about what has made them happy or unhappy, successful or not, and so on. Some people know themselves well enough to have those insights without this kind of exercise, but many don't, and for them this exercise can yield surprising insights about themselves.

Success in this exercise requires the client's willingness to look inward and explore who she really is. You must employ curiosity, compassion, and patience to facilitate insight—and questioning and managing the dialogue effectively are the keys to facilitating insightful self-discovery.

Core Talents

Cashman (2009) developed the following exercise, which helps clients gain clarity about their strengths—the ways in which they can contribute most. Building on the lifeline exercise, we ask clients to look across those instances they identified as memorable experiences. We ask them to reflect on what those experiences say about the gifts they have to offer—those that are most likely evident in these memorable experiences. It's natural for people to want to contribute those gifts and talents that make them feel the best about themselves and what they do, so we assume those gifts are evident in the key experiences they recall. To do this exercise, ask clients to write short replies to the following statements:

♦ When I am at my best and making a difference for myself and others, this is what I am doing: _____.

◆   I am most proud of and like myself best when _____.

◆   I am most energized and engaged when _____.

◆   I receive rewarding feedback from others when _____.

◆   The talents and qualities that consistently show up in me are the following: _____.

This is a good exercise for a number of reasons. First, it is motivating and encouraging for clients to focus on what they do well (especially to the exclusion of what they don't do well). People generally like talking about themselves, particularly if it's about their strengths and successes. It's uplifting to them. It is positively reinforcing. It satiates their ego and builds self-confidence, and this is particularly true if they have been experiencing some challenges on the job or in their lives. It's a timeout from worry and stress when they can say to themselves, "Hey, you know what? I'm okay. No, I'm good. I do a lot of things right. I bring a great deal to the table."

Second, this exercise tends to energize people. It taps into their natural sources of energy, engages them, and builds their resilience. It helps them read their "owner's manual"—those life experiences that give meaning to their contributions. We have had clients who are positively reenergized by this exercise and encouraged to look deeper into themselves. It also gives them the strength to accept the things about themselves they need to develop further.

Third, this exercise is a perfect setup if you are coaching someone with low coachability (e.g., someone who resists hearing negative feedback or is arrogantly self-confident and has potentially crippling blind spots). By accentuating the positive first, you show these types of clients that you want to focus first on all the things they do well. This indicates that you are not simply looking to "fix" them but are seeing and respecting their existing strengths.

As you listen to their responses to these questions, look for patterns. Probe more deeply in areas where they have been vague or less certain about a capability, skill, or achievement. Help them flesh out their story so it is both compelling and concrete.

Core Values

In the approach developed by Cashman and Feldman, the next step is one of the most important—and often the most difficult. Identifying the client's core ideals and developing deep insight into what he truly values requires some further steps in self-discovery. In *Leadership from the Inside Out*, Cashman writes, "We all like to think we know where we stand and what we value, but knowing our authentic values—the standards and guiding principles rooted deep in our hearts and guts—is one of the most challenging aspects of self-discovery" (65).

One reason it can be challenging is that clients haven't been asked or haven't taken the time to become clear about their real values. We recommend this exercise because understanding the client's real values—not just those espoused and easy to rattle off and repeat—will aid the rest of the coaching process and allow you to revisit and gauge the congruence between the client's values, competencies, and behaviors. Here, again, we use Cashman's exercise to recommend that clients revisit their memorable experiences and the values that were evident in these experiences. With this deeper reflection in mind, ask your client to reflect on the following questions and write responses to them:

◆ What has life taught you about what is precious and valuable?

◆ What have the privileges—or traumas and losses—of your life taught you about what is most important?

◆ What would you most like to change in the world—and what is the value underneath this passion?

◆ What gives you the greatest meaning in your life and work?

◆ What is worth risking everything for?

Often this exercise yields something quite surprising and revealing to clients. The values they espouse—or, perhaps, superficially *think* are their values—give way to a deeper knowing and acknowledgment of what truly is important and what they stand for both as a person and as a leader. This revelation can sometimes be unsettling for clients, and it may take some time for them to integrate this deeper awareness. When this does happen, Cashman recommends reassuring clients that they are on the right track and encouraging them not to shy away from this emerging, deeper self-awareness.

Statement of Core Purpose

Finally Cashman and Feldman help clients to bring everything together in a statement of core purpose—that "sweet spot" where their gifts (core talents) are truly in service of what they stand for as a person and as a leader (core values). For the final piece of the equation, they ask clients to describe the ideal world they would like to help bring about. If they could live, work, and love in a world that they help to shape—one with ideal circumstances for themselves and for others—what would those circumstances be? This ideal world is the vision that drives them to contribute their talents in service of their values: their core purpose. Coaches can help clients construct the core purpose statement by capturing three to five of their key core talents, three to five of their key core values, and the description of the ideal world they'd like to bring about. Cashman uses the following format: "My core purpose is to use my (core talents) in service of my (core values) to bring about a world in which (ideal world)."

At this point, you can ask clients to read this as one contiguous statement—paying particular attention to their visceral cues and reactions as they read it through for the first time. This is the time to ask some probing questions such as:

♦ Trying this on for size—how does it fit? Is it too small? Too large? Just right?

♦ What about this statement resonates with your current sense of yourself? What does not quite resonate with how you know yourself to be?

♦ What about it appears challenging? Comforting or reassuring? Daunting or overwhelming?

♦ How does your work or leadership style reflect your core purpose?

♦ In what ways are your words and actions congruent with your core purpose and in what ways are they not?

♦ If you were living and working exactly according to your core purpose, would you be doing anything differently?

If the core purpose doesn't clearly emerge or resonate, you should resist the urge to move on; instead, continue to question and clarify. You will notice that clients often move through stages of deceptive simplicity and profound complexity before they can move to profound simplicity. This is normal at this stage of the process. This process is an evolving journey, and purpose continues to unfold throughout the client's life. Be ready for surprises during this step. Vulnerabilities as well as strengths will emerge, and you must be ready to address them. Be watchful for points where clients make emotional connections and show more energy about topics, because these points will be important during building commitment from the inside out.

Building Commitment from the Inside Out

If building awareness from the inside out is about clients understanding their core self, then building commitment is about them understanding the emotional engagement required to change. As we noted in chapter 12, no change or development is sustainable without envisioning what's possible if we commit to change and what's at stake if we maintain the status quo. The ability to imagine what's possible and what's at stake requires vision. It also requires a sense of urgency, thoughtful problem solving, and ultimately the decision to take action—and the resolve to begin acting as well as the perseverance to sustain it.

Change is difficult, especially transformational change. Most organizational change initiatives fail. Most diets fail. Most New Year's resolutions are unmet. Even when people face serious threats to their health, some cannot stop doing whatever they've been doing that is causing them harm. Yet people do learn. They do adapt. Most can develop their skills, some can overcome bad habits, and a few, over time, can change some deeper fundamentals about themselves—if they are motivated to do so. As we said in chapter 12, change is more likely to be sustained if clients have a strong sense of urgency about the need for change, if they are realistic about the commitments they are making, and if they can problem solve around the obstacles that inevitably will work against them. The following exercises can help clients build commitment from the inside out.

Envisioning the Path Forward

After clients have gone through building awareness, they should have clarity about who they are, what they truly value, what core skills they possess, and what stumbling blocks or weaknesses they need to overcome. Help them crystallize their enhanced understanding of themselves by asking them to envision the person they would like to become. The following questions are ones that Cashman recommends you ask at this point:

♦ The work you have done so far has helped you develop greater awareness about who you are, what skills you have, what your core purpose is, and what you need to change. Can you please summarize that for me?

♦ When we first started, we talked about your needs from this coaching engagement. Do you see them any differently now? If so, how would you now articulate your needs?

♦ Close your eyes for a moment and imagine that the coaching is finished and you have achieved all your goals. Imagine you have lived in alignment with your purpose in all domains of your life for many months now. What do you see? How does it feel? What now seems possible for you and the key stakeholders in your life?

♦ What will it take for you to achieve your goals? Are you committed to doing what's necessary to get there?

Then ask clients to write down three to five initial commitments they are willing to make based on what they have just envisioned. Have them focus on the most critical commitments necessary to achieve their goals. Identifying the commitments clients intend to make is not sufficient, of course, but it's an important starting point. Now we need to help clients explore those commitments further and do some reality testing.

Exploring Your Commitments

There are numerous avenues to take as you help clients think through their commitments. Fundamentally, however, you want to explore how realistic their commitments are, how urgently they feel the need to change, what obstacles they might encounter, and how they can overcome those obstacles. Here are some possible questions to ask. There is a sequential logic to these questions, but you don't necessarily need to ask them all or ask them strictly in sequence. Rather, they are suggestive of the kinds of questions you might ask.

- ◆ How successful have you been in making these kinds of commitments in the past and following through on them? If you haven't succeeded, what has gotten in the way? Why would it be different this time?

- ◆ How important to you and your life or work are the changes you are committing to? What will happen if you don't make these changes? Would the status quo be okay? What would you lose or fail to gain if you don't see this through?

- ◆ What would be the cost of making these changes? What would be the benefits?

- ◆ How urgently do you feel the need to make these changes? What if you didn't make the change until next year? What would you lose by delaying? What would you gain by making the change now?

- ◆ What could get in the way? What could prevent you from making these changes? How much control do you have over potential obstacles?

- ◆ What could prevent you from making the changes last? What could prevent you from sustaining the vision of yourself you are trying to achieve?

- ◆ How can you control, minimize, or prevent any of the obstacles you think you might face?

- ◆ Having thought all this through, how realistic are the commitments you want to make?

- ◆ What steps do you need to take now to make these commitments concrete and see them through?

- ◆ What do you need to do to maintain your commitments and sustain the change actions you are taking?

It's important to recognize that this is an intellectual exercise attempting to elicit an emotional response, and many clients will go through it fully intending to maintain their commitments but then be unable to do so because the exigencies of life and work get in the way. Life happens, and people get busy, and they respond to hour-by-hour problems, demands, issues, interactions, and events. Before long, their lofty commitments have fallen by the wayside. To help them, we recommend that they focus on only a few behavioral changes at one time—and maybe only one at a time. Help them think through how they will change just this one thing, and then follow up with them frequently. Some changes can be more dramatic because they are more public. A CEO who vows to be more communicative can ensure that her schedule offers numerous opportunities to communicate. She can enlist the aid of her assistant to help her reinforce her resolve and practice the actions necessary to sustain it. If a branch manager's commitment is to control his temper, you can seek his permission to ask some of his direct reports to speak to you confidentially now and then about how he is doing—and you can immediately call him on any situations where he has not controlled his temper.

During this step—building commitment from the inside out—you must try to engage clients' emotions. If this is nothing but an intellectual exercise, it will likely fail. We remind clients that it is always their choice either to continue doing more of the same or to make the changes that will improve their lives and performance. But if they don't feel an urgent need to change, then they will likely not have made an emotional commitment to the process. That's why the questions about the cost of not changing are so important. When you ask them what will happen if they don't keep their commitments, you need to see emotional engagement in their answer (creating tension between the positive and negative consequences is key). Otherwise, it may well be just talk.

Building Practice from the Inside Out

Building practice from the inside out means that clients are cognizant of the importance of doing the things they committed to do, are continuing to observe themselves, and are managing themselves on an ongoing basis. Cashman calls this the *path of discipline* because it means living their commitments on a sustained basis despite the exigencies of life and work. To practice from the inside out means that they are doing the things they said they would do; that they are doing those things consciously and consistently every day; and that they are aware of the change process they have embarked upon and remain cognizant of it continuously enough to sustain the change.

The discipline to build practice from the inside out can be supported by any tools that enhance client's self-awareness and attention to the changes they are trying to make. These tools might include journaling, meditating, reading materials related to the area of change, blocking time on their schedule for practice, self-retreats where they practice, working with peers or support groups, exercising while reflecting on changes, and so on. When we coach clients to build practice from the inside out, we are asking them to reflect and go inward with their dialogue. Many clients won't be in the habit of scheduling time away from day-to-day requirements and demands. Yet we would recommend the practices listed here as ways to improve self-observation and self-management. If you have clients who are having difficulty being disciplined or who are backsliding because they keep doing the things they have habitually done in the past, then a useful inside-out exercise for building practice is the trigger-response log.

Trigger-Response Log Exercise

Terry had a client (we'll call him Jim) who easily lost his temper at employees and occasionally lashed out at them in public. He knew that this behavior was problematic, but despite numerous attempts to react differently when something upset him, he was unable to change. This coaching was the company's last-ditch effort to save Jim as a manager. As part of the process, Terry asked Jim to describe a number of recent situations in which he lost his temper: what happened, who was there, what caused it, how Jim reacted, what happened afterward, and so on. Then he asked Jim to think specifically about what triggered his outbursts. Jim brainstormed a list of the things that typically "set him off." Then Terry asked Jim to keep a log of his flare-ups: to write the situation down every time he lost his temper with an employee, identify what triggered it, and describe his response. After several months, Jim had refined his understanding of what triggered the outbursts. Once they had a better understanding of his triggers, Terry helped Jim think through different responses to them. He asked Jim to continue keeping the trigger-response log, to make himself more aware of the triggers, and to try to react differently to them. Eventually Jim was able to recognize when the triggers occurred, learn how to anticipate them, and react differently when they occurred. Within a year, this inside-out method of building practice helped Jim curb the behavior that had placed him on a path to derailment.

Engaging the Inner Achiever

Some people are naturally high achieving and, in essence, compete with themselves. If they ran a mile in 5 minutes and 37 seconds yesterday, they will push themselves to run it in 5 minutes and 36 seconds today. No matter what the field of endeavor, they are determined to continually improve their performance. They may also be competitive with other people, but the truest measure of achievement for them is that they constantly strive to beat their own best times. If a client is like this, then you can engage his inner achiever to build practice from the inside out. It can be as simple as asking, "How did you do?" and then "How do you want to do it next time?" or "What do you want to improve next time?" Inner achievers already ask themselves these questions and will already know the answers. However, during the coaching process it can be helpful for you to act as a sounding board and encourage them to keep practicing and perfecting—and sharing their results with you. People who don't have an inner achiever probably will not respond to this practice, and for them it may be better to build practice from the outside in, which we discuss in chapter 14.

Building Accountability from the Inside Out

Whether or not people are motivated by an inner achiever, they can probably relate to the idea of an internal critic or stakeholder, the conversation we have inside our heads about our progress, our shortcomings, and our opinions in general. One of our clients refers to the internal dialogue and the disparate voices as "the band in the basement." Some people have active bands and some less so. Regardless, in order to move from their current reality to their vision, clients must have a healthy, active, internal feedback loop, one that allows them to learn from experience and find intrinsic motivation to remain in (or join) the path of continuous learning.

The path of continuous learning involves gauging how their new behaviors align (or not) with the values, talents, and impact they desire. It's an important step in the coaching process because it helps them check for consistency between what they say their values, talents, and contributions are and their alignment with them. When clients are bringing their talents forward in the service of something greater (core purpose), they typically feel energized and impactful. If clients are out of alignment, they commonly feel drained, defeated, and inauthentic.

Building accountability is about helping clients develop the internal discipline to check in with themselves to ask how their behaviors align (or not) with their values, talents, and impact. It is also about helping clients take themselves continuously through the four-step change model throughout their journey. Asking, "How does the feedback I am getting from others or from my own observations deepen my awareness, renew or alter my commitment, or clarify the activities that require disciplined practice?" can provide new insight, renewed energy and commitment, and successive approximations in practice. Being accountable is about repeating the steps and acknowledging that development is a continuous, never-ending loop of building awareness (courage), commitment (vision), practice (discipline), and accountability (learning).

The richness of Cashman's inside-out and outside-in approach to coaching is not simply in the process and exercises we have described here; it is in the interplay of the inside-out and outside-in perspectives, as shown in figure 12. In the next chapter we will describe the outside-in complement to what has been described in this chapter. But first we will discuss three alternative approaches to transformational coaching: the psychoanalytic approach, the family therapy or system thinking approach, and the developmental approach.

PSYCHOANALYTIC APPROACHES TO COACHING

Psychoanalytically based coaching treads a fine line between coaching and therapy and should therefore not be attempted by anyone except a psychologist certified in psychoanalysis. Nonetheless, the concepts and frameworks used in this approach are illuminating and can be helpful to all coaches in understanding how clients relate to other people (including the coach); how they cope with others and the stresses of their work; and how their internal world influences their relationships, problem solving, and decision making, and thus how it affects their performance. This approach to coaching is highly contextual, as Seth Allcorn (2006) explains: "Understanding an executive independent of the workplace is not really possible. The executive's effects upon the organization and its members offer insights that may be used in coaching. Just as important is the effect of those with whom the executive works (superiors, subordinates, and employees) upon the executive. No executive is an island. He or she is always impacted by others, organizational history, and events" (p. 131). Also an important element of context is how the client relates to the coach and vice versa. In psychoanalytic coaching, this dyadic relationship becomes an instrument for reflective insight, as we will see.

Among the key concepts in psychoanalysis are the role of the unconscious in human behavior, the use of coping or defense mechanisms, and the phenomena of transference and countertransference. Sigmund Freud believed that people are largely unaware of the unconscious influences that shape how they relate to others and how they cope with stress. Of particular importance were an individual's relationship with his parents and siblings as well as various influences, such as a teacher he may have idealized, that affect how he constructs his self-image and tries to preserve it by unconsciously denying thoughts or feelings that are inconsistent with his self-image. One of the psychological mechanisms an executive might use to protect his affirmative view of himself is to project negative characteristics onto others. One of the executives Terry coached, for instance, characterized another executive in his firm as a "self-serving jerk who only looks out for himself." It's certainly possible that, unconsciously, Terry's client saw these behaviors in himself but denied it and preserved his self-image by projecting the negative characterization onto the other executive.

Coping Mechanisms

Denial and projection are examples of coping mechanisms. Other mechanisms clients may use include compensation (overcoming a weakness in one area by developing strength in another), avoidance (avoiding something that causes anxiety, discomfort, or stress), idealization (seeing only the positives in someone or something while ignoring the negatives), rationalization (creating logical reasons for mistakes or misbehavior), repression (hiding undesirable thoughts or feelings), provocation (provoking someone to attack so you can retaliate), and trivializing (making light of something large so it appears less important). Experienced coaches will no doubt have seen these kinds of behaviors in their clients. A psychoanalytic coach would recognize these behaviors as coping mechanisms and use them to uncover not only the unconscious motivations for using these defenses but also, and more important, what these mechanisms are defending—and why.

But even if you're not psychoanalytically trained, understanding and recognizing various coping mechanisms is a very useful skill. It can help you understand how a client is coping with stress or is in denial about her potential for failure—and you can use this knowledge to help your client grasp the reality of her situation. Furthermore, you can do this without probing her childhood, her relationship with her parents, or any traumas she might have experienced as a child. One of the great insights of psychoanalysis is that people often use coping mechanisms. Moreover, they use them unconsciously, and their behavior may be dysfunctional because those mechanisms, which likely developed in childhood, are no longer appropriate ways to act.

As a coach who is not psychoanalytically trained, you might recognize a coping mechanism your client is using, but instead of using it to explore the client's psyche you would use it to surface a dysfunctional behavior and help the client recognize that this is not an effective coping strategy. For example, imagine that your client is trivializing the fact that he failed to complete an assignment on time. A psychoanalytically trained coach might use that to probe the source of the client's fears and uncover a repressed traumatic memory from childhood that affects how the client is behaving today. A coach not certified in psychoanalysis might challenge the client's perceptions by asking implication questions: "I know you don't think it's important, but what if your boss does? What if your delay in completing this assignment is affecting your coworkers? You may be trivializing something that others don't believe is trivial." This can be a fruitful line of inquiry and challenge without delving into the client's childhood and without revisiting traumas that, if you are not a licensed psychologist, you are not qualified to deal with.

Transference and Countertransference

Another of the key concepts in psychoanalysis is transference and countertransference. Transference is a particular type of projection. It occurs when we project our perceptions of and behavioral dynamics with one person onto another. For instance, I may have had an absent father during my childhood. Because I lacked the wisdom and protection I should have had from my father, deep in my psyche I associate fathers with irresponsibility and my own fear that I am not secure or protected. As an adult, I enter the workforce and work for a laissez-faire manager who delegates many tasks but does not offer guidance on how to complete these tasks successfully. It's possible that I may transfer my feelings about my father—particularly anxiety, fear, and anger—onto this manager and begin to treat him as an absent father. As part of this transference, I would begin to project other characteristics of my father onto this manager, even if those characteristics were not appropriate, and I would behave toward him as though he were the father I needed and wanted in childhood but never got. If I were working with a psychoanalytically trained coach, the coach would help me surface this transference and recognize that I'm not treating my manager the way he is but instead the way I imagine him to be based on my wounded relationship with my father.

Countertransference occurs when the object of the transference responds in kind and acts the way the other person expects her to act. It's not uncommon in the world of therapy, for example, for patients to feel affectionate toward their therapists. By and large, therapists are kind and nurturing. They listen. They are there to help. If patients lack that nurturance in their daily lives, they may project onto their therapists the love and attention they want from the significant people in their lives. If therapists respond by accepting and returning the affection—by in effect playing the role of the nurturing loved one—they are countertransfering, which can have numerous unacceptable consequences, not least of which is compounding their patients' issues rather than resolving them.

Countertransference can also occur if I am coaching a business person who starts treating me as though I am an expert in business and I begin playing that role because I enjoy being thought of as an expert. Or it can occur if I am coaching a client who starts treating me like a friend, and I respond by becoming more like a friend, doing the sorts of things with him outside of the coaching relationship that friends typically do together. It could also occur if I am coaching a client who treats me like her therapist or marriage counselor—and I respond to her projection by assuming those roles. The challenge in countertransference is to have enough self-insight to recognize that it's happening and deal with it in an appropriate way. Usually, this means acknowledging to yourself that you've fallen into a trap and pulling yourself out of it—reminding the client, for instance, that you are not a therapist or a marriage counselor, or pulling back from the friendship activities and reinforcing the coach-client relationship and its boundaries, or refraining from offering advice or opinions of any kind when you lack the requisite expertise.

As this discussion suggests, another of the great insights psychoanalysis has given us is an understanding of the phenomena of transference and countertransference—and the recognition that these phenomena occur all the time. In fact, it may be impossible to prevent them from happening in any dyadic relationship. Invariably, people bring to each new relationship a set of experiences, assumptions, reactions, and emotions from all of their previous relationships, and they project some characteristics of people they've previously experienced onto the new person. This will happen to you whenever you start coaching someone new. As she tries to figure out who you are, she will project someone else's characteristics onto you and will behave toward you as though you were that previous person in her life. Likewise, you will project someone onto her and react toward her as though she were some previous client in your life. And all of this projection is likely to be unconscious. You can try to surface it in yourself by being reflective, by asking yourself these kinds of questions:

- ◆ Who does this client remind me of?

- ◆ If I were to label her, what words would I use?

- ◆ What category of client does she fit into?

- ◆ How do I think she will act? Or respond to me? What patterns am I expecting?

Answering these questions will help you discover what you may be transferring to her. Once you've built enough trust with your client and confidence that she has sufficient self-insight, you can also ask similar questions of her: "Who do I remind you of? If you were to label me, what words would you use?" And so on. The value of this exercise is to uncouple assumptions from reality, to test our understandings of each other, and strive toward an authentic acceptance of the other person.

FAMILY THERAPY AND SYSTEMS APPROACHES TO TRANSFORMATIONAL COACHING

Another coaching approach that requires considerable context setting is the family therapy or systems approach. Systems theory has its roots in mechanical and electrical engineering as the study of self-regulating systems. The most common example of such a system is a room thermostat. Thermostats measure the temperature. When you turn the dial to set the temperature you want, the thermostat is given a narrow range of acceptable temperatures. If the temperature falls below the set level, the thermostat signals the heating system, which turns on and blows warm air into the room. Once the temperature reaches the set level again, the thermostat signals the heating system to turn off. Key concepts in systems theory include homeostasis (self-regulating systems attempt to maintain stasis), feedback (the principal mechanism through which the system regulates itself), and circularity (self-regulating systems are closed loops). Among the first to apply systems thinking (or cybernetics) to human institutions (such as families) was Norbert Weiner (1988) in his book *The Human Use of Human Beings: Cybernetics and Society*.

Family therapy evolved from systems thinking, and it has grown into a vast and complicated field with many variations in approaches. However, the fundamentals remain the same. Among the key concepts in this approach to coaching are these:

1. You cannot consider the individual client apart from the organization. Individuals are part of the organizations in which they live or work. To understand the individual, you have to understand the organization. Consequently, to coach an individual, you have to coach the organization.

2. Organizations strive to maintain homeostasis. They resist change, which is why coaching individual clients to change is difficult. The system will resist their changes and attempt to return to the status quo. System theorists argue that this is why so many organizational change efforts fail.

3. Lasting change is more likely to occur if the change originates from outside the system or organization. A CEO who has been leading his company for some time has more difficulty initiating lasting change than a CEO brought in from the outside. Change initiatives that originate internally are often viewed skeptically as the latest management fad, whereas a compelling external consultant or management guru sometimes has the power to drive radical change in part because she is not part of the system. Similarly, a company that has been producing a successful but aging product for a long time is likely to resist introducing new products until external market forces (like a hugely successful competing product) intrude and force the company to innovate or die.

4. How a system came to be is not as important as how the system is operating now, especially its processes and information flow. In family therapy, for instance, the past is not important. What matters is what is happening now among family members. What do they believe, what roles do they play, how do they relate to one another, and what are the unspoken rules about how family members behave? In coaching, the client's past is not relevant; what matters is how the client is behaving now, and the assumption is that her behavior is largely a function of what's happening in the organization. As you can see, this approach is diametrically opposed to psychoanalysis.

5. Since systems consist of parts, linkages, processes, and information flow, you can start anywhere. In systems thinking, there is no point of origin, no place where you will gain the insight needed to understand everything else. There are no parental issues behind the client's use of coping mechanisms (as there might be in psychoanalysis). To understand your client, then, you just need to understand

how she fits in her organization, how the organization works, what underlying beliefs or myths influence how members of the organization behave, and so on.

This approach to coaching has a number of implications. If you can't understand individual clients apart from their organizations, for instance, then it stands to reason that individual assessments and skill- or trait-based taxonomies are of little value. A leadership assessment that measures a client's strengths and weaknesses based on a framework like *Lominger's Leadership Architect*® might therefore be interesting, but a systems-oriented coach would not find it of much value. In fact in this approach to coaching, any assessments, 360-degree or otherwise, that examine a client outside of his organizational context would not provide useful insight. Consequently, for system-oriented coaching the needs compass we introduced in chapter 3 would have to be modified so that each of the four poles encompassed a whole-systems view.

Another implication of the family therapy or system approach to coaching is that change can generally not be driven solely by a client, no matter how motivated that client might be. To effect transformative change in your client, you would have to effect a transformative change in the organization. Unless the structure and dynamics of the organization change, a client's individual attempts to change will be resisted by systemic influences that, by their nature, will try to enforce homeostasis. Imagine, for instance, that you are coaching a client who is overcontrolling and does not delegate important tasks to his staff. The staff feels disempowered, and some of the best people are leaving. If you are a system-oriented coach, you would assume that the locus of the problem is in the organization, not in your client. You would try to determine what in the organization is causing your client to behave that way. You might discover that it is the norm in this organization for bosses to be hands-on and exercise their authority, that the founder of the company was that way and other leaders have, in effect, adopted the founder's leadership paradigm. Or you might discover that failure is punished in this organization and people have learned to avoid accepting responsibility. If your approach is to coach your client to be less controlling, you will likely fail because the dynamics in this system will militate against him giving up control. To effect transformative change, you may also need to coach his staff members and others in the organization to try to change the norms that are reinforcing the status quo.

Another key concept in family therapy and system thinking is that people in organizations assume various roles, and these roles define who they are, how they behave, and how others respond to them. In families, stereotypical roles might include the wise father and nurturing mother, the responsible big brother, the nurturing big sister, and so on. Departures from these stereotypes could include the absent father, the carefree father, the alcoholic father, the overworked mother, the socialite mother, the super mother, the know-it-all sister, the star brother, the sweet sister, the bratty sister, the doofus brother, and so on. In organizations, as well as families, common roles include the blamers, the scapegoats, the stars, the cheerleaders, the skeptics, and the stalwarts. There are the reliable people, the hardworking people, the misfits, the slackers, the heroes, the martyrs, the complainers, and the grunts. Whatever labels we attach to them, identifiable roles emerge in organizations, too, and people tend to conform to the norms and expectations of their roles. It is as though when we join an organization we are cast in a play, and once we learn our roles we tend to behave the way others expect us to behave. So a common practice in system-oriented coaching is to examine the role your client is playing relative to the roles of other people in the organization and how those roles shape individual and organizational behavior, even when the behavior is dysfunctional. Helping your client understand these roles is a step toward transformational change, although you have to recognize that one of the principal functions of roles is to preserve homeostasis.

It should be evident, even in this brief introduction to family therapy and system thinking, that this approach to coaching has much to offer. Particularly enlightening are the ideas that individuals and the systems in which they operate are inseparable, that people play roles and understanding those roles is essential to divining why they behave the way they do, and that systems are highly resistant to change. Therefore, to help your clients effect transformational change, change from the inside out, you must consider the system in which they operate and know how and why that system is inclined to resist those transformational changes—unless you also change the system.

DEVELOPMENTAL APPROACHES TO COACHING

Finally, and we will discuss this approach very briefly, there are various psychological theories about how humans develop, and another approach to transformational coaching is to follow one of the developmental frameworks. Theories of human development have a long history beginning with Sigmund Freud and Jean Piaget and Erik Erikson, who was the first to articulate a stage theory of adult development. Stage theory is the concept that humans develop in a series of identifiable stages. Based on their own research, later theorists like Daniel Levinson and Lawrence Kohlberg proposed their own theories of the stages of life (Kohlberg's work focused on stages of moral development), and each of these theories is illuminating, but the theorist whose work has probably been most adapted to coaching is Robert Kegan (1982), particularly from his book *The Evolving Self: Problem and Process in Human Development*.

In this book, Kegan argues that "if you want to understand another person in some fundamental way you must know where the person is in his or her evolution" (p. 113). Why is this important? "Because the way in which the person is settling the issue of what is 'self' and what is 'other' essentially *defines* the underlying logic (or 'psychologic') of the person's meanings. Since what is most important for us to know in understanding another is not the other's experience but what the experience means to him or her, our first goal is to grasp the essence of how the other composes his or her private reality." So the central concept here is that coaches cannot understand their clients unless they understand where those clients are in their evolution, in their development as human beings.

In *The Evolving Self*, Kegan identifies five stages in human development. From birth to fully formed adult, those stages are the incorporative self (separation from the mother), the impulsive self (development of autonomy), the imperial self (development of the ego), the interpersonal self (incorporation with others), and the institutional self (incorporation with systems). According to stage theory, as we move into each successive stage, our evolution becomes static for a period. We embrace the new stage and grow comfortable with it. But as we mature, the stage becomes unstable. Sooner or later, we shed the stage we are in, like a snake shedding its skin, and move on to the next stage, where our development stabilizes anew.

Evolving from one stage to the next involves a transformational shift in our perception of ourselves and others, as well as a shift in the way we construct knowledge. Interestingly, when we are firmly ensconced in each stage, we can't perceive the stages beyond us, so our evolution through successive stages is, in fact, a raising of our consciousness.

A number of authors have proposed different theories of human development, including some who offer convincing arguments that women's development differs from men's (Gilligan, 1993; Belenky et al., 1997). Coaches who use a developmental approach with their clients typically try to identify which stage their clients are currently in, which gives them a perspective on why clients are behaving the way they are (because that is how they currently perceive the world) and why they might not be aligned with their roles or the organization's expectations of them. Having that insight helps coaches determine what they can do to help facilitate the client's growth from her current stage to the next stage of development, which often requires a transformational change on the client's part.

The greatest contribution of stage development theory to coaching lies in the concept that adult development is not only evolutionary but that it proceeds in stages, that people construct a view of reality based on the stage they're in, and that growth from one stage to the next involves a quantum shift in their perception of themselves and others. Coaching may involve an extensive series of exercises and discussions with clients to help them understand the stage they are in, grasp that there is a stage ahead of them, and begin the journey from their current stage to the next. This is by no means an easy journey, especially if clients lack sufficient self-awareness and psychological insight or if they are comfortable in their current stage and well-defended psychologically. Quantum shifts of this nature are generally preceded by agonizing discomfort and the sense that the world as the client knew it is no longer valid.

CHANGE FROM THE INSIDE OUT

The four coaching approaches we have discussed in this chapter are meant to bring about transformational change. They provide what amounts to a guidebook for coaches, a map to help them help their clients traverse rocky psychological terrain as they grow—from the inside out—toward a self that is more authentic, more integrated, and more masterful. In early maps of the arctic region, mapmakers imagined that four rivers led from the North Pole to the outer edges of the arctic. Likewise, we can imagine these four coaching approaches as rivers leading outward from our clients' core to the outer shores, and our challenge as coaches is to help them make that journey. We may choose to follow any of the four rivers as long as we are capable navigators of the river we choose. When the journey has ended, if we have done our job and our clients have had the courage to take an honest look at themselves and their core purposes, then we leave them along the shores of greater self-awareness and mastery, having been fundamentally transformed.

Beware, however, of undertaking these journeys without the requisite training and certification. Although we can learn much from psychoanalysis, family therapy, and adult development theory, we have no right to practice these methods unless we are qualified. If we attempt it, we risk running the ship aground, having done more harm than good. Coaching from the inside out can be highly transformational, but in the process it can also disinter a client's demons, and if you aren't competent to fight those demons, you'd best not go there. In the next chapter, we will talk about coaching from the outside in, which may or may not be as transformational as inside-out coaching but is more familiar ground for many coaches and can still be a highly effective way to help clients develop themselves and their skills.

14

Performance Coaching
(from the Outside In)

Sometimes, the goal of coaching is to help clients improve their performance by modifying their behavior or way of thinking rather than by undergoing a deep transformation. They may already be capable performers, but they have a few rough edges or some interpersonal challenges, they are receiving feedback they should respond to but don't know how, they have been through a comprehensive assessment of their skills and discovered some areas of weakness they would like to improve, or they believe they are stalled in their current position and would like help to get themselves back on track. When you work with such clients, you might use some of the tools and processes of inside-out coaching, which we discussed in the previous chapter, but it's more likely that your primary approaches will involve coaching from the outside in.

In chapter 13, we introduced a coaching metaphor originated by Kevin Cashman in his book *Leadership from the Inside Out*. In this book, Cashman presents an approach to leadership development that involves two complementary perspectives: developing leaders from the inside out by focusing on their core values, strengths, and purpose, and from the outside in by focusing on external influences, such as their work environment, feedback and reinforcement from others, their performance metrics, and so on. Cashman argues that effective leadership development (and coaching) comes from integrating these two perspectives—going from one to the other in a kind of infinite loop, as shown in figure 11. The inside-out approach that we discussed in chapter 13 has the potential to result in a transformational change in clients; the outside-in approach we discuss in this chapter is more likely to result in behavioral change. Combining the two is often the most effective approach coaches can take.

Coaching from the outside in means helping clients understand how others perceive them as well as their performance effectiveness and development needs within the context of their team and organization. If inside-out coaching amounts to an *internal* 360-degree assessment, then outside-in coaching is the *external* stakeholder 360-degree assessment. When we coach from the outside in, we use different practices and tools than we use when coaching from the inside out, but coaching is rarely linear, as figure 11 illustrated, so you may very well begin with inside-out coaching, then shift to outside-in as you explore how other people perceive something the client just said about herself, and then return to inside-out coaching depending on what is happening in the coaching dialogue and how prepared the client is to do some thoughtful self-examination.

Clients with high coachability—those who are psychologically minded and open to self-exploration—often prefer to begin with inside-out coaching. However, clients with low coachability, such as those who are not psychologically minded or who work in organizations where professional development is a low priority, may not be prepared to launch themselves into the kind of highly personal exploration that is required in the inside-out approach. It may be best for these clients to start with coaching from the outside in. For them, beginning with 360-degree assessments or external data sources, such as employee engagement surveys, may actually offer a safety net that enables them to develop more self-insight at a leisurely pace. Moreover, if you need to build rapport with clients before delving into potentially threatening inside-out exploration, then starting from the outside in may be the best way to build a requisite level of coach-client trust.

FACILITATING CHANGE FROM THE OUTSIDE IN

The human change model we introduced in chapter 12 shows that for people to change they have to build awareness, then commitment, then practice, and finally accountability. This is an iterative, rather than a linear, process. As clients are building practice, they may become aware of a new change need. As they are trying—and perhaps failing—to build account-ability they may discover that they are not sufficiently committed and may need to re-build commitment. In chapter 13, we explored this change model and offered some practical tools and techniques that Kevin Cashman and his colleague, Janet Feldman, have developed for managing change using the inside-out coaching approach. Now we will elaborate on some of the tools and techniques they use based on the outside-in approach. The tools we present are obviously just a few among dozens of tools coaches can use during each phase of the change process.

Building Awareness from the Outside In

As you build a client's awareness from the outside in, you are invoking all of the parts of the needs compass except for the north pole (the client's self-perceptions). As we noted in chapter 3, the east pole of the compass includes others' observations of the client; the south pole, data from work products and performance metrics; and the west pole, your observations of the client. These outside-in perspectives are meant to build clients' aware-ness of how others see them (of how they appear within the work context in which they operate). At the beginning of the coaching process, it is not un-usual to find dissonance between inside-out and outside-in perspectives—that is, between how clients see themselves and how others see them. One of our principal goals in building awareness is to help clients develop a con-gruent and integrated view of themselves based on both perspectives. When clients do not have a congruent view of themselves and rely too heavily on self-perception to gauge their performance and impact, they usually deceive themselves by accentuating the positives and ignoring or dismissing the negatives—with derailment as a frequent consequence. Outside-in aware-ness building can alert clients to the potential for derailment and the correc-tive actions they need to take to avoid it.

In chapter 3 we talked about how you can use data from various kinds of surveys and assessments, and we listed the kinds of questions you might employ as you help clients explore how others see them and the implica-tions of how they are seen. Another exercise Cashman developed to build awareness from the outside in is one he calls the time capsule.

Time Capsule

Ask clients to imagine that a complete portfolio of their work products—performance appraisals, resumes, organization charts, press clippings, articles, notes, cards, e-mails, office pictures, awards, and so on—were placed in a time capsule. Now ask them to fast forward five years and assume the role of a journalist who is writing a narrative about them based on their time capsule portfolio. The journalist's challenge is to identify the competencies, skills, and behaviors required to produce that portfolio (strengths) as well as the competencies, skills, and behaviors that appear to have been absent (potential areas for improvement). Ask the client to write that narrative either during a coaching session or as a homework assignment. When the narrative has been completed, ask the client to read it aloud. Probe by asking these kinds of questions:

♦ What key competencies and skills were needed to produce the results in this portfolio?

♦ What were this person's key strengths? Were any of those strengths overused?

♦ What commitments fueled this person's behaviors? What did he appear to expect of himself? What obligations did he feel towards others?

♦ What were this person's underlying values, intentions, and motives?

♦ What could this person have done better? What competencies or skills did he need to build further?

Alternatively, ask your client, first, to create a summary of his work products portfolio, which either you or one of the client's trusted colleagues could read, and then, second, to write the narrative. When the narrative is done, read it to the client and then ask these kinds of questions:

♦ How does this resonate with you? Upon reflection, does this picture of strengths and potential areas for improvement seem accurate? If not, what would you change?

♦ Which comments are aligned with how you see yourself and which comments are not?

♦ Which important aspects of your contribution are recognized by others? Which are absent?

♦ What do people appear to misunderstand about you and your intentions?

♦ Do you agree with what people see as your strengths and needs for improvement?

You Play the Coach

A related outside-in awareness-building exercise is to ask the client what she would do if she were the coach. Ask her to review the surveys, assessments, and any other data you have gathered and then ask her these questions:

♦ If you were this person's coach, what would you observe about her? What would your impressions be?

♦ What does the data indicate about this person's strengths? What would you advise her to do to capitalize on her strengths?

♦ What does the data indicate about her development needs? What competencies or skills does she need to develop in order to be more effective?

♦ With which groups of people is she more or less effective? Superiors? Peers? Subordinates? Customers? People within her team? People outside of her team?

♦ What does she appear to enjoy doing? What does she not enjoy?

♦ If you were advising her, what advice would you give?

Like the time capsule exercise, the purpose of this exercise is to get clients to see themselves as others see them. The success of the exercise depends on clients' ability to see themselves as others see them, and to look objectively at the data and draw conclusions that are as unbiased as possible. You may need to assist in this process by asking questions like these:

♦ [Responding to an observation the client has made] Really? I think I would have seen it differently. What if...?

♦ Are you being too easy or hard on this person?

◆ What behavioral patterns do you see?

◆ How easy do you think it would be for this person—or anyone, for that matter—to make the change you are suggesting?

◆ You may be correct. This might have been a one-off situation, which isn't likely to be repeated. But what if it isn't?

◆ Summarize for me. What are the two or three key things this person needs to do differently?

Building awareness from the outside in requires objectivity and the ability to reconcile and integrate data from multiple sources. This stage may be disconcerting for clients—especially those who have strong egos or who have resisted hearing feedback—but it can also be liberating. Understanding how others see you requires critical examination and a willingness to be vulnerable, but it can also enable clients to lower their defenses and be honest with themselves, maybe more honest than they have ever been.

The time required for building awareness—from the inside out and outside in—is often greater than any other part of the coaching process, but it is part of the critical path in identifying the real coaching need (chapter 4) and ensuring that you and your client are working on the right issues. Your effectiveness as a coach will diminish if you do not spend adequate time on this important early part of the process. Be prepared to go back and forth between outside-in awareness building and inside-out awareness building until the client can reconcile her self-perceptions with the perceptions of others and the data found in surveys, assessments, performance evaluations, and other south pole indicators of the client's strengths and development needs.

Building Commitment from the Outside In

Commitment comes first from the self: from a client's conviction that he must change; from the urgency he feels about making those changes sooner rather than later; from his sense that this is not something he can put off; and from his commitment to take action, even if that action involves deviating from the path he has been taking to a path he's never taken. The commitment to change originates from within, which is why building commitment from the inside out is crucial. However, you can and should strengthen the client's commitment from the outside in, primarily by ensuring that the client grasps—at the gut level—the advantages of changing and the consequences of remaining where he is. Excellent tools to use are visioning and implication questions.

♦ Close your eyes for a moment and visualize what it will be like if you are successful at _____. What does that look like? What does it feel like?

♦ Now visualize what it will be like if you are not successful. If you continue as you are now, what will that look like next year? In two years? In five years? What does that feel like?

♦ What will happen if you don't change? What are the consequences of continuing as you are? [Then, after the client mentions one consequence] What else? What else?

♦ What will happen if you do change? If you succeed at _____, what will happen? What else will happen? What else?

The Mini-Survey

For one of the organizations that hired Korn/Ferry to provide global coaching services, we created a survey that included just two items to measure commitment from the outside in:

♦ Did the executive discuss her coaching goals with you?

♦ How often did the executive follow up with you regarding those coaching goals?

We shared these questions with our clients' stakeholders (boss, HR manager, colleagues, and direct reports) at the beginning of the coaching engagements and then administered the mini-survey to a random sampling of those stakeholders at the middle and end of the engagement—or more frequently if the initial outcomes showed that clients had not shared their goals and were not following up. The purpose of these questions was to reinforce the importance of enlisting others in our clients' development and to introduce more transparency into the process by asking others for help and feedback. As we told our clients, building commitment requires seeking the help and input from those around you.

The Coaching Team

A somewhat similar outside-in method for promoting commitment is to create a coaching team. Here, we ask the client to engage two of the most critical stakeholders throughout the coaching engagement: the client's manager and the HR partner. We have come to recommend this practice in nearly every engagement because one key success factor is the involvement and engagement of the client's manager or sponsor. If this person is fully engaged in the client's development, then we are much more likely to experience success and, moreover, more significant business impact.

Managers or sponsors often have more insight into the organization's strategic imperatives and will link individual development goals to them. In addition, when their manager plays an active part in the coaching process, clients take the process more seriously and understand that the benefits of being aware, committed, practiced, and accountable for changes are likely to improve their performance and enhance their opportunities in the organization.

Having the HR partner's active involvement in the process offers similar benefits. Clients know that they have the HR partner's dedicated support and know where they can get additional resources they may need to help in their development. And they can't help but be aware of the crucial role this person plays in tracking their progress and measuring them against the capabilities, performance, and growth of others at comparable levels who play similar roles in the organization. Needless to say, it can be highly motivational for a client when the two most critical people in the organization who influence his prospects are closely monitoring his progress toward achieving his development goals.

Time Capsule Reprised

We introduced the time capsule exercise in the previous section on building awareness, and it is a useful exercise here, too. To drive for deeper commitment, resume the time capsule exercise by reading the journalist's narrative again and identify where you find congruence or incongruence between skills, behaviors, or values of the person described. After reading the narrative, ask the client the following:

◆ What is the nature of the discrepancies—are they based on skills, behaviors, or values?

Having clients categorize the discrepancy is often a useful way for them to self-diagnose the problem and come to terms with its degree of challenge. Making behavioral changes and improving skills are generally far, far easier alterations to make than shifting core values. Continue with these questions:

♦   What core values are present that you should further leverage? What core values are lacking in the narrative, and what are the implications of that? Can you get where you want to go if you do not adopt and embrace those values?

This last question often leads to a frank discussion of the client's commitment to change and willingness to do what it will take to get there. In fact, it can often evolve into a key inside-out exploration of what the client really wants and whether she has the skill and the will to accomplish it.

Next ask:

♦   Which skills are present that you can further leverage? What core skills are missing or underdeveloped?

You need to go beyond a simple listing of the skills the person needs. We have had clients say, in effect, "Yeah, yeah, yeah, I know I need to be better at XYZ. I've known that for years." But being aware of the need for change and being committed to change are very different. When clients identify a skill development need, it's often best to follow with implication questions: "Okay, you've been aware of the need for years. Why haven't you acted on it? What's been preventing you from developing this skill? What will happen if you don't improve in this area? From a skills standpoint, you seem like you are stuck in a rut. What are you going to do to get out of it?" And so on. This is where you need to do some pushing (see chapter 10).

Continue with this approach:

♦   If you were this person's coach, what would you advise this person to do?

This question evokes one of our favorite coaching techniques—getting clients to coach themselves. When you ask them to step back and look at themselves as though they were detached from themselves and can see themselves objectively, they sometimes have insights they would not have had otherwise. Of course, it's impossible for people to truly see themselves objectively (we have far too many ego constructs and defense mechanisms in place for that), but most people know themselves well enough to identify things they need to change and the reasons why they haven't made those changes—at least superficially. But for this question to work, you may need to help them probe further by asking follow-up questions:

♦   [After the client offers a piece of advice] That's a good suggestion. Has this person tried it before? If so, why didn't it work the first time? What makes you think it could work now? What's different or what has changed since the person first tried this?

♦   That's good advice. Do you think this person will follow it? Why or why not? What will it *really* take for this person to be committed to this course of action?

♦   What are the next steps? What will it take for this person to turn a commitment into a reality? What could get in the way? And how will this person overcome it?

♦   What else?

It's helpful if you ask the kinds of "Columbo" and "What Else" questions we described in chapter 8. These questions help clients explore their initial answers more deeply. If you are skillful in asking these kinds of questions, you can move them to a depth of understanding and commitment that is well beyond where they will have been initially.

Commitments Revisited

Finally, if you completed the initial commitments exercise during the stage of building commitment from the inside out, then revisit those commitments. Ask clients some of these questions and have them revise their commitments accordingly:

♦   What skills and values can you intentionally leverage and develop to grow your proprietary leadership difference?

♦   Specify the core values you wish to bring into greater focus. How do you create greater transparency and engagement in these values for yourself and others?

♦ Specify the specific core skills and capabilities you wish to bring into greater alignment. What behaviors would reflect greater alignment of these skills in delivering on your commitments?

♦ What behaviors can you alter, modify, or initiate to bring about your desired impact?

Building Practice

In chapter 12 we referred to building practice as the *path of discipline*. The goal in this phase of the human change process is to consistently practice the new behaviors, to build and improve upon the new skills, and to integrate and live the new values. This takes discipline, continuous awareness ("Am I doing what I committed to do?"), and integration. Each of these can be built from the outside in. Of course, discipline largely originates from within the client, but coaches can help build practice in some concrete ways. Among the best practices we have discovered are preparation, process, partners, and reinforcement.

Preparation

A client whose development goal is to become a more confident public speaker prepares by carefully planning his next presentation. He spends many more hours creating and rehearsing than he did previously. He prepares and practices to the point where he can confidently step up to the podium and deliver a more engaging, better organized, and compelling presentation than he's ever done before. He builds practice through thoughtful preparation until it becomes habitual for him to thoroughly plan his presentations.

A client whose change goal is to overcome an aversion to confrontation prepares for difficult conversations by outlining what she expects the other person's arguments will be and carefully constructing her own pros and cons. And she prepares for the emotional side of confrontation by doing some deep-breathing exercises she's learned in a yoga class. Another client prepares for a job interview by working with her coach. They videotape a mock interview so she can see how she's coming across and what she needs to adjust in her manner and responses to questions. These are examples of how clients can build practice through preparation. They might do some preparing on their own, or they might do it with their coach, family members, colleagues, or others. By using the discipline of preparation, they are practicing new skills and behaviors and acting on the change commitments they have made. In our experience, coaches can nearly always use preparation as a tool for helping clients build practice.

Process

Clients can also build practice by creating new processes or amending existing ones. Michael S., one of our clients who needed to improve his collaborative skills with his colleagues, built a process around sharing ideas with his colleagues before taking them to the executive committee. His process was a simple checklist that he added to the task list on his calendar. It reminded him that before he went to any meeting with new ideas, he would syndicate those ideas with his colleagues first and ask for their opinions and suggestions. He learned to build greater acceptance and cooperation from his colleagues. To his surprise, he found that he was able to improve upon his own ideas because, as he discovered, his colleagues often had useful and creative alternatives and reality checks when they discussed what he was proposing. If you can help clients like Michael develop or alter how they work, or what steps they take, or what procedures they follow, then you can help them build practice.

Partners

Sometimes, the best way for a client to build practice is to do it with a partner—her coach, her significant other, her boss, a trusted colleague, or someone else who is available at the right moments and is committed to her success. Serena B., for instance, signed on to a program designed to increase her vitality. She was among the many executives whose work and life commitments were stressful, and she had become overweight and was perpetually fatigued. Moreover, on her last annual physical she had learned of some physical symptoms that were the warning signs of more serious disease. But she found it difficult to stick with her exercise commitments, and she often ate foods that she knew were bad for her.

At her coach's behest, Serena's solution was to find a partner at work who could share her commitment and be a partner in every sense in her program. Not surprisingly, it didn't take her long to find someone. Linda H. had similar issues and shared her frustration. So the two of them joined a health club and committed to going to it together four times a week. They also starting having lunch together every day and jointly watched what they ate. Before long, they were good friends and depended on each other for mutual support and reinforcement. What each of them could not do alone they managed to do very well together. That's the value of having a partner while a client is trying to build practice.

Reinforcement
Lastly, a good outside-in technique for building practice is to find positive reinforcements for the desired behavior. Like the gold stars our teachers gave us when we did something right, positive reinforcements give us pleasure and are a measure of achievement, so we desire more of them, and this strengthens our will to keep doing whatever we are being rewarded for. It's important for people who are trying to change to have outside-in reinforcement when they do what they committed to do; conversely, if they fail to live up to their commitments, it is often useful for them to receive negative feedback. This is the familiar operant conditioning model of behavior modification, and although people are more complex and sophisticated than Pavlov's dog, operant conditioning does have its place in coaching. People are more likely to build practice if they receive positive reinforcement when they show the new, desirable behavior and negative reinforcement when they show the old, undesirable behavior. Similarly, clients are more likely to build new skills when they discover that practicing those skills results in improved performance and positive reinforcement from others.

Building Accountability
Clients who are on the path of continuous learning find ways to get ongoing performance feedback from the people in their domains who matter: customers, superiors, peers, subordinates, family members, and so on. Practicing accountability from the outside in is generally about measurement, so coaches can use mini-surveys throughout the coaching

engagement to measure progress; they can use pre– and post–360-degree survey results; they can record particulars about the coaching engagement that may include the presenting problem, the real coaching need, the stakeholders consulted, the number of hours spent together, the nature of the time spent together (confidential one-on-one sessions, observation of team meetings, public presentations), and so on as a way of building accountability into the coaching process.

Beyond accountability during the coaching engagement, however, it is important for clients to build accountability into their ongoing practice. Clients will need to measure the following: Are they successfully practicing the new behaviors? Is there evidence that they have developed new skills or enhanced existing skills? Are their values in practice aligned with their change goals? At the beginning of a coaching engagement, we often ask clients to think about what the changes they want to make will mean. What will be different? More importantly, what will be the evidence that they have successfully accomplished what they set out to accomplish?

THE BEHAVIORAL APPROACH TO COACHING

In his essay "People are Complex and the World Is Messy: A Behavior-Based Approach to Executive Coaching," David B. Peterson (2006) articulates one of the central concepts of behavioral coaching. "I have a simple yet fundamental assumption about coaching," he says. "The purpose is to change behavior. The core of my coaching boils down to one equally simple yet provocative question for the participant: What are you going to do differently? Implicit in that question is a focus on action and a focus on the future (rather than the past)" (p. 51). Also implicit in Peterson's simple question for clients is that they need to do something differently, that there is a gap between their current performance and their desired performance. Moreover, if clients already knew how to close the gap, they wouldn't need a coach. So inherent in behavioral coaching is the assumption that the coaching is a learning process for clients. Indeed, if the coaching succeeds, clients should have developed greater ability to identify the gaps themselves and know, at least directionally, how to change their behavior to eliminate the gaps. Behavioral coaching invokes coaches as teachers, although this does not necessarily imply that the coaching is directive. A substantial amount of behavioral coaching can be done non-directively.

Behavioral coaching typically begins with an information-gathering and diagnostic phase in which you seek to understand:

♦ What the client's boss and the organization expect of your client—which is usually expressed as goals but may include behavioral, attitudinal, and skill-level expectations.

♦ How your client has been performing—which may include assessments, performance appraisals, performance feedback, employee surveys, and other people's perceptions of your client gathered via interviews.

♦ The gaps between your client's current and desired performance and behaviors.

♦ How your client perceives herself and the gaps she wishes to close.

We use the needs compass (chapter 3) to develop a comprehensive perspective on the client's current performance, her goals or performance targets, and her needs (the gap between current and desired performance levels). This diagnostic also identifies the behaviors the client needs to change. From here, behavioral coaching follows the human change process. We use the diagnostic to build the client's awareness and help her gain insight into the areas she needs to improve and why they need to be improved. Then we test her commitment to change and use inside-out and outside-in methods to help her strengthen her commitment. Then we coach to help her build practice (developing her skills and abilities) and accountability (helping her measure success and reinforce the new behaviors).

Behavioral coaching has evolved from the principles of behaviorism as developed by Ivan Pavlov, John Watson, B. F. Skinner, Albert Bandura, and others. Among the most important of these principles are *stimulus-response* and *reinforcement*. Through conditioning, the behaviorists argue, people learn to respond in conditioned ways to repeated stimuli, much as Pavlov's dog was conditioned to salivate when researchers rang a bell prior to feeding him. Once the dog was conditioned, he would salivate whenever the bell rang, whether or not he was fed. Similarly, if an employee in my division never approaches me except to ask me for favors, and I've grown annoyed with it, I will start to feel annoyed when he's walking toward me even if he doesn't speak to me. Behaviorists believe that numerous stimuli in our environment influence us to respond in certain ways—and we are usually not conscious of those influences. So if you are coaching a client who is behaving problematically, particularly if he has a pattern of problematic behavior, then it's useful to look for the stimulus that is eliciting his behavioral response. Linking the stimulus with the response is a helpful way to make clients more aware of what's causing their behavior, and awareness is the first step toward change.

Behavior becomes conditioned if it is reinforced. If I receive a commendation every time I do exceptional work, then the commendation reinforces my willingness to work hard and produce exceptional work. I like getting commendations, so I will strive to do exceptional work on future projects. My boss may also tell me I've done a great job and acknowledge the exceptional quality of my work in front of my peers, which makes me feel good about myself. The commendations and acknowledgements are extrinsic reinforcements, whereas feeling good about myself is an intrinsic reinforcement. Both types of reinforcement are useful in coaching. When we ask clients to change their behavior, we need to help them create feedback mechanisms to let them know how they are doing. Along with feedback, they need positive reinforcements of the changed behavior.

One of Terry's clients (we'll call him Sam) had lost a sizable performance bonus the preceding year because he was rated lowest among his peers on collaboration. During the coaching, Terry helped Sam determine what he was doing that his peers deemed uncollaborative, and Sam learned what he needed to do differently to become more collaborative and be seen that way. As he practiced the new behaviors, Sam asked for feedback from his boss and some of his peers. Terry observed him and also gave him feedback on how he was doing. When he did well, he got positive reactions and approval; when he backslid, he got negative reactions and disapproval, mainly in the form of questions about "what went wrong." Over a period of time, he also got positive reinforcement from improved interactions with his peers, pats on the back from his boss, and the satisfaction he felt from working in a more collegial and productive environment. When he later received a substantially higher rating for collaboration with his peers, Sam also got strong positive reinforcement in the form of the performance bonus that he'd failed to get the year before.

We might ask whether intrinsic or extrinsic reinforcements are more powerful, and among psychologists there are opposing views. It may not matter. The key for coaches is to ensure that clients will have the new, desired behaviors reinforced in their environment. Reinforcements help make change permanent. In the absence of positive reinforcement, clients will likely revert to their former patterns of behavior.

Reinforcements may be positive, as the story about Sam illustrates, or negative, like the frown on the district manager's face when I tell her that the team will not complete the project on time. That frown—coupled with other frowns from that manager—is something I want to avoid, so I'll be motivated to push the team harder to get the work done on time. In many coaching situations, clients will come to the table with less-than-stellar performance reviews, discomforting feedback, or assessment and survey results that indicate the need for change. These negative reinforcements can be powerful motivations for change, but in our experience even harsh feedback may not be enough to sustain behavioral change because the damaging behaviors are often habitual and are reinforced by numerous other influences in clients' environments. So it is important to ensure that the desired behaviors are rewarded and reinforced while the undesirable behaviors are extinguished by negative reinforcements over a long period. How long? It depends on how urgently clients feel they need to change and how committed they are to staying the course.

The core concepts of the behavioral approach to coaching are important, not only in understanding human behavior, but also in understanding change. In the last chapter, we described the family therapy or systems thinking approach to coaching, which stresses that to change people you have to change the system in which they operate. What the systems approach recognizes is that systems are replete with behavioral reinforcements that strive to maintain homeostasis. To help people change, you have to remove or inhibit these reinforcements, which is extraordinarily difficult, and put powerful reinforcements in place that will help clients sustain change and counter the systemic barriers they will surely encounter.

THE COGNITIVE APPROACH TO COACHING

In an article on cognitive coaching, Jeffrey E. Auerbach (2006) writes, "As a coach, I'm a thought partner. As a thought partner, I help my clients think with more depth, greater clarity, and less distortion—a cognitive process. Coaching is largely a cognitive method" (p. 103). The perspective among those who follow the cognitive approach to coaching is that people's moods, attitudes, and behavior are largely the product of how they think about things, and if their thinking is flawed, then the best way to help them is to show them how to think correctly. According to this approach, all that clients need to transform is the way they think.

Cognitive coaching grew from rational-emotive therapy, which psychologist Albert Ellis developed in the 1950s. Ellis believed that many of people's problems stemmed from errors in their thinking, and he created the ABC model to illustrate this. The A stands for an Activating experience, C for an emotional Consequence, and B for a Belief about the activating experience. Ellis believed that people often leap from A to C without understanding that B is the real culprit. In other words, they connect the activating experience with the emotional consequence. For example, I turn in my project report to my boss. Later, when I haven't heard from him, I poke my head in his office and ask if my report is okay. He looks up with a scowl and says, in a dismissive tone, "Yeah, it's fine." I am crushed. I return to my office and can't do anything productive the rest of the day. I worry that he thinks I'm incompetent and wonder if I'm about to be fired. I'm so anxious I can't sleep that night. According to Ellis, the activating event was my boss's response to my question, the consequence of which is my insecurity. But I failed to see that the real cause of my distress was not my boss's response to my question but rather my flawed beliefs that (1) he was scowling because he thought I had done poor work and (2) I need to worry if all of my boss's interactions with me are not uniformly positive and upbeat. In fact, he may have been scowling for reasons that had nothing to do with me. Maybe he'd had a family argument that morning. Or someone cut him off in traffic. Maybe he liked my report but I just caught him at a bad moment. The point is that my mental leap from his response to my anxiety is not rational. Furthermore, it is unrealistic to expect that all of my interactions with my boss will be upbeat. Some interactions—maybe most of them, in fact—are bound to be neutral. And some, hopefully only a few, may be downbeat and negative if, for instance, he was expecting more than I (or the rest of our team) could deliver, if he is under pressure from his boss, or if he is simply having a bad day.

Cognitive coaches look for distortions or inaccuracies in thinking that could be causing their clients anxiety, emotional distress, or poor decision making. Many of these distortions are well-known logical fallacies.

♦ **Overgeneralizing**. Assuming that one instance of something is evidence of a pattern. "She debated that point endlessly in our meeting. She must be argumentative."

♦ **Arguing from silence**. Assuming that someone's silence is proof of their position. "He didn't say anything about my proposal, so he must support it."

♦ **Arguing from ignorance**. Assuming that something is true because it hasn't been proven false (or vice versa). "Jeanne didn't say we couldn't go forward with our plan, so she must be okay with it."

♦ **Assuming the worst**. Assuming that if something bad happens something worse will follow. "They just cancelled our Portland contract. Next they'll cancel all of our contracts and we won't ever regain market share in the northwest. You know what that will do to me?"

♦ **False dilemma**. Assuming that there are only two possible outcomes or options when in fact there are many. "Either we accept Marc's conditions or we'll have to throw out everything we've done so far and start over."

These are just five of more than one hundred logical fallacies that have been identified. In their dialogues with clients, cognitive coaches listen for fuzzy or flawed thinking and then help clients understand how they are jumping to conclusions (in Ellis's terms, connecting the activating experience with the emotional consequence), and how to think correctly about what they experienced (understanding why their beliefs about the activating experience are wrong). The assumption is that once clients understand why their thinking was flawed and know how to think correctly, the causes of their distress will vanish and their lives and performance will improve. Cognitive coaches are, in effect, teachers of rational thinking.

Another important concept in cognitive coaching is that people create mental maps to help them interpret experience. These maps are sometimes called schemas or mental models. In effect, they are unconscious templates for understanding things and knowing how to respond to them, mental constructs for understanding how the world works. One of my mental maps might be something like "anyone who talks about his own accomplishments is a braggart and should not be trusted because he's only out for himself." When a new colleague joins my group and displays some awards he's won at previous jobs on the wall of his office, I become suspicious toward him because my mental map tells me that this is the appropriate way to respond. Mental maps are the unwritten rules whereby I make sense of the world and other people in it. Each of us has hundreds of them in our head, and they guide us—usually without us being aware of it—as we react to events, changes in our environment, new information, and interactions with other people. In cognitive coaching, the coach would try to help clients become aware of their mental maps, especially when those maps are the source of—or are contributing to—the problem.

A particular kind of mental map is called *self-talk*. These are the usually unspoken messages you give to yourself about yourself. *I'm a winner. I'm a loser. I'll never get this right. I will get this right. I might as well give up. I'm determined to see this through. I'm too old for this. I'm too inexperienced. I can't do this. I can do this. I look great. I look awful.* And so on. Self-talk can be elevating, or it can be crippling. Henry Ford is often quoted as saying, "Whether you think that you can, or that you can't, you are usually right." Collectively, self-talk like this is an articulation of your self-image. You may be aware of some of the messages you give yourself—but generally not all of them. Cognitive coaches, sensing that clients suffer from poor self-image, may try to surface the crippling self-talk and help clients change the script. We have coached many clients who had low self-esteem, and this is generally the approach we took.

The cognitive approach has much to offer coaches. Whether you are coaching from the inside out or the outside in, it can be very useful to help clients appreciate that how they think about the world (and themselves) affects not only their emotional state but how they problem solve and make decisions, how they interact with others, and how they respond to the myriad of unfolding events and circumstances occurring daily in their lives and in the world of work.

APPRECIATIVE INQUIRY AND POSITIVE PSYCHOLOGY

One of the more recent applications of psychological theory to coaching is appreciative inquiry (AI), which has grown out of the positive psychology and strengths-based movements. The essence of this approach is to heighten the positive potential in people and organizations by asking questions that help them identify what is most constructive, uplifting, and vital about themselves. Instead of focusing on what's wrong, you focus on what's right. Instead of identifying clients' weaknesses and coaching them on how to improve, you identify their strengths and coach them on how to do more of what they already do well. Instead of envisioning a bleak future and helping clients avoid it, you envision an ideal future and help clients attain it.

Coaches who practice AI believe that the process of asking questions is itself an intervention—that inquiry is the first step toward change. (We agree that asking questions raises awareness.) They also believe that words create reality, that language is an essential tool in crafting the desired state you want to reach, and that if you want positive change, then you need to use positive language. If you focus on success, you create more success; but if you focus on problems, you create more problems. In AI coaching, the coach asks questions like these:

♦ When you engage most effectively with people, what are you doing?

♦ What are you like when you are at your best?

♦ What are the most effective things you do as a team leader?

♦ What are you already doing well that you need to do more of?

♦ Imagine that from now on you could be the visionary leader you aspire to be. What would you have to do differently to make that happen?

These kinds of questions help clients discover a positive path forward, an aspiration to become the person they want to be. Clearly, this is in sharp contrast to the psychoanalytic approach where clients are trying to escape something crippling from their past. Appreciative inquiry has gained many adherents in the past few decades, but there remain a number of psychologists and coaches who believe that it's necessary to address clients' weaknesses as well as elements in their environment, behavior, or thinking processes that inhibit them and prevent them from achieving their full potential. We don't advocate one of these approaches over any of the others. They all have their strengths and applications as we seek to help clients improve their performance and, perhaps, to transform themselves from who they are to who they want and need to become.

INTEGRATING THE OUTSIDE IN WITH THE INSIDE OUT

We have noted a number of times that coaching is never a linear process. You may help clients build awareness and then move to building commitment, only to discover later that you have to return to building awareness. It is frequently the case, too, that in building practice clients falter, and you have to help them by returning to commitment building. And the process of building accountability may very well lead you back to building awareness.

So it is, too, with inside-out and outside-in coaching. With clients who are high in coachability, you may begin by coaching them from the inside out and then move fluidly to the outside in. Likewise, with low-coachability clients, you may begin with outside-in awareness building and then discover that they become open to inside-out commitment building. Effective coaching is an art, and like all arts it is fluid, creative, and iterative. Coaches need the skill to move seamlessly from awareness building to commitment building and back again—and from inside out to outside in—in a continuous loop that gives clients the right help in the right way at the right time. Moreover, the most capable coaches, in our opinion, are informed, multidisciplinary practitioners who are capable of using the tools and methods of many approaches to coaching but remain constantly aware of the line between coaching and therapy and don't cross it.

As we have emphasized throughout this book, helping clients is inherently an adaptive process because no two clients are alike, and you cannot coach everyone the same way. Just as some prefer to be coached directively and some nondirectively, some clients will be comfortable beginning with an inside-out approach to building awareness and some would be terrified. Some clients will respond better to the behavioral approach to coaching, others to cognitive methods, and still others to appreciative inquiry.

To coach effectively, you must be adaptive. If you begin in a way that frightens them, you may never build their trust (nor deserve it). Find the right starting point on the infinite loop and then move fluidly from one phase or perspective to another as the situation suggests and as clients respond to your ways of helping. Remember that clients possess greater wisdom about themselves and greater insight into what they can change and what, in their hearts, they know they really cannot. Support them as they take one step after another on a journey that, with or without your help, will always and inevitably be their own.

PART
4

Becoming an Adapative Coach

In this final part of the book, we examine what it takes to become an adaptive coach. Some of the potential coaches who have come to us at Lore and Korn/Ferry have arrived from the business world. They are former human resources professionals, managers who enjoyed coaching as part of their job, or retired executives who want to stay involved and believe they have a gift for developing people. Others arrive with degrees in psychology and years of experience as therapists. Neither profile is a guarantee that someone will become a successful executive coach. Those with business backgrounds often lack the knowledge and skills necessary to understand clients' real needs and guide them through the change process; those with psychological backgrounds often lack the business and organizational perspective necessary for them to understand their clients' world and offer relevant assistance. Ideal prospective coaches have one foot in both worlds. They bring an integrated perspective to coaching and are agile learners.

In chapter 15, The Informed Practitioner, we observe that the best coaches are well informed about business, leadership, organizational dynamics, human development, psychology, and the various approaches to coaching. Being an informed practitioner gives us the ability to adapt to our clients' needs and be more effective in the four types of coaching that organizations typically sponsor: knowledge and skills, developmental, corrective, and performance coaching. The appendix to the book includes an annotated bibliography of the best resources we have found to help adaptive coaches become more knowledgeable and skilled.

In the final chapter, Completing Your Own Journey, we note that our clients' journeys are to some extent also our own journeys—that in helping others gain insights about themselves we also discover insights about ourselves. Our journey is never complete because we never reach the point where we have nothing more to learn. Our ultimate quest is to discover the "I" inside—the authentic person who is the source of all the help we give others.

15

The Informed Practitioner

W hat is most notable about coaching today is the sheer number of people who call themselves coaches. The field was growing rapidly when we published the first edition of *Adaptive Coaching* in 2003, but the growth in the past nine years has been staggering, aided in part by the recession. When the economy turns down and people are being laid off, a number of those who have left jobs turn to coaching or consulting to make a living, and although it may present an opportunity for them, it is to some degree problematic for the coaching profession. In recent years, we met with a senior HR director in a large corporation, and he complained that most of the coaches who were seeking engagements with executives in his company were unqualified to coach. In effect, he said, they were practicing without a license, which begs the question, what are the qualifications, criteria, or requirements for becoming a coach?

Currently, there are none. Some organizations have lobbied for licensing, but no governmental entities have yet responded to the call. Consequently, there are no agreed-upon standards for coaches, no education or training requirements, no professional associations that can enforce standards. There are no residency requirements, no review boards, no testing, no annual recertifications, and so on. The International Coach Federation offers a certification program, as do some privately held coaching institutes, and many commercial firms that offer executive coaching have rigorous internal certification programs—but others don't. We are aware of one practitioner who certifies his coaches by telephone. In this environment, anyone who wants to be a coach can become a coach simply by having business cards printed saying that he's a coach.

Creating standards for the coaching profession would be challenging partly because there are so many different kinds of coaching, each with its own competency demands. Along with executive coaching, there is athletic coaching, fitness coaching, wellness coaching, life coaching, educational coaching (also called tutoring), career coaching, public relations coaching, transpersonal coaching, marriage counseling (a form of coaching), and psychological coaching (from therapists who have begun working in corporations as executive coaches but retain their psychological practices). Licensing discussions usually center on executive coaching, but the requirements that licensing would probably entail—educational minimums, standards of conduct, certification training, and performance standards—could also apply to wellness coaching, life coaching, career coaching, and so on. Where do you draw the line between the types of coaching that require a license and those that don't?

Despite this chaotic picture, one positive trend that has taken shape in the past decade is a movement toward greater professionalism, driven partly by the recognition among the most active executive coaches that coaching needs to become a profession and partly by human resources departments in companies that are screening potential coaches more rigorously and weeding out those who can't meet increasingly higher standards of acceptability and proven performance. If nothing else, these market forces will drive coaching toward higher standards and greater professionalism. Meanwhile, a picture is emerging in the coaching literature of the type of person who would be a highly qualified executive coach, and that person is being called an *informed practitioner*. Before describing what an informed practitioner looks like, however, we need to discuss the types of coaching organizations typically need.

ORGANIZATIONAL COACHING NEEDS

What organizations need from coaching differs depending on the purpose of the coaching and the circumstances of the person whom they want to have coached. We were approached, for instance, by a family-held manufacturing firm (we'll call them FHMF) that was looking for a coach with a particular set of skills. They wanted one of their younger family members (James) to assume responsibility for manufacturing. He had been with the business most of his life and was a successful manager. But FHMF also wanted to modernize its manufacturing operations and introduce lean manufacturing concepts into their production plants. They couldn't afford the time to send James back to school in lean manufacturing, and they didn't want to hire consultants. They wanted a coach, but not just any coach. They wanted someone who had proven experience in lean manufacturing, someone who could move onsite to their location for six to twelve months and act as James's coach and mentor in an immersive learning experience that would help FHMF transform their business.

At the other end of the spectrum was a client we'll call Suzanna. She was president of one of the operating companies of a large multinational distribution company (LMDC). Suzanna was a twenty-year veteran of the company and had risen through the ranks by leading from the front and being an aggressive competitor. She had exceptionally high expectations of her staff and was intolerant of mistakes. She had an entrepreneurial leadership style, which worked well for her early in her career, but she was becoming increasingly challenging to work with as she rose to the most senior ranks in the company, where collaboration and leadership through influence were the most important management skills. She did not value coaching (for herself especially), but the CEO and the board believed that if she did not receive help she would certainly derail. At their insistence, Suzanna accepted a coach, who realized in the opening moments of their first meeting that Suzanna would need a significant transformation in order to become the kind of leader the company needed her to be.

As these examples illustrate, what organizations need from coaching can be very diverse. FHMF needed a business and technical expert of a specific kind; LMDC needed a coach qualified in psychological interventions who could help a valued senior executive undergo a deep transformation in her leadership style. These coaching needs represent two of the four most common coaching needs organizations have: knowledge or skill coaching, developmental coaching, corrective coaching, and performance coaching. Figure 13 shows these organizational coaching needs, along with the information-gathering tools most appropriate for each need and the most common organizational response to each learning situation.

Figure 13: The Types of Organizational Coaching Needs

Quadrant 1: Knowledge and Skill Coaching

The first quadrant in figure 13 represents the kind of coaching required when organizations need to build someone's business or technical knowledge and skills. It is quite often done through internal mentoring programs or routine on-the-job training. Most large engineering companies, for instance, offer internal training programs in technical areas of expertise that their employees may not have acquired in college or with previous employers, and many cross-train new engineering graduate hires in areas of competence critical to their business, like project scoping and cost estimating. They also assign new hires to projects led or staffed by experienced people who can act as mentors. When organizations don't have the required expertise internally, they either hire experts as consultants, faculty, mentors, or coaches, as FHMF did for James, or they send employees to schools specializing in the expertise needed. External executive coaches who are experts in some business or technical areas may become involved in this type of coaching, but the vast majority of knowledge and skill development is done through on-the-job training.

The inner part of quadrant 1 in figure 13 shows the kinds of assessments organizations might use to determine an individual's development needs. Foremost in utility for this type of coaching are formal or informal skills assessments, which can identify gaps in knowledge or skills. Line managers and human resources professionals often use skills assessments along with some combination of position descriptions (including those next in an employee's career path), current performance appraisals, technical specifications for each position and level, and their own knowledge of the employee's strengths, weaknesses, and aspirations. They might also use competency assessments like Korn/Ferry's *Leadership Architect*® to identify skill areas where employees have the greatest development needs.

Quadrant 2: Developmental Coaching

The second quadrant in figure 13 is developmental coaching. Arguably, all coaching is developmental, but what we are referring to specifically in this quadrant is the kind of coaching organizations sponsor for their high-potential employees. Individual or cohort coaching often supplements other training and education programs intended to develop the next levels of managers and leaders in the organization. Developmental coaching typically includes a competency assessment as the basis for identifying employees' strengths and weaknesses as well as helping them form a more realistic picture of themselves. Organizations may also use skills assessments and, more rarely, psychological assessments to determine employees' development needs. Underlying all of the assessments are performance appraisals and on-the-job feedback, which helps organizations select the employees whom they consider to be high potentials.

In our experience as coaching solution providers, developmental coaching is one of the most common reasons organizations hire external coaches. Even if their human resources department has internal coaches, they generally lack the scope—and sometimes the expertise—to provide coaching for hundreds of high potentials. One of the principal capabilities coaches need for this type of coaching is the knowledge of various assessments and the ability to interpret the findings for their clients. For most commercial assessments, like the MBTI® or Lominger's *Voices®* or *Choices®*, this means completing a certification program in each assessment being used. Developmental coaching may involve some basic knowledge and skills coaching, mentoring, or on-the-job training (OJT) if employees are deemed to have knowledge or skill gaps. It can also move into corrective coaching if an employee is found to have a significant development need where an individual intervention is warranted.

Quadrant 3: Corrective Coaching

Corrective coaching is an individual intervention and is typically done when an otherwise effective executive has a significant flaw in operating style or behavior that is negatively affecting her performance or is otherwise disruptive to the organization, her subordinates, or the management team. Suzanne at LMDC is an example of an executive whose style was effective at one point in her career but is disruptive now. Problematic behaviors run the gamut from alcoholism to narcissism and self-aggrandizement and from exercising too much control to bullying and poor anger management. Organizations generally invest in corrective coaching in these situations only if the leader achieves results and is otherwise a strong contributor to the leadership team. However, unless the presenting problem is resolved, the leader is likely to derail.

To deal with these kinds of issues, organizations need coaches who are psychologically trained and certified, and if they use assessments they are likely to use psychological assessments like the *California Psychological Inventory®* (CPI) or a similar diagnostic tool. Competency assessments, performance appraisals, and interviews with key stakeholders may also be useful, but what this kind of coach typically relies upon most is his training and experience in helping people with psychological issues that may not require hospitalization or therapy but that are nonetheless debilitating enough to impair the person's effectiveness to a significant degree.

Quadrant 4: Performance Coaching

The fourth quadrant in figure 13 is performance coaching, which is often also called *leadership coaching*. This is the kind of coaching organizations usually provide to people in leadership or management positions who are not dysfunctional (which would call for corrective coaching) but who can benefit from coaching and mentoring as they are developing as leaders. As organizations develop their leaders, they may also provide high-level leadership development programs, but leaders primarily develop their skills through a variety of challenging assignments over the course of a career, as Morgan McCall, Michael Lombardo, and Ann Morrison describe in their book *The Lessons of Experience: How Successful Executives Develop on the Job* (1988). Leadership skills can be taught and coached, but the principal teacher is experience, so performance appraisals and feedback are the primary tools organizations use to help leaders improve their performance. That said, there is considerable demand for executive coaching that focuses on developing people's leadership capabilities.

THE COMPLETE COACH

Considering the broad spectrum of coaching needs organizations have, are any coaches qualified to provide all four types of coaching? Despite what some purveyors of coaching might argue, the answer is no. It would be rare indeed to find a coach with decades of experience and expertise in lean manufacturing who also had a doctorate in psychoanalysis or cognitive-behavioral psychology and years of therapeutic experience. In our experience managing a coaching practice, we have seen the full array of executive coaches: retired CEOs with years of experience running companies, who felt they had much to offer other senior executives; therapists who had spent decades doing psychological counseling and now wanted to work in the corporate world as executive coaches; human resource managers who had done internal coaching and loved it to the point of wanting to do nothing but coaching; and management consultants who believed that their strong suit was working with people.

They all bring unique capabilities and perspectives to executive coaching but will remain niche coaches unless they build their knowledge and skills in areas where they have less training. The retired senior executives typically have deep industry, management, and leadership knowledge, but

they often lack psychological insight and some of the rudimentary helping skills (like listening). The therapists bring psychological expertise and
expert helping skills, but they often lack business experience and—for all
of their knowledge of group dynamics—don't really understand how large
business organizations work. The HR managers know business organizations and understand talent management issues and strategies, but they
typically are not well schooled in psychological approaches, and they tend
to coach from an internal rather than an external perspective. The former
management consultants are business savvy and are usually good problem
solvers, but they often do not have deep insights into human behavior.

Occasionally, we meet the complete coach: the person with business
experience who has had leadership positions for a number of years, has
studied psychology and learned helping skills, and brings a broad spectrum
of knowledge, skills, experience, and perspectives to bear in any coaching
situation. These coaches may not be experts in lean manufacturing or some
other technical area, but they have been curious and committed enough in
their own development to learn about different psychological approaches,
group and team dynamics, leadership development strategies, assessments,
and organizational behavior, and they can bring different perspectives
and helping techniques to bear in a number of coaching situations. These
coaches are informed practitioners.

Their breadth and versatility enables them to adapt to their clients'
preferences and adapt their helping approach depending on how the client's journey unfolds and what the client wants and needs at each way-
point. They aren't experts in every psychological approach to coaching. No
one could be. But they know enough to understand the core concepts and
how to apply them without treading into areas they are not qualified to handle. They appreciate the nature of the trust their clients place in them and
understand the ethical standards they must uphold. Their versatility makes
them more useful to clients because they are not dogmatically following
one favored approach regardless of what is best for their clients. Instead,
they are informed and adaptive enough to feel confident taking a different
approach if that is what the client is more responsive to and if that is more
helpful in guiding clients on their journeys. Being an informed practitioner
makes you more adaptable in your approach to coaching, and this is the
most responsible way to call yourself a coach.

16

Completing Your
Own Journey

The self-reflective nature of coaching reminds us of Nietzsche's (1966) often-quoted aphorism that when you gaze long into an abyss, the abyss also gazes into you. Nietzsche was warning those who fight monsters that they may become monsters themselves. Coaching is not so perilous an avocation, but it is impossible to coach clients confronting their own demons without being affected by the experience. If you are coaching from an authentic place within yourself, if you are empathetic and can identify emotionally with your client's struggle, if you truly have helping hands and a helping heart, then some part of the client's journey will also be your own.

Those of us who write about coaching often neglect this vital part of the coaching process. We focus so much on serving clients that we forget that coaching is also a journey for the coach. As we help others develop, we arc also developing. As we strive to give them insights about themselves, we invariably discover insights about ourselves. And in reaching into our well of knowledge about human psychology, leadership, and performance, we also find some nuggets of truth that apply to us. As developmental psychologist and coach Jennifer Garvey Berger (2006) observed: "Developmental theories—while useful in our work with others—are also very helpful in our work on/with ourselves. Whenever I teach or consult about developmental theory, even if the focus is on helping others, questions inevitably arise about what this means for the coach as he walks his own developmental path" (p. 101).

Coaching is inherently self-reflective, and, if you are psychologically minded and committed to your own development, as most coaches are, then this is a blessing because it enables you to satisfy not only your curiosity about others but also your curiosity about yourself—and curiosity is one of an effective coach's greatest traits. The best coaches are born curious—about what makes people tick, about how people get stuck and how we can help them get unstuck, about the various theories landmark psychologists have posited about human nature, about the complex and sometimes mysterious workings of organizations, about the nature of leadership and the characteristics and behaviors of good leaders, about how leadership can go awry, and about ourselves as coaches, as professionals, as human beings.

We have an ethical obligation to put the client's journey first, but that does not mean that we sublimate our own journey. What happens in our hearts and minds is critically important because it affects how we coach, how we relate to our clients, and how authentic we are when we sit across from them and ask, "How can I help you?" At the core of our journey is a search for authenticity, for a genuine self who can listen, reflect, question, and advise from a place devoid of bias, dogma, and self-interest. It isn't always easy to get there because we are human beings, after all. In our lesser moments, we project an image of ourselves that is more certain than we know ourselves to be and less flawed than we wish we were. And why not? What client would want to be coached by someone who wrestles with uncertainties or needs approval to shore up self-confidence? Just as clients assume that their physician is healthy and their therapist psychologically fit, they assume their coach knows the pathways to success and is an experienced and capable guide.

Your capability is honed not only in your study of human development and your experience with clients but also in the crucible of self-reflection. To complete your journey as a coach, you must also do your own work, peeling away the layers of your own onion, as it were. Whatever else coaching is, it is also a process of self-discovery, especially if you are actively and consciously reflecting on your own journey as well as your clients' journeys. This kind of introspection can be wondrously gratifying and insightful if you are honest enough with yourself to permit egoless inquiry.

CLIMBING TOWARD THE RECEDING SUMMIT

As we all know, coaching can be immensely satisfying. In good coaching sessions, your clients will have uncovered something about themselves that had been hidden, or they will have discovered alternatives to a dysfunctional way they had been acting, or they will have gleaned some insights about their team and learned how to better lead the people they are responsible for. You will have observed the moments those insights occurred with the quiet satisfaction of the guide whose skill made it possible. It can be a heady experience, particularly when it is reinforced by appreciative clients. And while it is important to celebrate those successes and feel confident in your coaching abilities, it is also important to guard against too much self-congratulation. You can become so pleased with these victorious moments that you detach from your clients and lose sight of the genuine outcomes of your coaching, which may or may not be as splendid as you believe. You can begin to feel that you have mastered coaching, that you have reached the pinnacle of your profession. Once that feeling takes hold, your development has stalled. You have arrived at the terminus.

Part of your journey entails separating your impact from your ego, like separating the egg white from the yolk. Following a coaching session, it is important to debrief the experience by stripping away those feelings of self-satisfaction, which are gratifying but can also be deceptive, and look objectively at what occurred and why. We have found that the following storytelling exercises help facilitate this process:

♦ If you were to write up this coaching session as a story—told from the client's point of view—what would the story be? Who was the protagonist? The antagonists? How did the suspense build, and how was it relieved? What were the climactic moments in the story? How were the tensions resolved or not? What did the hero learn or fail to learn? And where might the story go from here? Cast yourself as an observer of the story but not a participant. What does this story reveal about the client's journey?

♦ Next, if you were to write up this coaching session as a story told from your point of view, what would the story be? You are the hero of this tale, but try to look at the story as though you were observing someone else. What did the hero do? What challenges did she face? Where did the hero stumble—

and where did the hero triumph? What were the obstacles or traps, and how did the hero overcome them? How did this story end? Where could the hero go next?

This storytelling exercise is an excellent way to view the coaching experience dispassionately. When we do this, we realize that the narrative running through our head before we did the exercise is quite different from the narrative running afterward. Moreover, if you ask your clients to construct a story based on their experience of the coaching session, you generally discover that their story is very different from the story you imagined they might tell.

The purpose of this exercise is to develop a better understanding of what impact you are actually having, what steps yielded the outcomes you expected or ones you did not, and which insights for you were also insights for your client. The purpose is to give yourself a more realistic, less ego-driven estimation of where you were effective and where you could have been more so. Berger (2006), whose background is developmental psychology, wrote that "while developmental theories can be humbling (because it would be lovely—but unlikely—to think of ourselves at the pinnacle), they are also very hopeful" (p. 101). The joy of a coach's journey is that it never ends—that you are always climbing toward, but never reaching, the summit—that in your journey of continuous learning you simultaneously advance toward the summit while causing it to recede. And thank heaven for that.

THE PATHS UNTAKEN

When you mow the same lawn over and over, you develop a comfortable way to mow it. You learn the best place to begin, which direction to go, how to get around the trees and shrubs, and where you will have to use a weed trimmer instead of your mower. It is likewise in any human endeavor. As we coach people repeatedly, we learn which approaches work better for us, which questions evoke the best responses, which stories to tell at which points along the way, and so on. In the commonplace act of honing our craft, we fall comfortably into routine and predictable patterns and grow increasingly used to the paths we have repeatedly taken. So it is that we may not pursue–or even fail to recognize—alternative approaches that could have taken the dialogue in a different direction and perhaps yielded even better results for our clients.

Coaches often don't think about those alternatives, so when we are debriefing coaches after some sessions, we find it instructive to explore not only the paths they took but also the ones untaken. We do it by asking questions like these:

◆ Tell me about a pivotal moment in that coaching dialogue. What happened? What did your client discover?

◆ How did you arrive at that point? What did you do next? What could you have done differently?

◆ You chose to confront your client and challenge his perception of the president's comments. What could you have done instead?

◆ Your choice at that point was to have her think about her need for control, which seems like a good choice. But what are some alternatives? What else could you have done?

◆ From what I understand about his company, it seems like the culture discourages direct conflict in meetings. Could you have introduced some systems thinking at that point?

◆ You said she is minimizing the potential impact of that decision, especially on her remote team members. What could you have done to help her think more realistically about her choices?

◆ I like the direction you took that conversation, but where else could you have taken it?

The point of this exercise is to help coaches reflect on the paths they chose—and explore the ones they didn't. It is not meant to be a critical conversation as much as an open dialogue about alternative possibilities. We have presented it here as a supervisory dialogue, but it can also be a conversation you have with yourself, perhaps on the airplane flying home or during a quiet moment after dinner. It is an opportunity for you to reflect on a client session and think about what else you might have done or what you might have done differently. By asking yourself those what if questions, you surface possibilities you may not have seen during your dialogue with clients and may discover intriguing directions to go in next time you're in a similar situation. Exploring the paths you have not taken is as important to your journey as examining the paths you took.

THE "I" INSIDE

If you are like most coaches, you sometimes share something about yourself with your clients. A story, perhaps. A lesson you learned. Something you experienced at school or at work. Something you are proud of or something you regret. A challenge you faced and how you met it. Or something you failed to do and what that cost you. What you reveal about yourself to your clients—and what you choose not to—is part of the persona you project.

Later, as you think about what you have shared with clients, it is worthwhile to reflect on where your stories, learnings, advice, and revelations have come from. When you needed them, those recollections came to mind. They were important to you. They helped you illuminate part of your client's journey—and perhaps part of your own. Your choices reveal a great deal about you and who you are. They are shadows of the "I" inside. Understanding and accepting your "I" inside, that person you are at the core, is crucial if you are to project an authentic self to your clients.

The purpose of this journey is not to find blemishes or wallow in insecurities. It should be undertaken with loving kindness for the person you are and respect for the gifts you can offer to others. When it is undertaken in that spirit of acceptance, the authentic self you discover is a gift you give to yourself. And it makes you a better coach.

REFERENCES

Allcorn, Seth. 2006. "Psychoanalytically Informed Executive Coaching," in Dianne R. Stober and Anthony M. Grant, eds., *Evidence Based Coaching Handbook*. Hoboken, NJ: John Wiley & Sons.

American Management Association. 2008. "2008 Talent Development Survey." *Talent Management* (July).

American Psychiatric Association. 1994. *Diagnostic and Statistical Manual of Mental Disorders*. 4th ed. Washington, DC: American Psychiatric Association.

Auerbach, Jeffery E. 2006. "Cognitive Coaching," in Dianne R. Stober and Anthony M. Grant, eds., *Evidence Based Coaching*. Hoboken, NJ: John Wiley & Sons.

Bacon, Terry R. 2011. *The Elements of Power: Lessons on Leadership and Influence*. New York: AMACOM Books. Also see *www.theelementsofpower.com*.

Bacon, Terry R. 2011. *Elements of Influence: The Art of Getting Others to Follow Your Lead*. New York: AMACOM Books. Also see *www.theelementsofpower.com*.

Belenky, Mary, Blythe Clinchy, Nancy Goldberger, and Jill Tarule. 1997. *Women's Ways of Knowing: The Development of Self, Voice, and Mind*. 10th anniversary ed. New York: Basic Books.

Berger, Jennifer Garvey. 2006. "Adult Development Theory and Executive Coaching Practice," in Dianne R. Stober and Anthony M. Grant, eds., *Evidence Based Coaching Handbook*. Hoboken, NJ: John Wiley & Sons.

Berglas, Steven. 2002. "The Very Real Dangers of Executive Coaching." *Harvard Business Review* (June).

Blanchard,Ken, and Don Shula. 1995. *Everyone's a Coach*. Grand Rapids, MI: Zondervan Publishing.

Bohm, David. 1996. *On Dialogue*. London: Routledge.

Bohm, David, Donald Factor, and Peter Garrett. 1991. "Dialogue: A Proposal." Accessible at *http://world.std.com/~lo/bohm/0000.html*.

Campone, Francine. 2008. "Connecting the Dots: Coaching Research—Past, Present and Future," in David B. Drake, Diane Brennan, and Kim Gortz, eds., *The Philosophy and Practice of Coaching: Insights and Issues for a New Era*. San Francisco: Jossey-Bass.

Cashman, Kevin. 2008. *Leadership from the Inside Out: Becoming a Leader for Life*. 2d ed. San Francisco: Berrett-Koehler Publishers, Inc.

Cashman, Kevin. 2009. "720° Coaching and Development: The Dynamic Interplay of Inside-out and Outside-in Approaches." Conference Board presentation (January 28).

Cialdini, Robert B. 2006. *Influence: The Psychology of Persuasion*. Rev. ed. New York: William Morrow.

Coutu, Diane. 2002. "How Resilience Works." *Harvard Business Review* (May).

Deloitte. 2011. "Talent Edge 2020: Building the Recovery Together—What Talent Expects and How Leaders Are Responding" (April). Accessible at *www. deloitte.com/assets/Dcom-UnitedStates/Local%20Assets/Documents/IMOs/ Talent/us_talent_talentedge2020employee_042811.pdf*

Egan, Gerard. 2009. *The Skilled Helper: A Problem-Management and Opportunity Development Approach to Helping*. 9th ed. Pacific Grove, CA: Brooks/Cole.

Executive Coaching Forum. 2008. *The Executive Coaching Forum's Handbook*. Accessible at *www.executivecoachingforum.com*.

Feldman, Janet, 2010. Personal conversation with Laurie Voss, November.

Fenner, Peter. 2007. "Listening and Speaking from No-Mind," in John J. Prendergast and G. Kenneth Bradford, eds., *Listening from the Heart of Silence: Nondual Wisdom & Psychotherapy*, Vol. 2. St. Paul, MN: Paragon House.

Flick, Deborah L. 1998. *From Debate to Dialogue*. Boulder, CO: Orchid Publications.

Gilligan, Carol. 1993. *In a Different Voice: Psychological Theory and Women's Development*. 29th printing ed. Boston: Harvard University Press.

Goldsmith, Marshall, Laurence Lyons, and Alyssa Freas, eds. 2000. *Coaching for Leadership: How the World's Greatest Coaches Help Leaders Learn*. San Francisco: Jossey-Bass/Pfeiffer.

Goleman, Daniel. 1995. *Emotional Intelligence.* New York: Bantam.

Hamrick, Charles. 2008. "Focus on Cultural Elements in Coaching: Experiences from China and Other Countries," in David B. Drake, Diane Brennan, and Kim Gortz, eds., *The Philosophy and Practice of Coaching: Insights and Issues for a New Era.* San Francisco: Jossey-Bass.

Hart, Vicki, John Blattner, and Staci Leipsic. 2001. "Coaching Versus Therapy: A Perspective." *Consulting Psychology Journal 53*, no. 4 (fall).

Hirsh, Sandra Krebs, and Jean M. Kummerow. 2007. *Introduction to Type in Organizations.* 3rd ed. Mountain View, CA: CPP, Inc.

Hoffer, Eric. 1963. *The Ordeal of Change.* New York: Harper and Row.

Kampa-Kokesch, Sheila, and Mary Z. Anderson. 2001. "Executive Coaching: A Comprehensive Review of the Literature." *Consulting Psychology Journal 53*, no. 4 (fall).

Kegan, Robert. 1982. *The Evolving Self: Problem and Process in Human Development.* Boston: Harvard University Press.

Kilburg, Richard. 2000. *Executive Coaching: Developing Managerial Wisdom in a World of Chaos.* Washington, DC: American Psychological Association.

Lombardo, Michael M. and Robert W. Eichinger. 2006. *FYI: For Your Improvement, A Guide for Development and Coaching.* 4th ed. Minneapolis: Lominger International, a Korn/Ferry Company.

Lore International Institute. 1997. *Coaching Effectiveness Survey.* Durango, CO: Lore International Institute.

Lore International Institute. 2000. *Survey of Influence Effectiveness.* Durango, CO: Lore International Institute.

MacFarquhar, Larissa. 2002. "The Better Boss." *The New Yorker*, April 22–29.

Maslow, Abraham. 1998. *Toward a Psychology of Being.* 3rd ed. New York: Wiley.

McCall, Morgan W., Michael M. Lombardo, and Ann M. Morrison. 1988. *The Lessons of Experience: How Successful Executives Develop on the Job.* New York: Free Press.

Merriam-Webster's Collegiate Dictionary. 1999. 10th ed. Springfield, MA: Merriam-Webster.

Michaels, Ed, Helen Handfield-Jones, and Beth Axelrod. 2001. *The War for Talent.* Cambridge, MA: Harvard Business School Press.

Nietzsche, Friedrich. 1966. *Beyond Good and Evil: Prelude to a Philosophy of the Future.* Walter Kaufmann, trans. London: Vintage Books.

O'Reilly, Charles A., III, and Jeffrey Pfeffer. 2000. *Hidden Value: How Great Companies Achieve Extraordinary Results with Ordinary People.* Cambridge, MA: Harvard Business School Press.

Peltier, Bruce. 2010. *The Psychology of Executive Coaching: Theory and Application.* 2nd ed. New York: Routledge.

Peterson, David B. 2006. "People Are Complex and the World Is Messy: A Behavior-Based Approach to Executive Coaching," in Dianne R. Stober and Anthony M. Grant, eds., *Evidence Based Coaching.* Hoboken, NJ: John Wiley & Sons.

Saporito, Thomas. 1996. "Business-Linked Executive Development: Coaching Senior Executives." *Consulting Psychology Journal 48* (spring): 96–103.

Stober, Dianne R. and Anthony M. Grant, eds. 2006. *Evidence Based Coaching Handbook: Putting Best Practices to Work for Your Clients.* Hoboken, NJ: John Wiley & Sons.

Tobias, Lester L. 1996. "Coaching Executives." *Consulting Psychology Journal: Practice and Research 48,* no. 2 (spring): 87–95.

Weiner, Norbert. (1988) *The Human Use of Human Beings: Cybernetics and Society.* Cambridge, MA: De Capo Press. This book was originally published in 1950.

Young, Jeffrey E., and Janet S. Klosko. 1994. *Reinventing Your Life.* New York: Penguin.

RESOURCES FOR ADAPTIVE COACHES

This appendix provides an annotated bibliography of excellent resources for adaptive coaches, but it is by no means complete. There are tens of thousands of books available on business, organizational dynamics, leadership, adult learning, emotional intelligence, and other topics related to effective executive coaching, not to mention the scores of handbooks and guides to hundreds of assessments coaches might use. However, the books we have listed here are among the finest resources we know that are useful to adaptive coaches who need to build their knowledge in these particular areas.

Adult Learning

Learning in Adulthood: A Comprehensive Guide, 3rd ed. Sharan B. Merriam, Rosemary S. Caffarella, and Lisa M. Baumgartner. Jossey-Bass, 2006. A book that's become a standard text in adult learning. Among its best features is a survey of major areas of thought around how adults learn. Written for educators but useful for coaches in thinking about how best to help clients grow.

The Adult Learner, Seventh Edition: The Definitive Classic in Adult Education and Human Resource Development. Malcolm S. Knowles, Richard A. Swanson, and Elwood F. Holton III. Taylor & Francis, 2011. One of the classics in adult learning featuring Knowles' theory of andragogy with its focus on self-directed, autonomous learners. A must resource for coaches who adopt a learning approach to helping clients develop.

The Skillful Teacher: On Technique, Trust, and Responsiveness in the Classroom, 2nd ed. Stephen D. Brookfield. Jossey-Bass, 2006. Although primarily aimed at teachers of college students and adults, this book is useful for coaches, especially those who coach groups or teams or combine person-centered counseling techniques with some form of instruction.

Behavioral Approaches to Coaching

Behavioral Coaching. Suzanne Skiffington and Perry Zeus. McGraw-Hill Book Company, 2003. One of the best books to read for an introduction to behavioral approaches to coaching. Zeus is head of the Behavioral Coaching Institute, which promotes scientifically validated coaching methods and use of assessments in producing behavioral change.

Contemporary Behavior Therapy, 5th ed. Michael D. Spiegler and David C. Guevremont. Wadsworth Publishing, 2009. Written by two clinical psychologists, this book is for therapists, not coaches, but it can give coaches a solid introduction to major contemporary behavioral and cognitive approaches to helping clients.

The Complete Guide to Coaching at Work. Perry Zeus and Suzanne Skiffington. McGraw-Hill Book Company, 2001. An earlier work by Zeus and Skiffington (authors of *Behavioral Coaching*), this book overviews behavioral coaching approaches, particularly in a business setting, for coaching executives and teams. One chapter on managers as coaches.

Business Resources

Behavioral Theory of the Firm, 2nd ed. Richard M. Cyert and James G. March. Wiley-Blackwell, 1992. A classic book on business and organizational theory. More academic in approach but an insightful look at the dynamics of business organizations and how they make decisions.

Business, 11th ed. William M. Pride, Robert J. Hughes, and Jack R. Kapoor. South-Western College/West, 2011. An introductory textbook on business. A useful overview of business functions for those with little experience in business.

Corporate Lifecycles: How and Why Corporations Grow and Die and What to Do About It. Ichak Adizes. Prentice Hall, 1988. A useful understanding of how organizations grow, mature, and decline. Particularly helpful for coaches working with founders or entrepreneurial CEOs—or leaders in large, bureaucratic companies.

The Evolution of Management Thought, 6th ed. Daniel A. Wren and Arthur G. Bedeian. John Wiley & Sons, 2008. A superb history of management thought from early civilizations to the modern era. Most useful for MBA students but good context-setting for coaches, especially those who work with executives.

Understanding Business, 9th ed. William Nickels, James McHugh, and Susan McHugh. McGraw-Hill/Irwin, 2009. An introductory textbook on business. Excellent for coaches who have no background or experience in business.

Coaching Overviews

Coaching Models: A Cultural Perspective: A Guide to Model Development: for Practitioners and Students of Coaching. Diane Lennard. Routledge, 2010. A good overview of many coaching models, with an emphasis on readers developing their own approaches from an informed perspective.

Evidence Based Coaching Handbook: Putting Best Practices to Work for Your Clients. Dianne R. Stober and Anthony M. Grant, eds. John Wiley & Sons, 2006. An excellent collection of essays on evidence-based coaching methods (as opposed to belief-based methods). Evidence-based coaching rests on a foundation of scientific and proven principles (whereas belief-based coaching derives from a coach's unproven beliefs about how to coach). Cognitive and behavioral methods, for example, are evidence based.

The Handbook of Knowledge-based Coaching: From Theory to Practice. Leni Wildflower and Diane Brennan, eds. Jossey-Bass, 2011. A robust collection of essays on different approaches to coaching and issues related to coaching. Noted for its emphasis on putting theories into practice. An excellent resource for coaches of all kinds.

The Philosophy and Practice of Coaching: Insights and Issues for a New Era. David B. Drake, Diane Brennan, and Kim Gortz, eds. Jossey-Bass, 2008. An outstanding collection of essays on the theoretical and practical bases for coaching.

The Psychology of Executive Coaching: Theory and Application, 2nd ed. Bruce Peltier. Routledge, 2010. An incisive overview of the major theories of psychology applied to coaching. For psychologically minded coaches or readers wanting a broad understanding of how psychology applies to coaching, it doesn't get much better than this.

Coaching Resources

FYI for Learning Agility™. Robert W. Eichinger, Michael M. Lombardo, and Care C. Capretta. Lominger International: A Korn/Ferry Company, 2010. Over the course of a career, learning agility has been proven to be a strong predictor of success in leadership roles. This book explains the fundamentals of learning agility and offers numerous developmental remedies for executives needing to increase their learning agility. A key resource for coaches who use any coaching approach.

FYI for Teams: For Team Members, Team Leaders, and Team Coaches, 2nd ed. Cara C. Capretta, Robert W. Eichinger, Michael M. Lombardo, and Victoria V. Swisher. Lominger International: A Korn/Ferry Company, 2009. An excellent resource for team assessment and coaching. Full of practical tips on improving team performance.

FYI, For Your Improvement: A Guide for Development and Coaching for Learners, Managers, Mentors, and Feedback Givers, 5th ed. Michael M. Lombardo and Robert W. Eichinger. Lominger International: A Korn/Ferry Company, 2009. One of the best collections of practical tips for leaders and managers based on Lominger's proven model of leadership competencies—The Leadership Architect®. This book, and the Leadership Architect® sort cards, are an invaluable resource for coaches using an assessment and competency tool to help leaders identify their strengths and weaknesses and work on the gaps.

The Coaching Kaleidoscope: Insights from the Inside. Manfred Kets de Vries, Laura Guillen, Konstantin Korotov, and Elizabeth Florent-Treacy eds. Palgrave Macmillan, 2010. A very scholarly look at coaching from European practitioners, particularly those associated with INSEAD. Excellent collection of essays on coaching.

The Skilled Helper: A Problem-Management and Opportunity-Development Approach to Helping, 9th ed. Gerard Egan. Brooks/Cole, 2010. Written for counselors and therapists but extraordinarily helpful for coaches as well. One of the finest instructional texts on the processes and techniques of working with clients. Covers the fundamentals of helping relationships and the essential skills of anyone engaged in helping.

Tricky Coaching: Difficult Cases in Leadership Coaching. Konstantin Korotov, Manfred Kets de Vries, Andreas Bernhardt, and Elizabeth Forent-Treacy, eds. Palgrave Macmillan, 2012. One of the most useful resources we have seen for executive coaches. Numerous stories of difficult clients told by experienced coaches highlighting the challenge the coach faced, the approach taken, the coaching dilemma, and commentary.

Cognitive Approaches to Coaching

A New Guide to Rational Living, 3rd ed. Albert Ellis and Robert A. Harper. Wilshire Book Co., 1975. One of Ellis's classic self-help books about irrational beliefs. Addresses issues like fear of failure, unreasonable need for approval, self-discipline, overcoming depression, conquering anxiety, and refusing to be happy.

Cognitive Behavior Therapy: Basics and Beyond, 2nd ed. Judith S. Beck and Aaron T. Beck. The Guilford Press, 2011. The most widely adopted textbook on cognitive behavior therapy in the world. Considered a standard text in this branch of psychotherapy.

Cognitive Therapy Techniques: A Practitioner's Guide. Robert L. Leahy. The Guilford Press, 2003. A highly regarded and practical collection of cognitive therapy techniques for clinicians. Useful for coaches as well.

Overcoming Destructive Beliefs, Feelings, and Behaviors. Albert Ellis. Prometheus Books, 2001. Another of Ellis's classics about rational emotive behavior therapy. All about constructing self-helping thoughts, feelings, and beliefs and eliminating self-destructive behaviors. A key resource for coaches following cognitive helping methods.

Rational Emotive Behavior Therapy: A Therapist's Guide, 2nd ed. Albert Ellis and Catharine MacLaren. Impact Publishers, 2005. A slim guide to practicing rational emotive behavioral therapy. Intended for therapists but useful for cognitive coaches, too.

The Practice of Rational Emotive Behavior Therapy, 2nd ed. Albert Ellis and Windy Dryden, eds. Springer Publishing Company, 2007. Another Ellis book for practicing therapists on rational emotive behavioral therapy. This has specific advice for treating individuals, couples, families, and so on.

Cultural Differences

Culture, Leadership, and Organizations: The GLOBE Study of 62 Societies. Robert J. House, Paul J. Hanges, Mansour Javidan, Peter W. Dorfman, and Vipin Gupta, eds. Sage Publications, 2004. The most comprehensive study of cultural differences ever undertaken. Builds upon Hofstede's work and provides even more cultural differentiators.

Cultures and Organizations: Software of the Mind, 3rd ed. Geert Hofstede, Gert Jan Hofstede, and Michael Minkov. McGraw-Hill, 2010.

Culture's Consequences: Comparing Values, Behaviors, Institutions and Organizations Across Nations, 2nd ed. Geert Hofstede, ed. Sage Publications, 2001. Examines more than fifty countries on five dimensions of cultural difference: power distance, uncertainty avoidance, individualism vs. collectivism, masculinity vs. femininity, and long-term vs. short-term orientation.

Developing Global Executives: The Lessons of International Experience. Morgan W. McCall, Jr. and George P. Hollenbeck. Harvard Business School Press, 2002. Written by two leadership development experts who focus on the unique knowledge and experience requirements for developing global executives. An outstanding volume for coaches working in multicultural environments.

Diversity in Coaching: Working with Gender, Culture, Race, and Age. Jonathan Passmore, ed. Kogan Page Limited, 2009. A good collection of articles on coaching in particular cultures (e.g., China, Middle East, India, Russia, Japan) and such groups as African-Americans, Indians, alpha males, and women.

Global Diversity: Winning Customers and Engaging Employees within World Markets. Ernest Gundling and Anita Zanchettin, eds. Nicholas Brealey, 2007. Concrete advice for doing business in eight major world markets: China, Egypt, India, Japan, Mexico, Russia, United Kingdom, and United States. Excellent for coaches in these countries or for coaching executives who will be working globally.

Leadership in a Diverse and Multicultural Environment: Developing Awareness, Knowledge, and Skills. Mary L. Connerley and Paul B. Pedersen. Sage Publications, 2005. Focuses on developing greater multicultural leadership capability. A useful text for coaches working with clients who are moving into multicultural assignments and lack that experience.

What is Global Leadership? 10 Key Behaviors that Define Great, Global Leaders. Ernest Gundling, Terry Hogan, and Karen Cvitkovich. Nicholas Brealey, 2011. Good, practical resource for coaching global leaders.

Working GlobeSmart: 12 People Skills for Doing Business Across Borders. Ernest Gundling. Nicholas Brealey, 2010. Good discussion of the practical applications of cultural differences. Useful in coaching global executives or those working with people cross-culturally.

Dialogue

Dialogue: The Art of Thinking Together. William Isaacs. Crown Business, 1999. One of the best introductions to the art of dialogue from the director of the Dialogue Project at MIT. All coaches can benefit from Issacs' ideas on collective inquiry, confrontation, and clarification.

Difficult Conversations: How to Discuss What Matters Most, 10th anniversary ed. Douglas Stone, Bruce Patton, and Sheila Heen. Penguin, 2010. An excellent book on productive conversation, including thoughts on arguing, blaming, making false assumptions, problem solving, listening, and expressing yourself with clarity and power. Useful coaching skills and useful for teaching clients with a need for better communication skills.

Discussion as a Way of Teaching: Tools and Techniques for Democratic Classrooms, 2nd ed. Stephen D. Brookfield and Stephen Preskill. Jossey-Bass, 2005. A highly regarded text for teachers on using the discussion method in classrooms. Although not aimed at coaches, the techniques are useful in group and team coaching especially.

RC Series Bundle: On Dialogue, 2nd ed. David Bohm. Lee Nichol, ed. Routledge, 2004. A collection of essays on dialogue, including Bohm's initial essay, which launched this field. Fascinating work that goes to the source of conflict resolution through what Bohm called creative dialogue.

The Magic of Dialogue: Transforming Conflict into Cooperation. Daniel Yankelovich. Touchstone, 2001. Useful, practical techniques for engaging in collaborative dialogue.

Emotional Intelligence

A Coach's Guide to Emotional Intelligence: Strategies for Developing Successful Leaders. James Bradford Terrell and Marcia Hughes. Pfeiffer, 2008. Written for coaches, this book offers tips for teaching emotional intelligence to clients—as well as for developing the coach's own emotional awareness. A good resource for coaches, whether or not emotional intelligence is the focus of the coaching.

Coaching for Emotional Intelligence: The Secret to Developing the Star Potential in Your Employees. Bob Wall. AMACOM Books, 2006. Written for managers, this book has instruction on how to give feedback and how to coach, which will not be useful for most coaches. But the chapters on corrective coaching are useful.

Emotional Intelligence. Daniel Goleman. Bloomsbury Paperbacks, 2010. The book that started so much current interest in emotional intelligence. A must-read book for coaches.

Emotional Intelligence 2.0. Travis Bradberry and Jean Greaves. TalentSmart, 2009. Designed to help readers improve their emotional intelligence. Includes an online EI assessment. Offers practical tips for improving personal competence (self-awareness and self-management) and social competence (social awareness and relationship management). A good resource for helping clients develop their emotional intelligence.

Go Suck a Lemon: Strategies for Improving Your Emotional Intelligence. Michael Cornwall. CreateSpace, 2011. Thirty-two strategies for improving your emotional intelligence, most presented through the author's personal stories and examples. A breezy, non-didactic look at EI, as suggested by the book's title. Interesting for its stories.

Handbook for Developing Emotional and Social Intelligence: Best Practices, Case Studies, and Strategies. Marcia Hughes, Henry L. Thompson, and James Bradford Terrell, eds. Pfeiffer, 2009. A collection of seventeen articles on emotional intelligence. Outstanding and informative, this book is written for coaches, counselors, therapists, and educators. Practical, scientific, and comprehensive, a great resource for coaches.

Intimate Relationships, 6th ed. Rowland Miller. McGraw-Hill, 2011. Not about emotional intelligence, per se, but a highly regarded textbook about relationships, with contributions from psychology, sociology, family studies, communication, and neuroscience. Well-grounded in research and an excellent text on relationships, especially for coaches who come from business but have no formal education in psychology or human behavior.

The Handbook of Emotional Intelligence: Theory, Development, Assessment, and Application at Home, School, and in the Workplace. Reuven Bar-On and James D. A. Parker, eds. Jossey-Bass, 2000. One of the most scholarly compendiums of essays on the research behind and uses of emotional intelligence. For coaches who want in-depth knowledge of this subject.

Working with Emotional Intelligence. Daniel Goleman. Bantam Books, 1998. This book focuses on the competencies of people with high emotional intelligence. Less theoretical and more applied than his initial book on this subject.

Family Therapy

Essential Skills in Family Therapy, Second Edition: From the First Interview to Termination. JoEllen Patterson, Lee Williams, Todd M. Edwards, Larry Chamow, and Claudia Grauf-Grounds. The Guilford Press, 2009. A textbook for beginning family therapists. Process oriented, covering basic administrative and client management skills as well as therapy. Insightful for inexperienced coaches who want to take a systems view of coaching.

Family Therapy: An Overview, 8th ed. Herbert Goldenberg and Irene Goldenberg. Brooks/Cole, 2012. A highly regarded, in-depth look at family therapy. More psychological in orientation, with a comprehensive look at different schools of thought and approaches to family therapy. For coaches needing a graduate-level understanding of this field.

The Family Crucible: The Intense Experience of Family Therapy. Augustus Y. Napier and Carl Whitaker. William Morrow Paperbacks, 1988. An older but still insightful book made up almost entirely of vivid case studies illustrating family therapy at work.

Group Coaching

Coaching the Team at Work. David Clutterbuck. Nicholas Brealey, 2007. A good introductory text on team coaching, more for new coaches than experienced coaches.

Effective Group Coaching: Tried and Tested Tools and Resources for Optimum Coaching Results. Jennifer J. Britton. Wiley, 2010. Another good introductory text on team coaching. Covers practical steps for starting a group coaching practice, including marketing.

Group and Team Coaching: The Essential Guide. Christine Thornton. Routledge, 2010. A deeper look at group dynamics and system thinking. Includes advice on coaching dysfunctional teams.

Group Coaching: A Comprehensive Blueprint. Ginger Cockerham. iUniverse, 2011. A practical guide to group coaching, including case studies and tips from experienced group coaches. An excellent resource for coaches of groups.

Facilitative Coaching: A Toolkit for Expanding Your Repertoire and Achieving Lasting Results (Essential Tools Resource). Dale Schwarz and

Anne Davidson. Pfeiffer, 2008. A cornucopia of techniques for coaching individuals or groups. A great resource for all coaches. Includes a CD with seventy exercises plus tips and tools for using them.

Group Process

Blackwell Handbook of Social Psychology: Group Processes. Michael A. Hogg and Scott Tindale, eds. Wiley-Blackwell, 2002. An excellent collection of academic essays on group behavior, social status, leadership, influence, conformity, group structure, attitudes, norms, and so on. Blackwell also publishes a similar handbook on intergroup processes.

Group Dynamics, 5th ed. Donelson R. Forsyth. Wadsworth Publishing, 2009. Widely respected textbook on group dynamics. Research-based and full of case studies, this is one of the most comprehensive books available on this subject. For coaches who want a deep understanding of organizations, groups, and teams or who use system thinking in their coaching.

Group Dynamics for Teams, 3rd ed. Daniel J. Levi, ed. Sage Publications, 2010. An excellent introduction to teamwork and the issues teams face: leadership, power, social influence, conflict, problem solving, decision making, creativity, and diversity.

Groups That Work: Structure and Process, 2nd ed. Paul H. Ephross and Thomas V. Vassil. Columbia University Press, 2005. Uniquely valuable contribution because it focuses on working groups—those formed to produce a product. Useful for organizational coaches who frequently work with standing teams or committees.

Paradoxes of Group Life: Understanding Conflict, Paralysis, and Movement in Group Dynamics. Kenwyn K. Smith and David N. Berg. Jossey-Bass, 1997. Unique in its emphasis on dysfunctional groups or teams. How and why groups get stuck: the paradoxes of groups and group behavior. A very helpful resource for coaches dealing with dysfunctional teams or organizations.

The Abilene Paradox and Other Meditations on Management. Jerry B. Harvey. Jossey-Bass, 1988. A slim, insightful, and entertaining book about group think and other craziness in management and organizational behavior. In our view, required reading.

Human Development

The Evolving Self: Problem and Process in Human Development. Robert Kegan. Harvard University Press, 1982. Kegan's classic book on the meaning-making stages of development throughout one's life. A must-read for coaches interested in human development.

Theories of Development: Concepts and Applications, 6th ed. William Crain. Prentice Hall, 2010. An excellent introduction to various theories of human development from Piaget on. Serves as a broad introduction to the topic.

Leadership

Elements of Influence: The Art of Getting Others to Follow Your Lead. Terry R. Bacon. AMACOM Books, 2011. Research-based examination of the techniques leaders use to influence others to do their bidding. Identifies ten positive influence techniques and four negative techniques. Includes a self-assessment of influence effectiveness.

Handbook of Leadership Theory and Practice: A Harvard Business School Centennial Colloquium. Nitin Nohria and Rakesh Khurana, eds. Harvard Business Review Press, 2010. A thick, academic collection of essays on various leadership topics by some of the most renowned thinkers on the subject. A graduate-level course on leadership research and current perspectives.

John P. Kotter on What Leaders Really Do. John P. Kotter. Harvard Business Review Books, 1999. A slim volume, one of the classics on leadership and general management. Gives coaches an informative and easy-to-read overview of the challenges and principal tasks of leaders and managers.

Leadership: Understanding the Dynamics of Power and Influence in Organizations, 2nd ed. Robert P. Vecchio, ed. University of Notre Dame Press, 2007. An anthology of some of the classic writings on leadership by many of the leaders in the field. One of the finest collections of essays on leadership. Practically required reading for anyone who coaches leaders.

Leadership from the Inside Out: Becoming a Leader for Life, 2nd ed. Kevin Cashman. Berett-Koehler Publishers, 2008. A full explication of Cashman's inside-out and outside-in approach to leadership development, which we summarized in chapters 13 and 14. This book is excellent for executive coaches but useful for anyone wanting to know more about the dynamics of human development and transformative change.

Leadership: Theory and Practice, 5th ed. Peter G. Northouse, ed. Sage Publications, 2009. An outstanding introduction to the many approaches to understanding leadership, including traits, skills, style, situational, contingency, path-goal, exchange theory, and so on. For coaches interested in the many ways of looking at leaders and leadership effectiveness.

Leading Change. John P. Kotter. Harvard Business Review Press, 1996. One of the classics on leading change in organizations. Essential for coaches working at senior levels in companies.

On Becoming a Leader, 4th ed. Warren Bennis. Basic Books, 2009. Another of the classic books on leadership by the dean of leadership gurus. Indispensable for coaches of leaders.

The Bass Handbook of Leadership: Theory, Research, and Managerial Applications, 4th ed. Bernard M. Bass with Ruth Bass. Free Press, 2008. Virtually an encyclopedia of thought on leadership. A valuable resource summarizing much of the thought on leadership for the past four decades.

The Effective Executive: The Definitive Guide to Getting the Right Things Done, rev ed. Peter F. Drucker. HarperBusiness, 2006. Another classic on leadership and management from one of the finest management consultants of the twentieth century. A must read for executive coaches.

The Elements of Power: Lessons on Leadership and Influence. Terry R. Bacon. AMACOM Books, 2011. Companion book to Elements of Influence. This book analyzes the eleven sources of power leaders can develop that give them ability to be influential. Includes a self-assessment of one's power sources and practical suggestions for building each power source.

The Lessons of Experience: How Successful Executives Develop on the Job. Morgan W. McCall, Jr., Michael M. Lombardo, and Ann M. Morrison. The Free Press, 1988. A classic book on how executives develop their skills on the job. Based on research and filled with details about the types of assignments and experiences that are most helpful. An essential resource on leadership development for coaches working with executives.

The New Psychology of Leadership: Identity, Influence, and Power. S. Alexander Haslam, Stephen D. Reicher, and Michael J. Platow. Psychology Press, 2011. Scholarly work on leadership as social identity, the leader as "we" instead of "I." This book is about leadership in context, so it is insightful for coaches taking a systems approach.

The Psychology of Leadership: New Perspectives and Research. David M. Messick and Roderick M. Kramer, eds. Routledge, 2011. A superb collection of scholarly articles on the personal characteristics of leaders, the factors that influence leadership effectiveness, and the effects of leadership positions on leaders themselves.

What People Want: A Manager's Guide to Building Relationships that Work. Terry R. Bacon. Davies-Black Publishing, 2006. A look at leadership and management from the perspective of those who are led or managed. Based on original research, this book identifies what people want from their managers and what they value most in the workplace. With numerous practical suggestions for improving workplace relationships, this is a helpful resource for coaches.

Organizational Theory

Diagnosing and Changing Organizational Culture: Based on the Competing Values Framework, 3rd ed. Kim S. Cameron and Robert E. Quinn. Jossey-Bass, 2011. An organizational culture assessment and change workbook based on the four-box competing values model. One useful framework for analyzing organizational culture.

Organizational Culture and Leadership, 4th ed. Edgar H. Schein. Jossey-Bass, 2010. Classic management tome about the interconnectedness of leadership and organizational culture. Good resource for coaching leaders of changing organizations or those with cultural malfunctions.

Organization Development: A Jossey-Bass Reader. Joan V. Gallos, ed. Jossey-Bass, 2006. Excellent collection of essays from prominent thinkers on organizational design, leadership, and change. Great resource for executive coaches working in large companies.

Organizational Assessment: A Step-by-Step Guide to Effective Consulting. Harry Levinson. American Psychological Association, 2002. The bible on assessing organizations from multiple perspectives and developing a consulting strategy. Very useful for coaches working with senior managers.

Positive Psychology/Appreciative Inquiry

Appreciative Inquiry: A Positive Revolution in Change. David L. Cooperrider and Diana Whitney. Berrett-Koehler Publishers, 2005. A brief introduction to appreciative inquiry and the 4D cycle (Discover, Dream, Design, Destiny). Essentially an implementation of positive psychology within an organizational design perspective.

Appreciative Inquiry Handbook: For Leaders of Change, 2nd ed. David L. Cooperrider, Diana Whitney, and Jacqueline M. Stavros. Berrett-Koehler Publishers, 2008. A very thorough introduction to appreciative inquiry with numerous exercises, examples, interview guides, reports, plans, worksheets and slides. Includes an appendix of classic articles on appreciative inquiry. An indispensable resource for practitioners and coaches looking for practical ideas.

A Psychology of Human Strengths: Fundamental Questions and Future Directions for a Positive Psychology. Lisa G. Aspinwall and Ursula M. Staudinger, eds. American Psychological Association, 2003. A collection of scholarly articles on the philosophy of and research behind positive psychology. Good resource for coaches who want more depth on positive psychology and the psychological thinking that preceded it.

Authentic Happiness: Using the New Positive Psychology to Realize Your Potential for Lasting Fulfillment. Martin E. P. Seligman. Free Press, 2003. One of the classic books from the father of positive psychology. Coaches of all kinds should be aware of positive psychology and its usefulness in helping some clients.

Flow: The Psychology of Optimal Experience. Mihaly Csikszentmihalyi. Harper Perennial Modern Classics, 2008. Fascinating book on the phenomenon of flow—that timeless and joyful state of optimal experience and performance. A good read even for non-coaches.

Learned Optimism: How to Change Your Mind and Your Life. Martin E. P. Seligman. Vintage, 2006. Another classic from Seligman. This one on how pessimists can learn to be optimistic. A good resource for coaches.

Practicing Positive Psychology Coaching: Assessment, Activities and Strategies for Success. Robert Biswas-Diener. Wiley, 2010. Slender book on implementing positive psychology in coaching. Practical, with exercises coaches can use with clients.

Positive Psychology Coaching: Putting the Science of Happiness to Work for Your Clients. Robert Biswas-Diener and Ben Dean. Wiley, 2007. A guide for coaches who want to help their clients implement positive psychology in the workplace. Numerous practical suggestions.

The Power of Appreciative Inquiry: A Practical Guide to Positive Change,
2nd ed. Diana Whitney and Amanda Trosten-Bloom. Berrett-Koehler Publishers, 2010. The most comprehensive guide to using appreciative inquiry
in organizations.

Psychoanalytic and Psychodynamic Approaches to Coaching

Executive Coaching: A Psychodynamic Approach. Catherine Sandler.
Open University Press, 2011. A wise, informative, and brief introduction
to key psychoanalytic (psychodynamic) concepts and their use in coaching. Uses multiple case studies to illustrate concepts like the unconscious,
empathy, defense mechanisms, and transference/countertransference.

Executive Coaching: Systems Psychodynamic Perspective. Halina Brun-
ning, ed. Karnac Books, 2006. A collection of scholarly articles on the systems psychodynamic approach to coaching. Interesting exploration of the
unconscious dynamics in organizations.

Organizations in Depth: The Psychoanalysis of Organizations. Yiannis
Gabriel. Sage Publications, 1999. The application of psychoanalysis to
organizations. Interaction of individuals and organizations, psychoanalysis of organizational culture, and the emotional life of organizations. One
chapter on core psychoanalytic ideas and theories is especially useful for
coaches new to this approach.

*The Unconscious at Work: Individual and Organizational Stress in the
Human Services.* Anton Obholzer, Dr. Vega Zagier Roberts, and Members
of the Tavistock Clinic "Consulting to Institutions" Workshop, eds. Routledge, 1994. Application of Freud's theories to organizational life. Written
for the human services but applicable to all industries. A wide-ranging exploration of unconscious forces operating within organizations.

System Thinking

An Introduction to General Systems Thinking, 25th anniversary ed. Gerald
M. Weinberg. Dorset House, 2001. Excellent general introduction to the
core concepts of system theory. Originally published in 1975; updated for
this edition. Weinberg was one of the pioneers in this field.

General Principles of Systems Design. Gerald M Weinberg and Daniela
Weinberg. Dorset House, 1988. Focuses on the dynamics within systems

that drive stasis. Very useful for family therapists and coaches with a systems view of helping.

The Systems View of the World: A Holistic Vision for Our Time, 2nd ed. Ervin Laszlo. Hampton Press, 1996. One of the primary texts in the field of system thinking by one of its leading experts.

Thinking in Systems: A Primer. Donella H. Meadows. Chelsea Green Publishing, 2008. Slim but excellent introduction to systems thinking. Has a very accessible style and many examples and illustrations. Great resource for understanding systems and coaching using system thinking and family therapy.

Transpersonal Psychology

Integral Psychology: Consciousness, Spirit, Psychology, Therapy. Ken Wilber. Shambhala, 2000. Wilber is a prolific author in the field of transpersonal psychology. One of the pioneers in integrating Western psychology and Eastern spiritualism, he seeks in this book to bring together diverse perspectives on consciousness and the integration of mind and brain. This book is more theoretical than practical but is useful as an introduction to Wilber's philosophy.

Journey of the Heart: The Path of Conscious Love. John Welwood. Harper Perennial, 1996. Welwood's bestseller about building intimate relationships. Considered a classic on fixing broken relationships.

Paths Beyond Ego: The Transpersonal Vision. Roger Walsh and Frances Vaughan, eds. Tarcher, 1993. A good compilation of articles on transpersonal psychology from some of the dominant thinkers in the field.

Psychotherapy and Spirit: Theory and Practice in Transpersonal Psychotherapy. Brant Cortright. State University of New York Press, 1997. An excellent analysis of transpersonal psychology applied in therapeutic interventions.

Toward a Psychology of Awakening: Buddhism, Psychotherapy, and the Path of Personal and Spiritual Transformation. John Welwood. Shambhala, 2002. Welwood is another of the pioneers in integrating Western psychology and Eastern spiritualism. The emphasis is on spiritual development and includes chapters on psychotherapy in a spiritual context.

INDEX